FREE SPEECH
IN THE
COLLEGE COMMUNITY

FOR KAREN

FREE SPEECH
IN THE
COLLEGE COMMUNITY

ROBERT M. O'NEIL

INDIANA UNIVERSITY PRESS
BLOOMINGTON AND INDIANAPOLIS

The paper used in this publication meets the minimum requirements
of American National Standard for Information Sciences—Perma-
nence of Paper for Printed Library Materials, ANSI Z39.48-1984.
Manufactured in the United States of America

Library of Congress Cataloging-in-Publication Data

O'Neil, Robert M.
Free Speech in the college community / Robert M. O'Neil.
p.   cm.
Includes bibliographical references.
ISBN 0–253–33267–2 (cloth : alk. paper)
1. Academic freedom—United States. 2. Freedom of speech—
United States. 3. Freedom of information—United States.   I. Title.
LC72.2.O54   1997
378.1'21—dc21   96-47161

1   2   3   4   5   02   01   00   99   98   97

CONTENTS

INTRODUCTION

Should speech on the university campus be freer than speech on the streets and in the malls and parks? Most of us assume it should be. Conventional wisdom would give maximum protection to academic expression, if only because of the unique setting in which it occurs. The very mission of a college or university depends upon broad latitude for viewpoints in the pursuit of truth and understanding. So of all places in society where people may express controversial views, should not the university campus be the most open and speech the freest?

The answer, curiously, is both yes and no—and for reasons that are equally central to the mission of higher education. The nature and status of campus speech offers an intriguing paradox. Many messages within the academy are indeed optimally protected. Professors, for example, enjoy a far greater freedom to speak and write and pursue research than their counterparts in business or even other professions. Yet in other situations, the very nature of academic discourse actually imposes higher standards than does the general community, with the result that some forms of campus speech may actually be less free than are comparable communications in the larger world.

It might be helpful to begin by examining several of those areas where campus speech is constrained in ways that go beyond the rules of society at large. Three specific interests come to mind and illustrate the paradox. Integrity in scholarship is the first such special interest, and it is central to the nature of academic communication and expression. So high are the standards of honesty and originality in scholarship that plagiarism may well be the most heinous of academic offenses. The misuse of someone else's research or even the failure adequately to acknowledge a debt to another scholar invites drastic sanctions with the universal support of the academic profession. Tenured professors can be, and have been, dismissed for proven acts of plagiarism, even if no harm resulted to the scholar whose work had been misappropriated.

The contrast is striking between the way the academic world views such acts and the standards of the larger society. "Plagiarism" does not exist as a civil cause of action, much less as a crime. The closest one comes under the general law is the battery of civil (and, in extremis, criminal) remedies for copyright infringement. Yet the standards for proof of infringement are far more stringent, requiring evidence not only of access but of copying as well. For example, much academic plagiarism—such as using the work of others, even without permission or proper attribution—would be deemed "fair use" and would thus not be actionable under the copyright laws. Only the most extreme forms of plagiarism would infringe copyright.

The differences between the two standards are thus quite striking. Yet this contrast reflects values that are central to the mission of the academic community. At the heart of condemnation of plagiarism is the scholar's special duty in the use and attribution of the scholarly work of others— an interest that goes far beyond the duties society imposes through copyright upon those who wish to use the intellectual achievements of others. Plagiarism is thus the most dramatic example of how special interests of the academic community restrict expression to a greater degree on campus than in the larger world.

A second, quite different example comes from the study of foreign languages and literature. If an instructor demands that students read assigned works in the original language and forbids them to consult English translations, violations of this rule surely warrant a grade reduction if not something more drastic. Obviously the general society imposes no comparable constraints; anywhere else, people who wish to read foreign works in translation are encouraged to do so. Yet the special academic rule that students stick to the original tongue reflects a unique set of interests in the study of foreign literature. Penalizing the use of ponies or trots makes perfect sense in the academy, though such a policy would be absurd off campus. Here, then, is a quite different but equally meaningful example of speech less generously treated within the academy.

A third example relates to the student honor system, a unique creature of the academic community. Under honor codes, students typically agree upon matriculation not to "lie, cheat, or steal." One who violates the code, even in a relatively minor way, risks dismissal or at least suspension. While such codes exist at many private universities, they are also found at such public campuses as the national service academies, the

University of Virginia, William & Mary, and others, mainly in the Southeast. Here again the contrast between the academy and the rest of society is marked: while "lying" may be morally reprehensible off campus, it is seldom an offense under the general law. There are specific, narrowly defined situations where speaking falsely may be penalized— for example, perjuring oneself by speaking falsely under oath or making false statements in an application for government benefits. Such untruths would readily trigger a campus honor code. But so would a host of other "lies" that violate no general civil or criminal laws.

Thus, in a quite dramatic way, the values inherent in certain campus communities impose on speech a higher standard than does society at large. The contrast reflects, quite simply, a special sense of integrity to which generations of students attending institutions with honor systems have pledged their adherence. There are, of course, some intriguing collateral issues—for example, how far such a commitment may serve to impose standards that might otherwise risk constitutional challenge. For now, it is enough to note that on some campuses "lying" may be treated far more harshly than anywhere else—and for reasons that are special to the academic community.

The other part of the paradox—situations where campus speech is more fully protected than in the outside world—may be more familiar. There is, of course, the special safeguard of academic freedom. Not only is there time-honored protection for what a professor says in the classroom; academic freedom may also extend to what professors say outside the classroom and to the speech of other members of the academic community, as we shall see in some detail in the chapters that follow. Academic freedom treats classroom speech as the core of protected expression for reasons that reflect the academy's unique pursuit of truth and understanding.

By reason of this core precept, certain expression that is integral to the teaching and learning process may be punishable off campus but not on campus. Academic freedom enjoys recognition not only in the policies of such organizations as the American Association of University Professors but from the courts as well. Two cases, which happen to involve the same state university many years apart, illustrate the special nature of academic speech.

Forty years ago the Supreme Court of the United States gave special protection to what a teacher says in the college classroom; the target happened to be a visiting lecturer at the University of New Hampshire, whose liberal political views (and specifically his lecture notes) became the focus of a McCarthy-era state attorney general. Chief Justice Earl Warren explained in this way the need for special solicitude:

> The essentiality of freedom in the community of American universities is almost self-evident. No one should underestimate the vital role in a democracy that is played by those who guide and train our youth. . . . Scholarship cannot flourish in an atmosphere of suspicion and distrust. Teachers and students must always remain free to inquire, to study and to evaluate, to gain new maturity and understanding, otherwise our civilization will stagnate and die.

In a concurring opinion Justice Felix Frankfurter (formerly a university professor) added his caution that "for society's good . . . inquiry . . . must be left as unfettered as possible" and that intrusion by external forces must be resisted whenever it "tends to check the ardor and fearlessness of scholars, qualities at once so fragile and so indispensable for fruitful academic labor."

More than three decades passed before the University of New Hampshire was again in court on such an issue—this time over a sexual harassment claim against a member of its faculty. Once again an academic freedom claim triumphed; university sanctions imposed on a professor because his classroom speech had upset some female students were set aside by a federal judge. Back pay and substantial damages were awarded, and the professor was reinstated. The university lost and lost badly, while the professor's classroom speech received a broad zone of protection.

Mention of academic freedom reminds us not only that campus speech and its treatment may differ from speech in the larger community but also that special factors within the academy may shape the scope of those differences. Not all speech that occurs on a college campus is equally entitled to such deference. Consider one case of professorial speech that has been recurrently troublesome to the academic community. Arthur Butz, an electrical engineering professor at Northwestern University, has for many years publicly proclaimed that the Holocaust never happened. He has repeatedly suggested in print and in speeches that six million Jews either suffered an epidemic or took their own lives during the late 1930s and early 1940s. Off-campus (and even internal) pressure to silence Butz has been intense since publication in the 1970s of his major book espousing Holocaust-denial theories. In the spring of 1996, this saga took a new twist: a national Jewish organization asked Northwestern to remove Holocaust-denial material Butz had posted digitally on his home page through the use of university computers.

Yet the university has steadfastly refused to seek Butz's dismissal, though it has felt no duty to favor him with promotion or unusual salary increments. Professorial statements of the Holocaust-denial kind, outrageous and shocking though they are to virtually all who read or hear them, fall within the parameters of academic freedom, if not of a citizen's right of free speech. If scholarly pursuit of knowledge is to be truly unfettered, society must be prepared to pay what may at times seem an exorbitant price by tolerating such extreme and provocative views. (Northwestern is a private university; it is thus not bound by the free speech guarantees of the Constitution. But as we shall see, the courts have addressed similar issues on public campuses and have reached similar conclusions.)

Butz thus continues, with impunity, to teach electrical engineering at Northwestern. Well and good for him, and for most other professors who may express comparably extreme views, on or off campus. But there may be limits to the scope of such protection even within the academic community. If a professor of English or politics or chemistry persistently declares that the earth is flat, such an aberrant view is protected by academic freedom as surely and fully as Butz's outlandish view about the Holocaust. But suppose the flat-earth adherent's academic field is, instead, geography. We might then have a quite different situation, in which even academic freedom may not completely shield the continued expression of such views. Even dismissal proceedings against a tenured professor would not be beyond contemplation.

What is the difference? For the geographer, unlike flat-earth proponents from other academic fields, academic freedom may not encompass statements that forcefully demonstrate incompetence in one's discipline. Therein lies an important implied exception to the scope of academic freedom and its protection for campus speech, even the speech of the professor and even—perhaps especially—in the college classroom (where the expectations of competence are of course paramount to the obligations of scholarship).

Let us return now to the case of Butz. Suppose that instead of electrical engineering, he has been hired to teach and study modern European history. We can and do tolerate a teacher of engineering who insists the Holocaust never happened. But would we treat with the same tolerance one whose expressed views on the Holocaust not only outraged alumni and donors but also conveyed to his own students a manifestly inaccurate version of the very subject he had been hired to teach? Of course, the times and places of his statements might affect the severity of the judgment; an offhand remark at a cocktail party would be far less egregious than a Holocaust-denial lecture to a required undergraduate history class.

At some point an institutional concern about competence would challenge the presumption of protection which academic freedom affords even the most extreme or provocative of professorial speech. Such a case—the Holocaust denier whose field is modern European history—would be more difficult than, and different from, the real Butz case, which already pushes academic freedom principles to the edge. We have no clear answers, because that most difficult of all cases has not arisen.

We do, however, have the first of several desiderata that may be generally helpful in defining the nature of campus speech. The subject matter of campus speech is occasionally pertinent, at least in relation to the speaker's assigned role within the academic community. The protections of academic freedom contain substantive limits reflecting those very values that justify exceptional tolerance for professorial speech in the first place. The geographer who insists the earth is flat and so instructs his students may forfeit the safeguards of academic freedom for flouting the very values on which a community of inquiry and scholarship depends. Subject matter is therefore relevant—highly relevant—in defining to this extent the scope of campus speech.

Several other factors may also offer useful guides. The location or place of campus speech has historically been meaningful. The classroom, as well as the laboratory, has always enjoyed a special status. Faculty offices, lounges, and similar locations may well be seen as extensions of the classroom. Yet there are many other campus sites where speech makes no greater claim to protection than would the same message off campus—the power plant, the dining-hall kitchen, the vehicle maintenance shop, and a host of other nonacademic places where the university connection is more incidental than meaningful. In between are hybrid sites—student lounges, athletic facilities, cafeterias, and other places where students sometimes extend classroom discussion but at other times engage in purely nonacademic discourse. Does it matter that such encounters physically take place on a college campus? Not always. Thus the role of place or location is partially but not universally helpful.

Moreover, the increasingly electronic nature of campus communication will diminish the role of the physical site. As more and more dialogue among faculty and between faculty and students takes place through e-mail and other digital media, the actual location of the speakers may become irrelevant. Even the concept of "classroom" may be sharply tested by the development not simply of courses that can be accessed instantaneously by computer anywhere in the world but also of entire degree programs. For the moment, "place" is still helpful in gauging the scope of campus speech—as long as we are prepared to revisit the issue a few years hence.

A third possibly helpful dimension is that of personal relationships. If one campus custodian verbally harasses or threatens another, the location of the exchange should make no difference; the measure of protection should be no more and no less than if the same encounter took place in a factory or an office building. Yet there are within the academic world other special relationships that may bear upon the scope of protection for expression. The student-teacher dynamic is probably most distinctive. Indeed, many professors and students probably believe that communications between them enjoy some type of privilege comparable to those between spouses or between lawyer and client or physician and patient. In the absence of special legislation conferring such a privilege—and none exists—student-professor communications, even of the most sensitive sort, are not legally privileged and thus are not exempt from discovery. Many years ago a justice of New York's highest court argued such a privilege should exist—the context was candid confessions of a student to a faculty adviser after a campus drug raid—but even he recognized the law did not provide such protection. In fact, as we shall see in the ensuing chapters, there are many situations in which relationships do have some bearing on the status of campus speech, though perhaps less visibly and dramatically than one might expect.

Finally, the nature of the institution itself may offer guidance in measuring campus expression. Private colleges and universities are by and large free to make speech as free (or as restricted) as they wish. Only in California, where the legislature recently stepped in to bar speech codes at secular private campuses, does the general law limit the ability of private institutions to decide how free speech ought to be. If, therefore, a church-related college wishes to impose higher standards on certain kinds of student speech (e.g., blasphemy, sacrilege), it is largely free to do so.

In the public sector, the Constitution fully applies. Campus policies are constrained by the Bill of Rights, specifically by the free speech and press clauses of the First Amendment. Thus, as we shall see, myriad restraints on campus speech have been struck down by courts because they abridged these constitutional freedoms. Campus codes addressed to racist, sexist, homophobic, and anti-Semitic statements have been repeatedly challenged and uniformly invalidated. What the courts have said in such cases may surprise many university presidents but provides a helpful conclusion here: while in some areas the standards governing campus speech differ from those of the larger community and may reflect distinctive interests of the academic community, in many other areas the standards are properly the same on as off campus. So it is with speech codes, among other types of campus expression.

In the chapters that follow, we begin with the subject of speech codes, not only because it has consistently been one of the liveliest of campus speech issues but also because it offers a valuable microcosm of many other topics. We turn in the second chapter to the equally basic subject of free speech and academic freedom for college and university faculty, drawing upon recent and notable cases of professors who have been outspoken on such sensitive matters as race and religion.

The third chapter addresses a host of rapidly emerging challenges in the electronic or digital world, as the computer becomes increasingly the medium of choice both for on-campus communications and for links between the academic community and the rest of the world. The off-campus speaker comes next, prompted by a rash of controversy attending the recent and usually unwelcome visits of Khalid Abdul Muhammad, a follower of Minister Louis Farrakhan. The fifth chapter examines a fascinating array of legal challenges to expressive activity by student organizations, from political protest to mandatory activities fees to racist fraternity skits.

The student press is the focus of the sixth chapter—what limits (if any) a university may set for regular student papers, the status of underground campus publications, and the recent rash of seizures of student newspapers containing controversial stories. The next subject is that of the arts on campus, an area that has been infrequently in the courts but has recently generated some intriguing disputes over the proper extent of artistic freedom in the academy.

The three concluding chapters address topics without which a book such as this one would not be complete. Since free expression clearly encompasses freedom in research, attention should be given to permissible limits on research activity, both by the institution and by the larger community. Religious expression on the public campus has been persistently troublesome and may become more so as the aspirations of student religious organizations intensify. Finally, though most of the legal issues affect public universities, the private campus is not immune from such concerns, as Stanford University recently learned when California lawmakers imposed First Amendment standards on private campus speech policies.

While many of these issues have been to court in recent times, few can be said to have been fully resolved. In each area, some of the most difficult issues remain surprisingly open. Those who guide and administer the nation's more than 3,000 institutions of higher learning face, almost daily, the daunting task of shaping policy and applying rules in ways that will best balance free speech and the needs of the campus community. It is this inescapable, eternal balancing process that makes so difficult and often painful the process which unfolds in these chapters. At the close of this study, we pause briefly to take stock of the current condition of campus expression.

FREE SPEECH
IN THE
COLLEGE COMMUNITY

I.

WHO NEEDS A SPEECH CODE?

Dr. Sarah Lamson, President
Covert College
Main Line, PA 19114

Dear Sally:

It sounds from your phone call over the weekend as though you're committed to having a speech code on your campus. If so, you'd be in good company. Stanford, Michigan, Penn, Wisconsin, Texas, and lots of other major universities have felt the same pressures and have reacted as you seem inclined to do. But there are two sides to the question, as I assume you realize from the fact you sought my views (knowing as you must how little enthusiasm I have for speech codes). Let me take advantage of your call by telling you more than you may really want to know on this subject—though not, I think, more than one *needs* to know if faced with the decision that now awaits you.

What I propose is to share with you a memo written recently by a senior member of our law faculty. She's more objective on this issue than I, and really looks hard at both sides of every question. What I asked her to do was give me a summary of the pros and cons on the speech code issue. But I also asked her to look at some of the reasons and pressures, since speech codes don't come out of a vacuum. She also agreed to look at alternatives that might achieve some of the same goals without raising quite so many difficult legal and policy problems.

While the memo that follows is entirely hers, she and I are generally in accord, at least on the main policy issues. We are also in complete agreement that what's done at Covert must be your decision and the faculty's and the board's, to which we may be able to contribute modestly, but which must in the end reflect your needs and realities and not those of any other institution.

Good luck, do the right thing, and keep us posted.

Very sincerely,
Samuel Stark

• • •

MEMORANDUM:
SOME THOUGHTS ON SPEECH CODES

Anyone who believes that campus speech codes reflect an artificial or imaginary condition are either ignorant or naive. There are, and have been for some time, very real and acute pressures upon American higher education, to which such codes offer a meaningful response. We need to understand those forces before we pass any kind of judgment on the codes themselves. We also need to ask whether speech codes are the only, or even the best, response. Then we need to explore alternatives that may be more appropriate for an academic institution, as well as being less risky or controversial. We begin, though, with the background conditions that have led so many colleges and universities—several hundred at least—to adopt speech codes and curbs in the past few years.

A. What Can a Speech Code Accomplish?

What is clearest about the impetus for campus speech codes is indisputably good motives. People who may differ sharply on the effect, legality, and even morality of such codes seldom disagree on the validity of the goals. Nor do knowledgeable observers disagree on the gravity of a condition that has widely affected higher education in the late 1980s and into the 1990s. In part the patterns are general and national.

When the Carnegie Foundation for the Advancement of Teaching surveyed university presidents for a study in the late 1980s entitled *Campus Tensions,* more than half the respondents noted that racial intimidation or harassment was a serious problem on their campuses. The National Institute Against Prejudice and Violence, which has the most detailed data base, cited at least 250 campuses at which acts of racial hatred occurred in the period 1986–89. The institute has elsewhere reported that one in five minority students encounters some form of physical or psychological racial harassment at least once a year.

There is some evidence that the national climate may be worsening. In the spring of 1993, the Anti-Defamation League of B'nai B'rith found that on certain statements (e.g., "blacks stick together more than others"), hostile views appear more often among people under age thirty than among those over fifty. Respondents in the middle-aged group seemed most tolerant. These data led one columnist to note with alarm: "A generation of bigots is coming of age."

The most powerful catalysts are, however, local campus events. The examples are legion. At the University of Wisconsin–Madison, it was the flaunting of a giant racist caricature to announce a forthcoming fraternity party. At Stanford, a few months later, it was the display of a Beethoven poster crudely defaced with stereotypic African features.

At another college it was the day African American students walked into a classroom to find that someone had written on the blackboard (in parody of the United Negro College Fund ad), "A mind is a terrible thing to waste, especially on a nigger."

At yet another campus it was the distribution of fliers to black students warning, "The Knights of the Ku Klux Klan Are Watching You." And so on through a truly sickening litany of racist, sexist, or homophobic slurs, caricatures, slights, even physical assaults.

At the University of Massachusetts–Amherst, which had resisted a speech code until late 1995 despite racial and ethnic tensions, it was apparently a cafeteria worker's use of an epithet in addressing a minority student that finally caused the Graduate Employee Organization to demand a code. Events at these and myriad other institutions across the country leave not the slightest doubt; anyone who disputes the existence of a persistent and substantial problem is simply blind to reality.

The critical issue is just how adopting a speech code might address— or redress—such conditions. Several hypotheses come to mind. For one, simply condemning racist, sexist, and homophobic statements may tend to reduce their incidence on campus. While we know that passing civil rights laws will not necessarily make bigots more tolerant, such laws undoubtedly deter or check the overt manifestations of bigotry.

Anecdotal or impressionistic data suggest that some positive effects may have occurred. University of Wisconsin–Madison officials reported initial improvement in the racial climate after the code was adopted, at least to the degree that racism became subtler. Stanford officials took some comfort from the fact that the speech code, once on the books, never actually needed to be invoked. So, at the very least, officially *banning* racist speech may succeed in *reducing* racist speech—though, as we shall see later, the overall record is quite mixed.

Whatever the impact on the insensitive speaker, speech codes may also benefit the victim of campus hate speech. Indeed, even if one assumed that banning slurs and epithets was a futile exercise, a case might still be made for such a ban to protect and vindicate vulnerable individuals. It is that goal of protecting victims of which University of Hawaii professor Mari Matsuda has written:

> Students who support universities through tuition and who are encouraged to think of the university as their home are involuntarily forced into a position of complicity with racism when their campus is offered to hate groups as a forum.

Such policies may also serve important symbolic functions. Simply adopting a code goes far to dispel any inference of institutional indifference or insensitivity. Such action at least puts the university on record as formally opposed to racism, sexism, and homophobia. Wisconsin's dean of students, Mary K. Rouse, wrote of her university's speech rule:

> By defining the limits of the University's tolerance, we can set a standard of conduct for the community. A disciplinary rule can be published and explained in orientation sessions for new students. In addition, such a rule helps define the legal edge of the University's ability to use disciplinary action in response to harassing speech, and makes clear that we must use nondisciplinary means to respond to most incidents of demeaning or insensitive conduct.

In a similar vein, University of Michigan law professor Catherine MacKinnon, a longtime proponent of codes, argues that the critical value of such policies is the evidence they offer of "the University choosing to side *with* the relatively disadvantaged and *for* equality. . . ." Those who hold this view insist that colleges and universities cannot simply be neutral. Doing nothing, in other words, is tacitly taking sides. By declining to adopt rules that curb ethnically demeaning speech, ostensibly neutral institutions are said to permit, and thus effectively condone, racism, sexism, anti-Semitism, and the like. If the institution remains persistently aloof from the conflict, continues the argument, it does not merely permit such attitudes to find expression but endows the views that embody those values with a kind of imprimatur; implicit in the perception of such offensive and demeaning speech is knowledge that the institution had the authority and capacity to intervene but consciously chose not to do so.

Even where such detachment may reflect the best of motives—concern for free expression, for example—speech code proponents argue that the institution has unavoidably put its prestige and authority on the wrong side of the ledger and has thus made prejudice (or at least its overt manifestation) more acceptable and respectable. The institution, the argument runs, "must issue unequivocal expressions of solidarity with vulnerable minority groups and make positive statements affirming its commitment to those ideals. Laws prohibiting racist speech must be regarded as important components of such expressions and statements."

Third, such rules may have more than simply symbolic value. They may also bear directly on the educational mission for which the university holds a core responsibility. Matsuda has written:

> The negative effects of hate messages are real and immediate for the victim. Victims of vicious hate propaganda have experienced physiological symptoms and emotional distress ranging from fear in the gut, rapid pulse rate and difficulty in breathing, nightmares, post-traumatic stress disorder, hypertension, psychosis, and suicide.

Such effects may quite naturally impede the learning process in ways for which the institution bears direct responsibility. The link has been well described by University of California–Berkeley law professor Robert Post, a sympathetic observer though not himself a code proponent:

> Racist expression interferes with education not merely because of general harms that it may inflict on groups or individuals or the marketplace of ideas, but also, and more intrinsically, because racist expression exemplifies conduct that is contrary to the particular educational values that specific colleges or universities seek to instill.

Not surprisingly, many of the recent speech codes reflect a direct link between restrictions imposed on racist or otherwise abusive language and the learning process, seeking to justify the ban mainly on educational grounds.

There is a quite different dimension, also educational. Racist epithets, slurs, and insults seem most remote, among all uses of language, from the rational discourse to which a university is devoted. Universities deal, first and foremost, in ideas. Yet, as the Supreme Court said of slurs and epithets over a half century ago in the course of holding that states might punish "fighting words,"

> Such utterances are no essential part of any exposition of ideas, and are of such slight social value as a step to truth that any benefit that may be derived from them is clearly outweighed by the social interest in order and morality.

Thus for the academic community to ban only those utterances that are at or beyond the outer limit of reason and logic and make no contribution to rational discourse might seem an appropriate way of preserving on campus the best values of academic dialogue, while at the same time serving other values of which we spoke earlier.

Finally, a practical motive, laudable as well, underlies some campus speech codes. The 1980s witnessed extraordinary efforts to achieve and to maintain modest increases in minority enrollments. The gains were at best fragile, especially during a time of dwindling federal financial aid for needy students. The competition among institutions became intense, not only in terms of financial support and academic program but quite as much in terms of campus climate and cultural environment. One publicized incident of racism—even one for which the institution bore no culpability (for example, a raid by a group of local vigilantes)—could erase the benefit of years of painstaking efforts to win confidence and commitment in the minority community.

Conversely, clear evidence of institutional concern—such as a strong speech code—might have more powerful appeal than improved aid packages or other tangible steps. The importance of such environmental factors was especially clear in enabling predominantly white institutions to compete effectively against the congenial and predictable climate of historically black colleges. This analysis should make clear that campus speech codes did not develop in a vacuum. They emerged from, and at times reflected, an urgent response to conditions that have been troubling not only to higher education but to the nation as a whole. Few institutions evinced any enthusiasm about curbing campus speech. Some administrators, with a sense of resignation, opted for a code as a response of last resort, a step to be taken only when lesser measures had failed either to sustain civility or to satisfy indignant victims of racism and other forms of bias. Yet adopt codes they did, and in numbers so substantial that the process of doing so must be viewed as one of the most significant developments in American higher education during the final decades of the twentieth century.

The case in favor of speech codes assumes many forms and may be stated in myriad ways. A particularly thoughtful formulation of the case came in a letter from a New York City attorney to the *New York Times* late in 1995. Entering the lively debate over the proposed University of Massachusetts code, E. David Hyland offered this perspective:

> What many speech code advocates are seeking is simple: a way of enlisting a whole community in creating an environment where people are not attacked and injured on the basis of their identity. While speech codes do not appear to be the answer, we must examine the roots of our prejudice and find ways of teaching each other to live without resorting to the kind of corrosive speech that hides underneath the "free exchange of ideas" umbrella.

B. Codes: How Does an Institution Get One?

Just as the arguments in favor of speech codes assume many forms, the resulting restraints on offensive campus speech also come in varied sizes and shapes. During the decade of active code-making, three basic models emerged. In broad outline, they are the fighting words approach, the emotional distress theory, and the nondiscrimination/harassment option. The most comprehensive survey of speech codes, conducted by the Freedom Forum First Amendment Center in 1993 and replicated in the spring of 1996, identified a wide array of campus policies that may reach racially and otherwise offensive speech—directed, for example, against threats of violence, hazing, harassment, libel, obscenity, disruption, and breach of the peace. Many such policies long predated the current fascination with speech codes and were adapted to meet newer concerns. Our focus here is not with the myriad policies and rules that could conceivably be brought to bear on offensive expression, but rather with those codes that came into being in the late 1980s and early 1990s in direct response to pressures and forces of the type we have just surveyed.

It is for that reason we concentrate here on the three types of speech-targeted policies that were most widely in favor during this critical period.

Banning certain deeply offensive epithets or phrases as "fighting words" has respectable legal support. Over a half-century ago, the United States Supreme Court unanimously sustained the conviction of a religious activist who had insulted a New Hampshire policeman with language so intemperate and provocative it seemed likely to incite to immediate violence. Under those conditions, said the court, states and cities might treat such language as "fighting words," beyond the protections of the First Amendment.

Though later cases have reached different results—the high court has not sustained a fighting words conviction since the 1942 case—lower courts have continued to apply the doctrine to genuine incitement and provocation. When it came time to draft campus speech bans, the fighting words theory offered a plausible precedent. Following this precedent, the University of California late in 1989 adopted a policy which would treat as student misconduct

> the use of "fighting words" by students to harass any person(s) on University property, on other property to which those policies apply . . . or in connection with official University functions or University-sponsored programs.

"Fighting words" were defined as

> those personally abusive epithets which, when directly addressed to any ordinary person are, in the context used and as a matter of common knowledge, inherently likely to provoke a violent reaction whether or not they actually do so.

The scope of taboo language includes but is not limited to "derogatory references to race, ethnicity, religion, sex, sexual orientation, disability, and other personal characteristics." The policy adds that fighting words constitute harassment

> when the circumstances of their utterance create a hostile and intimidating environment which the student uttering them should reasonably know will interfere with the victim's ability to pursue effectively his or her education or otherwise to participate fully in University programs and activities.

In sharp contrast to the California approach is one taken about the same time by the University of Texas at Austin. A settled principle of tort law allows one person to recover damages from another for the "intentional infliction of emotional distress." The classic case is the sadist or joker who sends a telegram announcing the death of a close relative, which the recipient believes, and suffers a heart attack. If the sender of the telegram is sued and damages are sought, courts have never been deterred by the fact that "speech" is involved. While the heart attack case is clearly the most appealing, recovery has been allowed for truly reckless communications even without proof of direct physical harm.

This precedent seemed helpful to the faculty committee charged with seeking a policy at Texas. The rule they designed, and the administration adopted, made it a university offense to

> engage in racial harassment of any student, whether the harassment takes place on or off the campus. Racial harassment is defined as extreme or outrageous acts or communications that are intended to harass, intimidate or humiliate a student or students on account of race, color or national origin and that reasonably cause them to suffer severe emotional distress.

Several differences between these two policies deserve comment. Whereas the California rule reaches a broad range of protected groups, the Texas policy addresses only issues of race, color, and national origin. Even more important, the Texas rule requires proof of two elements that might or might not be present in a California case—intent to humiliate or harass and proof that some harm has in fact resulted. In California, one may be punished for words that are "likely to provoke a violent reaction, whether or not they actually do so." In Texas, by contrast, there must be actual proof that the words did "cause [the victim] to suffer severe emotional distress," though the harm need not have been physical.

The issue of intent reflects another important difference. Under the Texas rule the actor must have *meant* to harass or intimidate the victim. In California, a misguided joke might trigger the policy; it is enough that the actor "should reasonably know" of the probable effects, whether or not such effects were intended. These differences are not simply cosmetic or stylistic. They may, in fact, have constitutional import, since the California policy could well reach kinds of speech that Texas (and the courts) would view as protected.

The third approach is the one most commonly used by universities wishing to ban racist and other demeaning speech. Its focus is on discrimination or harassment, whether or not the speech code is technically an extension (as it often is) of the general equal opportunity or nondiscrimination policies. Michigan's approach (eventually struck down by a federal court) was fairly typical. The policy adopted by the Michigan regents in late 1988 carried the title "Discrimination and Discriminatory Harassment by Students in the University Environment." The preamble linked this new speech policy to earlier provisions that banned racial and other forms of bias on the Ann Arbor campus. The proscribed acts and comments were identified throughout as indicia of discrimination. The guidelines that explained the new rule cited "discriminatory behavior" as the sole rationale.

Stanford's approach (also later invalidated by a court) may have been a bit subtler but was philosophically similar. The university's policy against "discriminatory harassment" proscribed expression if it

> is intended to insult or stigmatize an individual or a small number of individuals on the basis of their sex, race, color, handicap, religion, sexual orientation, or national origin; and . . . is addressed directly to the individual or individuals whom it insults or stigmatizes [by "fighting" words or nonverbal symbols].

Again, the key element—not simply as a jurisdictional talisman but as the real focus of institutional concern—was speech or conduct that discriminates against vulnerable members of the campus community. It was rising concern for the welfare of these persons that evoked the institutional response and undoubtedly shaped the nature of the response.

A more recent code, proposed in the fall of 1995 by the University of Massachusetts Graduate Employee Organization, also turns on harassment. Beyond "threat and intimidation," harassment may be either verbal or physical conduct "that a reasonable person, with the same characteristics as the targeted individual or group . . . would find discriminatorily alters the conditions under which [he or she] . . . participates in the activities of the University, on the basis of race, color, national original or ethnic origin. . . ." The policy adds that

> verbal conduct may include, but is not limited to, epithets, slurs, negative stereotyping, threatening language, or written or graphic material that serves to harass an individual or group of individuals.

This policy would apply to all members of the campus community (except visitors, such as off-campus speakers) and would clearly reach in-class as well as extracurricular speech. Its breadth and scope suggest the degree to which a term such as *harassment* is capable of reaching whatever expression the drafters of the code feel must be reached.

While other patterns have been used, most speech codes reflect one of the three models outlined here. Some policies combine approaches, much as Stanford focused chiefly on discrimination but added a passing reference to fighting words and even included a hint of emotional distress (though without Texas's demand for proof of intent and harm). The variations are not without significance, both in testing the policy and in defining its scope. Yet the underlying common elements and goals transcend such differences.

C. What's Wrong with a Speech Code?

The drafting of campus speech codes brought forth the best and the worst from the U.S. academic community. Some of the early policies were quite simply overzealous. Witness, for example, the infamous University of Connecticut rule (struck down by a federal court) which listed as examples of forbidden harassment

> use of derogatory names, inappropriately directed laughter, inconsiderate jokes, anonymous notes or phone calls, and conspicuous exclusion from conversations and/or classroom discussions . . .

If few speech codes were quite so bold as Connecticut's in seeking to reach otherwise protected speech, many were simply vague and open-ended in ways that invited creativity on the part of deans and disciplinary committees. Take the University of Pennsylvania as a case in point. Many Americans wondered in the late spring of 1993 how a Penn undergraduate could have been charged under the speech code for having shouted "water buffalo" toward a group of African American young women outside his dorm window. The code may not hold the complete answer, but it does help. Penn's policy (later narrowed) had been one of the broadest. It simply forbade "any behavior . . . that stigmatizes or victimizes." The premise of the charge seems to have been that calling anyone a "water buffalo," while invoking the proximity of the Philadelphia Zoo, might well "stigmatize or victimize," if that is all one need prove. In the end, the charge was dropped, though only after national ridicule nearly derailed the nomination of Penn's president, Sheldon Hackney, to head the National Endowment for the Humanities.

Penn is hardly alone in falling short of precision. Nearby Haverford College adopted a rule that broadly proscribed many types of discrimination, then added with remarkable candor, "precise criteria for identifying discrimination or harassment are hard to establish." Iowa State University defines harassment or hazing as "any act which intimidates, annoys, alarms, embarrasses, ridicules, or produces psychological or physical discomfort." Harvard's policy makes the definition of forbidden harassment largely subjective, since "the experience of racial harassment may not be so clear-cut and can thus be confusing and disorienting." The task of definition is inherently and inescapably difficult.

Even the best of legal minds have been humbled by a drafting assignment which, in fact, many universities did entrust to their ablest scholars of constitutional law. Moreover, some institutions seem to have abandoned the quest for certainty in part because key terms such as *harassment* lacked sufficient consensus or common understanding. Other institutions, feeling an urgent need to act, did the best they could with this daunting task. The issue before us now is whether that best was good enough, either in law or in policy.

A starting point may be to assess the effect of such policies. Opinions differ on the degree to which codes actually succeed in reducing racist and ethnically demeaning expression. Intensive study at the University of Wisconsin–Madison, for example, found modest correlation between enactment of the code and a period of diminished hostile behavior and expression—though leaving open the question of causality. There seems to be no reliable evidence of the extent to which an improved campus climate can be traced or credited to the enactment of a speech code.

There is, moreover, some tentative evidence of two negative phenomena. One is the rise in expectations that may occur among protected groups after adoption of a speech code but that may be largely unrequited if enhanced civility does not soon follow. Thus, even if racial conditions do not deteriorate, there may be a sense of lost momentum among vulnerable groups in the absence of marked improvement.

Even more serious, there is substantial risk of backlash among those at whom speech codes are directed. Such policies may not only fail to change attitudes for the better; they may actually stiffen the resistance of hard-core racists, sexists, and anti-Semites. Dr. Thomas Jennings, in a recent and exhaustive study of three institutions, found some such evidence at Stanford. He reports:

> Some students perceived a backlash against "progressive" opinions among a large segment of the University community, and they linked the political correctness debate with the adoption of [the Stanford speech code]. In other words, some "progressive" black students believed that following the adoption of [the code], "conservative" students at the University were empowered to speak out more during a time when it became fashionable (nationally and locally) to criticize political correctness. Some black students believed that racial relations had not changed as a result of [the code], and that relations might have grown more tense and more separate. A black administrator believed that the adoption of [the code] helped galvanize the more conservative political members of campus to speak out about their concerns.

Speech codes could become counterproductive in two other ironic ways. American Civil Liberties Union (ACLU) president Nadine Strossen has warned that laws against racist speech can create a discretion in their use that makes the intended beneficiaries of such laws "likely targets of punishment"—a phenomenon that actually occurred under the British Race Relations Act during the 1960s. The other downside risk is one of which Strossen also warns—that "censorship measures often have the effect of glorifying racist speakers" to the extent that "racist speakers may appear as martyrs or even heroes." Thus, there is a genuine danger that speech codes may not simply fall short of a laudable goal but in fact may even undermine that goal.

Backlash or not, risks on both sides inhere in taking a highly visible course of action, especially in response to expressed needs and feelings of vulnerable campus groups. The dilemma is acute: If the university adopts a speech code but conditions do not improve (or actually deteriorate), the institution may experience rising and frustrated expectations. If, on the other hand, the university declines to act and race relations deteriorate, it will also be faulted for failing to take the one step that many may believe would have helped.

Under either scenario, little would be gained by arguing (whatever the record would show) that taking the other course would have been no better and might even have been worse. Perhaps all that can be said is that one ought not to embrace a speech code with any certainty of perceptible impact or tangible results. And proponents may well concede that results are not the central goal in any event.

Apart from results, there are other risks of interpretation. Consider a few of the improbable, almost certainly unintended, situations to which some codes have been applied. Among the first cases filed at the Madison campus under the University of Wisconsin's code (all eventually dismissed) were the complaint of a white student that he had been called a "redneck" by another white during a student senate debate and complaints against a campus newspaper for running a cartoon that allegedly offended Christians.

Perhaps the most poignant example of misdirection involved a white dental student at the University of Michigan. He attended the orientation session of a preclinical class that was widely viewed as one of the hardest courses in the second-year program. After the class broke into small groups, he said that "he'd heard that minorities had a difficult time in the course and that he had heard they were not treated fairly." The professor in charge, a minority person, filed a complaint against the student under the speech code. She claimed the comment was unfair and might jeopardize her chances for tenure. The student was unavailing in his plea that he was sympathetic and was only trying to be helpful. After being "counseled" about the existence of the code, he agreed to write a letter apologizing for making such a statement without adequately verifying the allegation (which he said he had heard from his roommate, a black former dental student).

Such experiences do incalculable harm and go far to dispel two claims that code proponents make—first, that such rules are really aimed at the dormitory and the lockerroom and thus need not affect the learning process; and second, that the speech likeliest to be curbed is largely devoid of content or idea. Several of the Michigan cases show how easily rules designed to deal with extracurricular speech may spill over into the classroom. Quite apart from the fact that no campus code seems to have been so limited in its scope, the process of application is almost certain to follow provocative language wherever that language occurs—with classrooms, libraries, and laboratories inevitable sites of controversy.

The proponents' other premise—that hate speech involves no idea or viewpoint—seems even more tenuous. Ideas or beliefs are in fact central to the use of most slurs, epithets, and the like. If there were no message, there would be no threat; we would simply laugh and walk on. The very source of our concern—the reason victims of such language are so deeply hurt and offended—is that ideas of the most pernicious sort are involved, and are intended to be conveyed. Like many challenging and provocative ideas, they are potentially dangerous. Thus it will simply not do to dismiss speech codes as though they were unconcerned with thoughts or ideas or values. There is a fundamental difference between hateful thought and mindless hate. Speech codes cannot address one without reaching the other.

One might now observe that such matters as language, scope, effectiveness, etc., are relatively trivial and miss the main issues. Fair enough. Two basic concerns about what's wrong with speech codes remain to be addressed—the one, that they may abridge free speech and thus violate the Constitution; the other, that lawful or not, they are simply measures inappropriate for a university. The two issues are of course interrelated. Each deserves distinct treatment.

The constitutionality of speech codes remains a matter of debate, though such policies have fared poorly in the courts. The starting point is that all public colleges and universities are bound by the First Amendment. That means they must tolerate much speaking and writing that may not be pleasing to many of their students, faculty, alumni, trustees, and others. Case after case has reaffirmed this principle with regard to student protest, campus newspapers, radical student groups, and outspoken faculty. While private campuses are not directly governed by the Bill of Rights, many pride themselves on observing standards of expression at least as high as those their public counterparts must meet. Thus the guiding principle for virtually all institutions of higher learning is that free speech must be protected, even when the speech for which freedom is sought may be offensive or disruptive or at variance with the campus mission.

Speech code proponents do not simply repudiate the First Amendment or claim a blanket exemption from the Bill of Rights. There are, as we noted earlier, some solid and seemingly supportive precedents. Not only had the Supreme Court in 1942 upheld a fighting words conviction. A decade later the justices sustained state "group libel" laws aimed at racist propaganda and at the groups that disseminated it. (These laws, in fact, had been passed right after World War II largely at the urging of a young law professor, later the eminent sociologist David Reisman. His goal was to arm governments in this country to resist any repetition of the Nazi propaganda that had paralyzed European governments a decade before.)

By the 1980s, there were major signs of change in the courts. Racists in white sheets had successfully challenged many local bans against the Ku Klux Klan and other hate groups. When the American Nazi Party sought to march through the heavily Jewish Chicago suburb of Skokie and city officials denied them a permit, the Nazis (aided by the ACLU) found relief in both state and federal courts. Then at the end of the decade, the Supreme Court twice struck down flag-burning laws because they made criminal the expression of unpopular ideas. So when the testing of campus speech codes began, resort to the old cases was already tenuous. Immediate court challenges were almost certain, given the intense controversy that preceded board action at the major institutions. Those challenges did in fact occur and by the early 1990s had cast substantial clouds over all such codes, at least on public campuses.

There have been at least five cases. One, brought against the University of Connecticut to challenge the "inappropriate laughter" policy, brought an unreported judgment against the code. The three reported federal cases all arose in the Midwest, against the University of Michigan, the University of Wisconsin, and Central Michigan University. They can be treated as a group on the basis of shared constitutional issues. In the fall of 1989, a federal judge in Detroit held simply that the Michigan regents had abridged freedom of speech. The judge looked well beyond the terms of the code in concluding that the policy reached constitutionally protected speech. Especially revealing was the code's accompanying guide, which told students "you are a harasser when . . . you laugh at a joke about someone in your class who stutters" or when "you comment in a derogatory way about a particular person or group's physical appearance . . . or their cultural origins. . . ." This document persuaded the court that "the drafters of the policy intended that speech need only be offensive to be sanctionable." (The judge was assured the guide had been withdrawn before the case came to trial, though no public announcement had ever been made to that effect.)

The key to this judgment was evidence that the Michigan policy had been applied to speech which clearly would have been protected off campus. Notable (along with the case of the sympathetic white dental student described earlier) was the experience of a social work graduate student who expressed in class his belief that homosexuality was a disease for which a counseling program should be fashioned. The student was charged under the code with harassment on ground of sex and sexual orientation. A formal hearing was held. The hearing panel found the student guilty of sexual harassment but not of harassment on the basis of sexual orientation. Despite the partial acquittal, the judge had heard enough:

> The fact remains that the . . . authoritative voice of the University on these matters . . . saw no First Amendment problem in forcing the student to a hearing to answer for allegedly harassing statements made in the course of academic discussion and research.

Several other cases, including that of the white dental student, reinforced the judge's conviction that the policy was overly broad because "the University considered serious comments in the context of classroom discussion to be sanctionable under the policy." The university administration's own consistent reading of the policy thus confirmed its excessive reach.

One such judgment would have been nearly fatal to the speech code movement. This court went on, however, to find the policy unacceptably vague; "looking at the plain language of the policy," he concluded, "it was simply impossible to discern any limitation on its scope or any conceptual distinction between protected and unprotected conduct."

Distinct though they are, these two grounds clearly reinforced one another, as is often the case in free-speech litigation. (A simple example may illustrate the difference between vagueness and overbreadth. If a city passes a law that no one may say "hell," "damn," "God," or "Christ" within the city limits, that is quite precise and thus not at all vague. It is, however, clearly overly broad because it bans much speech that is fully protected. If the same city forbade "all speech that is not protected by the First Amendment," by definition the law could not be overly broad. Yet it would be intolerably vague; even experienced constitutional lawyers could not tell with confidence what could and could not be said within the city limits. Thus vagueness and overbreadth are analytically quite different concepts, even though they often accompany and reinforce one another, as in the Michigan speech code case.)

On to Wisconsin. Some months after the Michigan case, another suit was filed in federal court there, alleging that the regents' speech code was similarly unconstitutional. The emphasis in Wisconsin was much more on the "fighting words" rationale for curbing campus speech; the university had insisted the policy was covered by the old Supreme Court case. But the judge disagreed, since "the rule regulates discriminatory speech whether or not it is likely to provoke a [violent] response . . . [and] covers a substantial number of situations where no breach of the peace is likely to result." Thus the fighting words doctrine offered little support to code drafters. Any attempt to validate the code through balancing of interests seemed pointless; to this judge, balancing would be allowed only with respect to laws that were neutral toward the content of speech. That could hardly be said of the Wisconsin (or any other) speech code, the essence of which is to single out for harsher treatment a particular kind of message. Whether the message is hateful does not matter; the point is simply that speech codes limit expression on the basis of the message and are inescapably content-based.

The Wisconsin federal judge addressed another issue that has been persistently troublesome. Proponents of speech codes often claim that racist epithets and slurs claim no First Amendment protection because they convey no ideas. The court responded:

> Most students punished under the rule are likely to have employed comments, epithets or other expressive behavior to inform their listeners of their racist or discriminatory views. In addition, nothing in the . . . rule prevents it from regulating speech which is intended to convince the listener of the speaker's discriminatory position. Accordingly, the rule may cover a substantial number of situations where students are attempting to convince their listeners of their positions.

Finally, there was again the issue of vagueness. The Wisconsin judge reached a conclusion similar to that reached in the Michigan case:

> The UW rule is unduly vague because it is ambiguous as to whether the regulated speech must actually demean the listener and create an intimidating, hostile or demeaning environment for education or whether the speaker must merely intend to demean the listener and create such an environment.

The inherent ambiguity was compounded by the varied approaches that different campuses adopted, and by the contrast between the code's provisions and the examples that accompanied its publication. The judge acknowledged he could have resolved the ambiguity by going one way or the other—but that was a task for regents and lawmakers, not for federal courts.

Two more recent chapters involve quite dissimilar institutions. At Central Michigan University, the men's basketball coach was discharged for using the word *nigger* in lockerroom exhortation of his mostly black team. He went to federal court, challenging both his dismissal and the validity of the university's "discriminatory harassment" policy. The judge found key provisions of the policy unacceptably vague. He had special disdain for the ban on "any behavior . . . [either] verbal or nonverbal behavior . . . intentional or unintentional . . . [that] subject[s] an individual to an intimidating, hostile or offensive . . . environment. . . ." This policy was no clearer than the University of Michigan code which the same court had struck down a couple of years earlier, and fared no better.

The coach's victory turned out to be Pyrrhic. His discharge was eventually upheld on general public employee speech grounds. The court ruled that his use of a racial epithet, even for hortatory purposes, and even acceptably to some of his black players, did not enjoy First Amendment protection apart from the unconstitutional policy the university had invoked. So in the end the coach won the speech code battle but lost the employment war for reasons that always lurk behind such a case.

Of the three reported federal cases, the one from Central Michigan was the only one to reach a higher court. In the summer of 1995, the appeals court upheld the district judge on both counts. The code, said the appeals court, was fatally flawed because it "reaches a substantial amount of constitutionally protected speech. . . . [Its] language . . . is sweeping and seemingly drafted to include as much and as many types of conduct as possible." The university was, however, within its rights to fire a coach for bad judgment rather than bad language. The court concluded:

> The First Amendment protects the right to espouse the view that a "nigger" is someone who is aggressive in nature, tough, loud, abrasive, hard-nosed . . . at home on the court but out of place in a classroom setting. . . . What the First Amendment does not do, however, is require the government as employer or the university as educator to accept this view as a means of motivating players.

Meanwhile, a quite different kind of case was taking shape at Stanford University, site of one of the most widely touted codes. Stanford's code— though never enforced—drew so much criticism during its drafting that the California legislature adopted a law, the so-called Leonard law, holding nonsectarian private colleges and universities to the same student free speech standards as California's public campuses. Since Stanford's code had been the primary impetus for the law, it was hardly surprising that Stanford became its first battleground. A state judge struck down the code, applying First Amendment precepts as the law prescribed. In the spring of 1995, the Stanford administration decided not to appeal, however much it disagreed with the ruling, and the Stanford code passed into history.

Meanwhile, the pertinent principles of law off campus were also changing. About the time the Wisconsin case came down, the U.S. Supreme Court took a case testing the constitutionality of a city ordinance that banned, among other symbolic displays, racially motivated cross burnings. To the surprise of many observers, the justices were unanimous in striking down the law, albeit on two quite different theories. Four justices would have set it aside on vagueness principles very much like those we saw in the speech code cases.

The majority, however, broke new ground. For them the key flaw was the law's focus on content or message or viewpoint, even within an area of speech (fighting words) that could have been curbed even without regard to content. The city could have banned the burning of all materials, including crosses, but could not selectively ban only those cross burnings that were prompted by racial bias or animus. That was viewpoint discrimination, which now for the first time ran afoul of the First Amendment even in the context of otherwise unprotected speech.

This decision seemed to sound the death knell for most campus speech codes. The University of Wisconsin regents, who were struggling to repair or revive their code after losing in federal court, abandoned the effort in September. On a close vote, with vigorous dissent, the regents accepted the advice of their attorney that even a revised code might well abridge free speech. Other institutions also read a clear message, that few codes drawn along such lines could survive the Supreme Court's broader First Amendment ruling. Many colleges and universities either repealed speech codes or allowed them to languish.

A few universities, still committed to such efforts, sought to adapt to the changing law. Michigan continued for some time trying to revise its code, though placing greater emphasis on conduct and not speech. Rutgers, which had adopted one of the strongest codes, now limited the reach of the policy to speech that could be criminally punished under state law. But most of the codes were either given a decent burial by formal action or were allowed to expire quietly and unnoticed.

A canvas of the law brings us to the final and in many ways the most compelling objection to speech codes. Apart from legality and practicality, growing numbers of observers ask whether a university has any business banning certain messages. Of course there are limits on campus speech. If a student cheats on an exam or plagiarizes a paper and is threatened with dismissal, there will be little point in reminding the dean or committee that the act involved speech. Or if a student in a foreign language course gets a lower grade because a forbidden English translation of the major work has been used during a test, there is little solicitude for the student's undoubted right in any other context to read freely. In these and other situations, much like criminal conspiracies and solicitations under the general law, speech is being punished—but clearly not because of its message or viewpoint. Such easy cases do not help much in addressing the far harder question of curbing racist, sexist, and ethnically demeaning campus speech.

The central premise behind most speech codes is that certain messages are so harmful or so at variance with the goals of higher education that they do not belong on a college campus. Senior members of the academic community have heard this argument before. In the 1950s it took two ominous forms. One related to communist or "fellow traveler" professors whose views were said to be so dangerous and so antithetical to free and open inquiry that their presence on the faculty and in the classroom could no longer be tolerated. Sadly, some of the nation's preeminent universities acceded to such pressures and dismissed politically unorthodox scholars, sometimes on the pretext that they had refused to cooperate with legislative committees, but at heart because of their "dangerous" or "inimical" views.

During the same period, the nation encountered the issue in a quite different form. Some states adopted speaker bans, the effect of which was to bar communists and others of suspect views from appearing on public campuses in these states. Repealing such laws, even after they had outlived their usefulness, was politically risky. Only occasionally could judges be persuaded to set them aside on free speech grounds. Most persuasive was an argument that has been surprisingly little used in the speech code context: if a university bars one idea or viewpoint from the campus, it implicitly endorses all others. The only safe way to avoid such an inference of approval is to bar nothing and thus endorse nothing. So it is with speech codes: if the university is in the business of excluding or punishing certain messages or viewpoints, it is difficult to avoid implying that everything else has been officially approved. And such an imprimatur is precisely what U.S. universities have sought to avoid—at least since Thomas Jefferson established a university where error is permitted "so long as reason is free to pursue it . . ."

There is, moreover, a certain arrogance in assuming the capacity to determine what is "right" and what is "wrong" for campus consumption. Former Harvard president Derek Bok, a vigorous and consistent critic of such rules, asked:

> Whom will we trust to censor communications and decide which ones are "too offensive" or "too inflammatory" or too devoid of intellectual content? . . . As a former President of the University of California once said: "The University is not engaged in making ideas safe for students. It is engaged in making students safe for ideas."

There is a fundamental dissonance between controlling words and the very nature of a university as a place of free inquiry. Consider carefully the sort of example a college or university sets for its students by declaring officially that certain thoughts or viewpoints—however hateful and repugnant—are off-limits on its campus. Efforts to excise or punish abhorrent views imply that the normal modes of academic discourse—reason and persuasion—have failed, so that prohibition becomes by default the only viable option. The 1992 statement of Committee A of the American Association of University Professors, *On Freedom of Expression and Campus Speech Codes,* captures the point well:

> By proscribing any ideas, a university sets an example that profoundly disserves its academic mission. . . . [A] college or university sets a perilous course if it seeks to differentiate between high-value and low-value speech, or to choose which groups are to be protected by curbing the speech of others. A speech code unavoidably implies an institutional

competence to distinguish permissible expression of hateful thought from what is to be proscribed as thoughtless hate.

D. What Else Can Be Done?

If speech codes won't work or will cause more problems than they solve, what are the alternatives? Several quite different approaches deserve careful consideration by those who are truly committed to making college and university campuses more civil and hospitable places.

For starters, institutions can often be far more creative in using *nonspeech* rules. Many of the incidents to which speech codes have been applied might well have been addressed under such policies. If a racist or homophobe defaces a bulletin board with a swastika or spray paints "nigger" or "faggot" on a campus building, redress should not depend upon a speech code. If a university meeting is disrupted or a student is physically barred from entering the meeting, the viewpoint or bias of the disrupters should not be the measure of the institution's capacity to act. In fact, most of the speech-code targets that deserve to be punished can be reached through rules that do not bear directly on speech. And most incidents for which a speech code is said to be needed because they involve expression, not behavior, are probably not punishable. Thus the AAUP Committee A statement urged that "institutions should adopt and invoke a range of measures that penalize conduct and behavior, rather than speech. . . ."

Second, certain limited kinds of expression can be reached by policies which do mention speech but are narrower than speech codes. Sexual harassment is a prime example. Harassment may be verbal as well as physical, and there are perils in dealing with harassment that involves words alone. But courts and agencies have fashioned a substantial body of law for doing just that in the industrial workplace. Colleges and universities too are workplaces, where harassment (at least in the non-academic areas) should be as fully proscribed as would be the case in an office or factory.

Dealing with harassment in the academic context is far more sensitive and difficult, and really needs a volume of its own. AAUP and other groups are currently seeking to reconcile their views on freedom of speech or academic freedom on one hand and freedom from verbal as well as physical harassment on the other. The task will take some time and requires sensitive hands.

One other type of expression may be reached, on or off campus, without conceding too much to the censors. The American Civil Liberties Union, a staunch opponent of speech codes, has issued a policy statement insisting on maximum freedom for thought and expression. But the statement leaves room for "disciplinary codes aimed at restricting acts of harassment, intimidation and invasion of privacy." Illustrations are found in two of the statement's crucial footnotes:

> Threatening phone calls to a minority student's dormitory room, for example, would be proscribable conduct under the terms of this policy. Expressive behavior which has no other effect than to create an unpleasant learning environment, however, would not be a proper subject of regulation. . . . Intimidating telephone calls, threats of attack, extortion and blackmail are unprotected forms of conduct which include an element of verbal or written expression.

The point is quite simply that not all use of words, on campus or anywhere else, claims protection as free speech. The exceptions should be just that—exceptions to a general rule of protection. They should reflect familiar nonspeech university interests. They must be very narrowly defined and clearly proscribed. The procedures used for application and enforcement must avoid sweeping too broadly. Such policies as these need not and should not become backdoor speech codes.

Apart from rules and regulations, a university can take many steps to combat racism, sexism, and homophobia. At the very least, trustees and senior administrators can and should speak out promptly and boldly when incidents occur, making clear to the campus community that such expression is not compatible with the values of the institution. They might declare certain norms or standards—perhaps even in the form of a code, though without sanctions that would raise free speech concerns. The AAUP Committee A statement is helpful:

> The governing board and the administration have a special duty not only to set an outstanding example of tolerance, but also to challenge boldly and condemn immediately serious breaches of civility.

Stronger statements than these may be in order. Calling the use of epithets and slurs "totally unacceptable" or saying they "have no place on this campus" is not so coercive as to threaten anyone's freedom of speech. And of course, as we noted earlier, wherever a nonspeech rule has been broken by conduct such as spray-painting, defacement of property, or disruption of university events, there is no reason to be slow or shy about throwing the book at any offenders who can be apprehended. Speaking out is helpful, at the very least, and may lead to other measures.

Beyond the administration and board, groups like the faculty senate, staff council, and student government can play crucial roles in setting the tone of campus discourse. Their impact may ultimately be greater than that of deans, presidents, and trustees. Making clear that slurs and epithets are unacceptable to peers may go far, not only in deterring repetition but also in reassuring victims that someone else cares.

There is limited experience with a vastly different approach to reducing racist speech. Catharsis has been the approach for many years at Pomona College in southern California. Two decades ago students began scrawling emotional graffiti on a gray cinderblock wall. The college then gave this wall some cachet as the moral equivalent of London's Hyde Park corner. Students and others brought to the wall their passions and prejudices; for many years the ability freely to post racist and sexist and homophobic views in this form seemed to lessen face-to-face insults. Anyone who feared offense or insult could simply avoid reading the latest epithets. But new concerns arose in the spring of 1995. The proximity and intensity of the O. J. Simpson trial brought to the wall a new level of racial virulence, causing the administration to wonder for the first time whether the free speech wall could survive. A faculty-student committee explored the situation and created a committee to examine the wall and chart its future. Whatever its fate, the existence of such a forum for two decades seemed to have brought catharsis to at least one private college campus. It is an approach deserving of wider attention than it appears to have received.

In the end, institutions will almost certainly need to take active and visible roles in times of tension and animus. Above all, universities should approach racism, homophobia, sexism, and anti-Semitism through what they do best—education. Special programs and even courses may be developed with an eye to increasing intergroup understanding across campuses. Such educational efforts may even be made mandatory—certainly for groups like dormitory resident assistants and student personnel professionals who are on the front lines. Incoming freshmen might well be expected to read certain books that would aid understanding and tolerance, then to take part in discussions on key issues where insight is most needed—the horror of the Holocaust, current medical views of homosexuality, residual gender bias, historic genocide of Native American tribes, the brutality of slavery, and so on through a list that some might term "politically correct" but that would offer an invaluable supplement to each student's experience.

Beyond students, the question of mandating such exposure for others is more sensitive. As in any large work setting, nonacademic staffs might well be exposed to mandatory programs that enhance sensitivity. Graduate teaching assistants, who are both students and faculty, might be expected to take part in some such programs—not only because they are still learning about teaching but also because they are so close to undergraduates in so many curricular and co-curricular roles.

The roles and responsibilities of senior faculty members are inevitably more sensitive and complex. Perhaps it would be enough to offer programs on an optional basis, through teaching resource centers, and to encourage but not require senior professors to take part. For the moment, that may be as far as institutions ought to carry their educational responsibilities.

Finally, myriad policies and programs may enhance the institutional climate in other ways. Efforts to intensify the recruitment and support of minority and women students, with special attention to areas of most acute underrepresentation, offer a natural goal. Appointment to senior administrative roles of persons from vulnerable groups obviously conveys a crucial message of welcome and support. Special programs and facilities—an African American cultural center, a women's resource center, special places and programs for Hispanic and Asian students and others—all represent vital signs of hospitality and cordiality.

However much our most conscientious institutions may do along these lines, changing racist and sexist and anti-Semitic and homophobic views (and their expression) takes time. The process is gradual and painful. Many thoughtful people believe speech codes may help. Others believe with equal conviction that speech codes not only are not helpful but may hurt. At most, they are only part of a much larger and exceedingly complex academic environment.

II.

THE OUTSPOKEN UNIVERSITY PROFESSOR

A professor of philosophy who is Jewish writes in a magazine article that blacks have been less successful in school than whites—not because of racial bias but because "the average black is significantly less intelligent than the average white." A faculty colleague on the same campus who is African American charges at a state-sponsored arts festival that there has been "a conspiracy, planned and plotted and programmed out of Hollywood, where . . . Russian Jewry had a particular control over the movies, and their financial partners, the Mafia, put together a system of destruction of black people."

A senior professor of electrical engineering at a midwestern private university insists that the Holocaust never happened. He attributes the death of millions of Jews in Europe during the 1930s and 1940s to illness and suicide. An African American professor at an eastern state university tells his students he sees Zionism as one prime example of "reactive racism," his other example being Nazism.

A male professor of English at an eastern state university tells a magazine interviewer that sex between faculty and students may occasionally be beneficial to the student. "I'm talking about a female student," he explains, "who for one reason or another had unnaturally prolonged her virginity."

A senior anthropology professor at a state university on the West Coast tells undergraduate students in an introductory course that women have smaller brains than men and that gay men prefer jobs with women supervisors.

A teacher of German at a midwestern state campus shows his class a film about a homosexual schoolteacher in Berlin that includes male and female nudity and a scene in which one man urinates on another.

A lecturer in computer science at a California private university boasts that he carries illegal drugs to campus in his backpack, though he insists he does not use them while on campus.

• • •

Such cases, though highly visible, are remarkably rare on the academic scene in the United States, especially in a profession noted for holding and expressing strong views. These recent events cover the gamut—all parts of the country, all types of institutions, a variety of academic disciplines, in and out of class, and on issues ranging from sex to race to drugs to religion. Such cases attract attention far beyond their frequency, in part because they provide lively material for the media as well as for more specialized journals that cater to academic audiences. Such professorial pronouncements pose serious problems, both for the individual and for the institution. Indeed, in several of the cases just cited, public condemnation went as far as the governor of the state. Reprisal followed in each instance, testing basic principles of academic freedom.

We should hardly be surprised to find a few professors saying outrageous things. University teachers have a high propensity to speak out, sometimes boldly, on the most pressing issues of the day. Indeed, society expects its academic experts to hold strong views on current issues and to share these views with others. We would be deeply disappointed and would feel cheated if the professoriate remained silent on major issues. The fact is that most outspoken professors evoke little concern, and their comments are simply taken in stride. Yet there are times, as in the cases just cited, when professorial comments seem to cross the line of tolerable discourse.

While the examples noted here all occurred in the 1990s, the issue has deep roots. Even as the topics of controversy have varied over time, tension between professorial speech and societal values and norms goes back well over a century. In this century, the public views for which scholars were faulted consistently reflect the most divisive issues of the day—economic theory and the role of organized labor in the first third of the century, communism and the Cold War in the next third or so, giving way in the 1960s to the Vietnam War and racial justice issues that inflamed so many campuses and so deeply aroused much of the academic community.

Since the 1960s, the issues have been more eclectic, as the group of cases with which we began would suggest. Race, gender, sexual orientation, and religion seem to dominate the current caseload. There is no evidence that professors speak more freely today on such matters than was the case a decade or more ago; indeed, faculty are today probably more sensitive and more likely to restrain such comments. But the world in which they live and teach, both on and off campus, seems to have raised its expectations for professorial restraint.

What makes such cases difficult is the elusive line that must be drawn between protected and unprotected expression. Two separate systems shape this judgment. All college and university teachers are protected by principles of academic freedom, the dimensions of which we will explore shortly. In addition, the speech of those who teach in state institutions is protected by the First Amendment. Under both systems of protection, there are easy cases on one side or the other. Increasingly, however, both college administrators and courts have been troubled by the hard cases in between—cases in which professorial speech may offend or outrage or may seem utterly irresponsible to most observers but does not for that reason forfeit the protections of academic freedom and the First Amendment. Cases like those with which we began have pushed the safeguards of professorial speech to the limit. At the same time, the resolution of such cases offers guidance both to individuals and to institutions. The results are not always comfortable—though one would hardly expect comfort in a real world fraught with controversy.

Over the years, the academic profession has shaped for itself certain standards to govern professorial speech. There are certain clear cases at the extremes that define the spectrum; such clarity also helps to answer critics who charge that professors may never be disciplined, whatever they say or do. Plagiarism, for example, obviously involves expression. But this fact would give no comfort to a professor caught misappropriating the intellectual effort of another and publishing it as his own. (In its most extreme form, infringement of copyright supports not only civil damages but criminal penalties as well.)

Fraud or misrepresentation in science offers another example of professorial speech that is clearly subject to sanctions. The investigator who knowingly biases an experiment or deliberately reports false or misleading data from the laboratory merits universal condemnation and incurs severe sanctions within and beyond the academic community.

Here too the fact that speech is involved affords the malefactor no refuge or defense. So too the professor who uses words to foment a criminal conspiracy or to incite others to violence fares no better by reason of academic freedom than does any other citizen in trouble with the law. Of course the standards applied by the university are not identical to those of the general legal system; sometimes they are higher, while at other times they may be lower. The actual sanction a university deems appropriate will vary not only with the gravity of the offense but also with such factors as the offender's academic discipline. Not every violation of the general law bears equally upon every professor's fitness to teach. We would, for example, have far less tolerance for a convicted forger who teaches commercial law or legal ethics than for one whose field is English or physics. Even an offense that would be overlooked on the part of most professors—driving under the influence, for example—would have to be taken extremely seriously if the offender's field was driver and safety education or substance abuse. So it is with speech-related offenses; the extent to which an off-campus law violation should have consequences on campus requires a careful analysis of such factors and interests as these. Blanket formulas do not help.

We turn next to particular standards that govern professorial speech on controversial issues. Policies which the profession has shaped for itself offer helpful guidance, even if they do not answer all the hard cases. The American Association of University Professors more than a half-century ago (1940) adopted its basic Statement on Academic Freedom and Tenure. This statement has now been endorsed by over 150 national academic and professional organizations. Countless colleges and universities have by governing board action made it part of their own policies. As the cornerstone of a professor's right to speak and teach without fear of external or artificial constraint, this statement explicitly recognized the complex nature of scholars' roles in the larger community:

> When [faculty members] speak or write as citizens, they should be free from institutional censorship or discipline, but their special position in the community imposes special obligations. As scholars and educational officers, they should remember that the public may judge their profession and their institution by their utterances. Hence they should at all times be accurate, should exercise appropriate restraint, should show respect for the opinions of others, and should make every effort to indicate that they are not speaking for their institutions.

A corollary statement appeared later that year, co-sponsored by the Association of American Colleges. This document recognized that a university administration or board might

> feel that a teacher has not observed the admonitions [quoted above] and . . . that the extramural utterances of the teacher have been such as to raise grave doubts concerning the teacher's fitness for his or her position . . .

in which case charges might be filed in accordance with the association's policies on procedural due process and fairness.

A quarter-century later, after the trauma of the McCarthy era, with the academic community still haunted by memories of professors who had become political casualties because of what they had written or which groups they had joined or even whom they knew, AAUP revisited the issue and refined its standards. In a new statement directed expressly to off-campus speech ("Extramural Utterances"), the association reaffirmed the need for rigorous procedures in any formal inquiry into professorial speech. The 1964 statement added as a "controlling principle" that

> a faculty member's expression of opinion as a citizen cannot constitute grounds for dismissal unless it clearly demonstrates the faculty member's unfitness to serve.

This statement cautions, almost as an afterthought, that "extramural utterances rarely bear upon a faculty member's fitness for continuing service." Though it has never been the role of AAUP statements to offer examples or illustrations—preferring instead the refinement of policy over time through cases and investigative reports—this is one area in which such guidance might have been welcome.

The rub comes in applying such general precepts to individual, often complex, and difficult situations. In each of the cases we noted at the outset, critics within and beyond the academic community questioned the "fitness for continuing service" of the outspoken instructor. It may now be helpful to look more closely at several of these cases. Let us begin with Michael Levin, the Jewish philosopher who ventured so freely on the link between race and intelligence. He had been a member of the faculty of the City College of New York since 1969 and had held tenure for more than fifteen years at the time of the incident in question. He had never sought to impose on his own students any controversial views about race and intelligence.

It was, rather, in print—and in a range of publications, including letters to the *New York Times*—that Levin's provocative views appeared. What touched off the firestorm was a book review in a relatively obscure Australian magazine. It was there that Levin ventured the view that blacks had achieved less in education not because they were victims of racial bias or economic detriment but because "the average black is less intelligent than the average white." On this basis Levin sought, for example, to explain the undeniable underrepresentation of African Americans in the learned professions and in scholarly fields such as his own.

Response to news of this review, on and off campus, was angry and intense. The City College Faculty Senate adopted a resolution condemning Levin's views on race and intelligence. Hundreds of students, faculty colleagues, and staff members signed a petition, which soon appeared in the college newspaper, expressing their dismay about Levin's published views. African American state and city officials demanded City College take action at once.

The administration did respond. The college president, Bernard Harleston, a black psychologist, initially asked the Faculty Senate to appoint a special committee to "receive, investigate, and make recommendations concerning any charges of bias related activities" on the part of faculty members, specifically naming Levin as a possible target. Despite its earlier resolution of condemnation, the Senate now declined to investigate. When the president renewed his request several months later, the Senate again refused to act, its chairman warning that to convene such an inquiry might have a "chilling effect."

With off-campus political pressure continuing to mount, Harleston felt he had no choice but to investigate on his own. He constituted an ad hoc committee, which he charged to examine Levin's writings in the context of "review[ing] the question of when speech both inside and outside the classroom may go beyond the protection of academic freedom or become conduct unbecoming a member of the faculty, or some other form of misconduct." In announcing the creation of this body, Harleston added a comment which may have been inadvertent but was later to haunt him and fellow administrators in the months that followed:

> the process of removing a tenured professor is a complicated one. . . .
> Tenure is the life blood of the College. [Levin's] views are offensive to the

basic values of human equality and decency and simply have no place here at City College.

After deliberating for nearly nine months, the committee reported its tentative conclusion that Levin's writings might have had a detrimental effect on his classes. But before any action could be taken pursuant to this finding, the internal process ground to a halt when Levin filed suit in federal court against the college and its president. He claimed that the creation of the ad hoc committee and its charge, among other factors, denied rights of free speech that were guaranteed by the Constitution.

Levin's lawsuit addressed two other concerns. One was the creation of so-called shadow sections in introductory philosophy. After Levin's writings had become a cause célèbre on campus, Dean Paul Sherwin of the Humanities Division asked the philosophy chairman to assign someone else to teach Levin's basic course. The chairman adamantly refused. Such a request, he protested, was "immoral, illegal, and an unwarranted interference in the discretionary powers of a department chairman." The dean then took matters into his own hands. Before the next semester began, he wrote to every student enrolled in Levin's basic course. The dean's letter cautioned that students might be, or might become, aware that Levin had "expressed controversial views." Should any students wish to transfer out, the dean now offered them a new section, created for just that purpose—an option that eleven students eventually chose. (In the letter to the students, Sherwin reaffirmed a level of confidence he had earlier expressed in Levin as "an able classroom teacher who is fair in his evaluation of students.")

Levin's third charge in the federal lawsuit was that the City College administration had failed to protect the decorum of his classes. Several of his lectures had been disrupted, he had received occasional death threats, and he was periodically the target of anti-Semitic slurs and remarks. Materials posted on his office door had several times been set afire. On one occasion a group of twenty demonstrators invaded Levin's classroom, armed with a bullhorn, chanting and shouting; the class had to be terminated. Thus there was reason for apprehension. Yet the president and others insisted they had done all that was humanly possible to ensure peace on a volatile campus, and specifically to safeguard Levin's teaching. Levin remained dissatisfied and sought damages for what he claimed was inadequate security.

A nonjury trial in the federal district court brought complete vindication for Levin on all three counts. A sympathetic judge addressed each of the issues. He saw the case as symptomatic of a far larger problem, so he took this occasion to link Levin's plight with national trends:

> This case raises serious constitutional questions that go to the heart of the current national debate on what has come to be denominated as "political correctness" in speech and thought on the campuses of the nation's colleges and universities.

The judge then addressed each of Levin's specific claims. The inquiry targeted to his writings, in the absence of any conduct likely to support major sanctions, inevitably stigmatized Levin within the academic community. So selective a focus on the published views of a professor also abridged his freedom of speech because it was "admittedly predicated solely upon his protected First Amendment expression of ideas."

The creation of the "shadow sections," the judge ruled, was also constitutionally flawed. There was no claim that Levin had ever, in class, made any possibly demeaning comments about race and intelligence. No students had ever complained or sought to transfer out of Levin's courses. Thus the effect of sending students a letter like Sherwin's was not only to raise doubts and create a stigma—quite likely reducing Levin's enrollments—but also to "officially [condemn] his ideas as controversial and dangerous to the welfare of his students and the educational process in the College at large. . . ."

Finally, the judge sided with Levin on the issue of classroom security. The failure to provide better protection for Levin's classes effectively curtailed his right to teach, almost as surely as though the administration had itself barred the doorway. In the end, the judge concluded, City College officials had created (and tolerated) a chilling effect on Levin's free speech and academic freedom, because of "and in retaliation for Professor Levin's First Amendment expression of ideas."

City College and President Harleston appealed. Levin's case was now buttressed by outside support in the form of a friend-of-the-court brief of the American Association of University Professors and several civil liberties groups. The brief found no need to take sides on Levin's views about race and intelligence. Nor did these groups speculate on other issues we will address later—whether, for example, an administrator can publicly condemn a professor's controversial views or can offer other options to students who have come forward to complain of in-class comments. What made Levin's case relatively easy for AAUP and others who came to his aid was the zeal of the CCNY administration— launching an investigation when the Senate declined to do so, creating shadow sections before a single student had complained, and publicly declaring that Levin's views "simply have no place here at City College."

As Levin's case reached the appeals court, it recalled another dispute on which this panel had recently ruled—the case of Professor Ernest Dube, a black psychologist who had equated Zionism and Nazism as forms of racism during a class at the State University of New York at Stony Brook. After he had been denied tenure, Dube filed suit in federal court, claiming that public outrage and pressure over his one comment had led SUNY administrators to deny him the promotion he would otherwise have attained. Public outrage there had been, in abundance. When New York governor Mario Cuomo heard about the flap, he issued a statement condemning "the failure of the University community to denounce Dr. Dube." The local Jewish community and a prominent legislator brought intense pressure on the campus administration to take corrective steps. The president did issue a statement distancing himself from Dube's views. The issue of tenure came up soon thereafter. The lower levels of the academic review process were sharply split, though slightly favorable. But the dean, the provost, and the president concluded, on the basis of Dube's rather meager publication record, that tenure was not warranted. The action was appealed to the state university system administration in Albany, which upheld the tenure denial.

Dube then took his case to federal court, where he claimed that his constitutional rights (including free speech) had been abridged. The trial judge refused to dismiss the suit, and the university appealed. The appeals court (which would soon hear Levin's case) dealt largely with procedural matters, but did address in passing the substantive issue of Dube's speech. In fact the free speech issue was not easy to reach. Dube had not really claimed he was denied tenure in retaliation for his controversial views. Rather, his focus was the public and external pressure, from the governor on down, which he claimed had forced the administration to capitulate at his expense. This theory, the court noted, was harder to prove and afforded a weaker basis for a constitutional claim. Even so, the appeals court felt a jury might find in Dube's favor on the "public pressure" issue and might therefore conclude he had been denied tenure "as a result of the controversy surrounding his teaching." This apparent victory turned out to be Pyrrhic for another essentially procedural reason: Dube had failed to show that he had a legally protectable interest in gaining tenure, so the case was sent back to the trial judge to address several remaining issues.

When Levin's case reached the same appeals court, the free speech issue was much readier for review. The ruling of the lower court was also cleaner; a trial judge had found fully in Levin's favor on all the substantive issues, quite unlike the preliminary procedural rulings from which Dube's appeal arose. Yet the *substantive* parallels were striking. After careful study of Levin's case, the court of appeals agreed on all counts with the trial judge that constitutional rights had indeed been abridged. On the shadow section issue, for example, the reviewing court seemed even more upset, noting that for a dean to invite students to leave a teacher's class "if he does not mend his extracurricular ways is the antithesis of freedom of expression." The targeted inquiry also troubled the appeals court, since the coupling of this inquiry with so much as a hint of loss of tenure created the kind of chill against which the First Amendment protects, even without formal sanctions.

When it came to granting relief, however, the higher court felt there was no need to issue an injunction against the college (as the trial judge had done) because the administration had threatened no further action. A declaratory judgment—a vindication of the plaintiff and a word to the wise—should suffice. Thus the case ended in the federal courts. Meanwhile, President Harleston had announced his intention to retire.

Harleston was not, however, to be permitted to leave office peacefully. As though in ironic confirmation of both parties' fears on the security issue, an inexplicable lack of police presence turned a late December rock concert at the City College gymnasium into a burial vault for nine young people from the adjacent community. That the year should end with the worst campus tragedy since the shootings at Kent State and Jackson State two decades earlier underscored the hazards of university administration, especially on such issues as security and safety.

Meanwhile, across the City College campus, the even more portentous saga of Professor Leonard Jeffries was unfolding. The parallels were uncanny. Levin and Jeffries were both Columbia University graduates who had been on the CCNY faculty for many years, and both were securely tenured. Both were uncommonly controversial, and both became objects of official City College action because of the public expression of highly provocative views about race. And in the end, both sought redress from the federal courts. But there the parallels end.

Leonard Jeffries, unlike Michael Levin, also held an administrative post. For several years he had chaired the college's African Studies Department. In 1984, while interviewing finalists for the directorship of international studies, he was quoted as asking one candidate, "Why does a Jew boy like you want to come to teach at this campus?" As a consultant to a state curriculum design project Jeffries had expressed avowedly Afrocentric views that some felt were disparaging to whites.

But it was the Empire State Black Arts and Cultural Festival, in the summer of 1991, that brought Jeffries and his views on ethnicity to national prominence. The speech he made there contained offhand jibes at prominent educators with whom Jeffries disagreed. He called historian Diane Ravitch "a sophisticated Texas Jew" and repeatedly caricatured her as "Miss Daisy." He accused Arthur Schlesinger, Jr. (who had resigned from the curriculum committee and whom Jeffries mistakenly believed to be Jewish), of participating in a Jewish plan to derail multiculturalism.

The core of the speech concerned the film industry, in which Jeffries found evidence of a need for more teaching about Afro-American culture in order to counteract neglect and stereotyping. He depicted for his audience

> a conspiracy, planned and plotted and programmed out of Hollywood by people called Greenberg and Weisberg and Trigliani. . . . Russian Jewry had a particular control over the movies . . . and their financial partners, the Mafia, put together a financial system of destruction of black people.

Reaction to the speech was immediate and intense. Governor Cuomo, then a leading prospect for the 1992 Democratic presidential nomination, exploded: Jeffries's statements seemed to him "so egregious that the City University ought to take action or explain why it doesn't." The next day a press aide muted the criticism but left no doubt about Cuomo's deep displeasure. New York senator Daniel Patrick Moynihan was only slightly less indignant: Jeffries, he urged, "ought to resign. If he does not, the trustees should."

Meanwhile, a prominent Bronx legislator urged his colleagues in the State Assembly to adopt a resolution that would bring about Jeffries's removal from the faculty. The executive director of the New York State Civil Rights Coalition (himself an African American) publicly lamented that Jeffries had not been rebuked earlier for his anti-Semitic and other offensive statements.

Jeffries, meanwhile, claiming there was a "media assassination of myself," was not without vocal support. Several widely publicized rallies took place soon after the Albany speech. One such gathering drew thousands of Jeffries's partisans to plead his cause in the press and in the public forum. Groups that had sponsored the cultural festival and thus provided the platform distanced themselves from the merits of his views on race and ethnicity but reaffirmed their belief in his right to express such views without fear of official reprisal.

Meanwhile, back in Manhattan on a campus already deeply divided by the Levin issue, the news from Albany was hardly welcome. A City College faculty committee had already taken Jeffries to task for public espousal of what he claimed to be black racial superiority. Calling such comments "outrageous and possibly offensive," this faculty group had stopped short of recommending disciplinary action, apparently hoping its admonition to an errant colleague would bring moderation. Clearly that hope had been misplaced.

President Harleston was now in an acutely uncomfortable spot. As an African American who had already taken Levin to task, he must be sensitive to parity, real and perceived. Thus he needed to respond, and he did so within a few days of the Albany festival. While deploring statements made by faculty or students that "undermine another racial or ethnic group," Harleston cautioned that "the college must ensure the right of its faculty and students to express their ideas without fear of institutional censorship." Some days later he added an important caveat obviously aimed at the increasingly volatile Jeffries case: "The right to free expression, and, indeed, to academic freedom, is not and cannot be absolute."

The Faculty Senate seemed readier to address the Jeffries issues than it had been to take on Levin. The Senate Executive Committee reviewed the Albany lecture and, like the earlier faculty group, confessed its discomfort about the views expressed there—but urged that no disciplinary action be taken. The full Senate took up the issue later in the fall and reached a similarly ambivalent conclusion. Jeffries was invited to, and did, address the Senate in his own behalf. After some deliberation, this body declared that it "disavowed and rejected" Jeffries's views on race and related matters. But it declined to recommend any formal sanction or censure.

Once again the campus administration was left to take its own course, and did so. When his colleagues in African studies voted to extend Jeffries's term as chairman for an additional three years, the administration cut the term to eight months. This step served notice of official concern about and displeasure with Jeffries, at least in his administrative role. The other shoe would soon fall. In the spring of 1992, the City University Board voted unanimously to replace Jeffries with a recently retired chair of African American studies at Yale. The new chair was given substantial latitude to develop graduate programs and to bring in more faculty members from other disciplines.

Perhaps inspired by Levin's experience as a plaintiff, Jeffries also went to federal court in search of redress. His claim was that the board's action to remove (or not continue) him as department chairman reflected solely the public outcry over his Albany speech and other extramural statements that had been similarly controversial. There was one vital difference between the two cases: whereas Levin had sought only injunctive and declaratory relief, Jeffries went much further and asked for damages of $25 million as well.

If the federal courts had been cordial to Levin's claims, they were positively effusive to Jeffries. The trial took three weeks, before a jury presided over by the same judge who, without a jury, had a few months earlier ruled in Levin's favor. Throughout the trial, Jeffries's lawyers maintained that the sole cause of his demotion had been the Albany speech. The complete videotape of the speech, more than an hour in length, was played for the jury. The college's lawyers sought to minimize, even to isolate, the impact of the speech. They stressed instead the aftermath and effect of the events in Albany (of which there was ample evidence), suggesting that the uproar had left Jeffries unable to guide his academic unit effectively.

Indeed, City College's attorney claimed that during the evaluation of Jeffries's qualifications to continue as chairman, officials were told they must not rely on the infamous speech; "everybody made clear," the lawyer recalled, "that the speech could have no part in the deliberation at all." In closing arguments, City College insisted the proximity in time between the Albany speech and the decision to seek a new chairman was pure coincidence, since officials had for some time harbored doubts about his competence and simply chose to act at that time.

Judge and jury were both understandably skeptical. As he sent them out, the judge told jurors that to find in Jeffries's favor, they must be persuaded that the Albany speech was a "substantial motivating factor" in the trustees' adverse action. That, apparently, was just what jury members were ready to find. They returned a verdict in two parts. First, they found that six named City College officials, including President Harleston, were legally responsible for depriving Jeffries of federally protected freedom of speech—that, in other words, they had decided to remove him from the chairmanship in retaliation for the views he had expressed publicly at the festival.

A few weeks later, the jury went on to assess damages, in an almost unprecedented vindication of an aggrieved professor. A total award of $400,000 included $80,000 against each of four City University trustees, $50,000 against the chancellor of the citywide CUNY system, and $30,000 against President Harleston. The dollar amount, while far short of the $25 million that Jeffries had sought, left no doubt of the jury's belief that the college had erred and that Jeffries had suffered in ways that deserved monetary redress.

One other shoe was yet to fall. The issue of Jeffries's status as program chairman remained in abeyance, though the college had assumed the position was open and had brought in a temporary chairman during the trial. But the federal judge believed that only the reinstatement of Jeffries would fully vindicate his rights. The judge cast a plague on both houses. Jeffries, he conceded, had made "hateful, poisonous and reprehensible statements" and had behaved in a "thuggish" way. But the college's actions had deprived him of constitutional rights that could only be redressed by complete restoration of the status quo. Moreover, the judge faulted the CCNY lawyers for a "dishonest" and perhaps even "cowardly" presentation of the case. In fact, the judge suggested that Jeffries could have been ousted from the chair by showing dereliction or even harm to the program. Instead, the college and its attorneys had, the judge believed, been "dishonest about their motivation." Thus, as a new school year opened, Jeffries seemed to have been fully vindicated, and the college appeared to have lost everything. Yet, as the *Washington Post* observed in an editorial captioned "Pity His Students," "The losers, aside from CCNY, are serious students of Mr. Jeffries's ostensible subject who are now stuck with Mr. Jeffries."

It did not, however, turn out quite that way. The legal system sometimes follows tortuous paths. There was still one court left, and City College pressed its appeal to this highest level. Late in 1994, the Supreme Court reversed, relying on a case it had recently decided involving an Illinois public health nurse. What the court said there it now applied to Jeffries: actions against disruptive public workers are not to be judged solely in hindsight but rather by giving administrators on the spot the benefit of the doubt. So the Jeffries case returned to the federal appeals court in a quite different posture. This court set aside its earlier judgment and dismissed all Jeffries's claims. City College now proclaimed "total and complete vindication." As the academic year ended the following June, Jeffries left the office from which he had effectively been removed, though he promised to press his quest for redress. The Supreme Court's refusal to rehear the case, however, closed a saga that had perplexed the academic community for nearly five years.

The Jeffries case had not quite yet run its course. The Black Studies Department had been under review for some time—and apparently for reasons that transcended concerns about the activities of its flamboyant leader. Thus, after the litigation had run its course, a new City College administration decided in the winter of 1996 that the time had come to downgrade the department to program status, a step which would result in modest financial savings. Other academic units had been closed, consolidated, or transformed. While some critics characterized the black studies action as a subterfuge to reduce the potential for future embarrassment, there was little likelihood it would be challenged in court. As the academic year ended, Jeffries and several of his colleagues protested to the media but faced the inevitable dismantling of what had once been so volatile and visible a department.

In the end, it is fair to ask what the Jeffries case means. As AAUP senior staff counsel Ann Franke observed, none of the courts really addressed the central issue—whether a reasonable fear of on-campus disruption, following an inflammatory off-campus speech, "justifies silencing an outspoken faculty member." The first round might suggest an affirmative answer; the second round implies the opposite. But the facts becloud any assessment of the merits. For one thing, the stakes were lower than in most such cases. There had never been any threat to Jeffries's academic status or tenure. The sole issue was his administrative role as department chair, a rotating assignment which is typically held for periods of three to five years, may or may not be renewed for a variety of reasons, and may even be terminated by the administration or the governing board (though often with some requirement of a hearing or other formal process).

The other difference lies in the scope of relief. Aggrieved faculty members usually seek reinstatement, sometimes accompanied by a declaration that they were wrongly treated and perhaps recovery of what the challenged action directly cost them in monetary terms. Jeffries's claim and the jury's award went well beyond any out-of-pocket losses; the amount he would have earned as chair, even in perpetuity, would have been but a small fraction of the generous award. There is one other factor that may deter extrapolation: *Jeffries* went far beyond institutional fault, imposing heavy personal liability and damages on six named officials. Personal damage awards against college and university officials are not unknown, but they are quite rare. In the dollar range of the Jeffries award, they are virtually unheard of.

We now move from race to what may be the most troublesome professorial speech issue of the 1990s—sexual harassment. The classic case is that of Professor Donald Silva of the University of New Hampshire. The case came to rest late in 1994 when the university reinstated the professor, reimbursed all his legal costs and awarded a substantial settlement—after a campus committee had found him guilty of harassment and sanctions had been imposed. The case began when several female students complained that Silva had used sexually suggestive (and offensive) analogies in his writing classes—e.g., focused exposition is like the sex act, and creativity resembles the gyrations of a belly dancer. After a faculty-student committee sustained the harassment charges, Silva was suspended and ordered to seek counseling at his own expense. He refused to do so and went instead to federal court. The judge found all the issues in his favor—both because the university's procedures were seriously flawed and because the evidence did not warrant sanctions for what Silva was reputed to have said in or out of class.

While the Silva case has attracted the most attention, it is not unique. Chicago theologian Graydon Snyder was charged with harassment about the same time for using in class (as he had done for years) a Talmudic tale in which a roofer is blown off a roof and falls on a woman, with whom he accidentally has sex. When a student complained about the use of this parable, Snyder was summoned before a hearing panel, which recommended probation and required him to seek counseling. The panel also had letters sent to every student and faculty member reporting that Snyder had been disciplined and describing the circumstances. Snyder sued in state court, but without success.

Meanwhile, the federal courts in California reviewed the case of another male instructor charged with harassment. Professor Dean Cohen had taught English for many years at San Bernardino Valley College. His teaching style had occasionally been faulted as "abrasive," though most students and colleagues found it challenging. His periodic use of four-letter words finally drew complaints from several female students. A hearing panel found Cohen guilty of harassment, required him to seek counseling, and further decreed that he must "become more sensitive to the needs of his students, and must alter his teaching style if he finds it impairs their ability to learn." Claiming that such an order gave no guidance but chilled his free expression in and out of class, Cohen went to federal court. The trial judge upheld the college's sanctions, though conceding that neither the harassment policy nor the decree was a model of clarity. What seemed to persuade the judge was the strength of the college's interest in providing a nonharassing environment for all students. The case has been appealed, with an array of organizations coming to Cohen's support on free speech and academic freedom grounds.

Not only the courts have struggled with sexual harassment issues. The American Association of University Professors found itself with two seemingly applicable—but clearly conflicting—policies. One was the old academic freedom statement, which declares professorial speech protected except for rare exceptions. The other was a newer policy, framed in 1990 by the Committee on the Status of Women, which targeted faculty speech on sexual matters that "contributes to an unprofessional academic or work environment or interferes with required tasks." Clearly the two approaches needed reconciling. The process was completed by the summer of 1995. The AAUP now offers a single policy recognizing that harassing conduct or speech may be punished if it is coercive or directly abusive, and in the "teaching context" only if it is "persistent, pervasive and not germane to the subject matter." No sanctions could arise from speech that simply creates a hostile "climate" or "environment," in or out of the classroom. Extension of harassment liability to situations like Silva's tasteless analogies, Snyder's unfortunate Talmudic tale, or Cohen's use of taboo words to get students' attention would not be permissible under such a policy. It remains to be seen how the courts will address the same tension.

In fact, as the courts begin to address these issues, policy guidance is needed across the board. The academic community does have some relevant "common law" norms, as well as some stated policies. When students complain that their professor has crossed the line between academic freedom and unacceptable speech, the university must respond. Take perhaps the easiest case—one so obvious it hardly deserves discussion, though it does help define the spectrum. Students complain they have signed up for a required course in mathematics only to find a third of every class hour preempted by professorial monologues on politics. If a person is hired to teach math, he or she may not then decide to teach something completely different. The administration has every right (indeed duty) to see that members of its faculty instruct in their areas of expertise and assignment. Of course if the institution feels it must take action to terminate the appointment of an errant lecturer, it must give adequate notice, follow rigorous procedures, and bear the burden of proof. Proving the requisite case may be fairly easy if the professor has been hired to teach X but instead insists on teaching only the completely different subject of Y.

When one leaves this easy and obvious case, answers become less clear. The most basic premise of academic freedom is that within very broad limits, in an assigned subject area, university professors may not be ordered what to teach and what not to teach to their students, and surely not what examples may or may not be used, what tone to take, what readings to stress, and so on. Defining the limits within these general principles has been recurrently challenging.

At the height of the Vietnam War, for example, many faculty members with strongly antiwar views "reconstituted" certain of their classes, turning what would otherwise have been discussions of philosophy or political science or even physics into seminars on the legality and morality of the war. Universities responded uncomfortably when students—or legislators—complained. The abstract principles were clear enough. AAUP policy provides that faculty members must in their courses "avoid persistently intruding material which has no relation to their subject." But the problems of interpretation were legion. Often the Vietnam War bore *some* relation to the subject of the course, even in the sciences. How much was too much under the rubric of "persistently intrude"? And what difference did it make if, in addition to discussing the Vietnam conflict, the professor conveyed personal views about its rightness or wisdom and implied a hope that students would espouse those views? Given the inordinate difficulty of these issues and the volatility of campuses at the time, it is not surprising the Vietnam era ended with little firm guidance.

Clearly the amount of time devoted to extraneous material is germane. A professor who never mentions the weather, or politics, or baseball, or his or her family might be intolerably dull. But if such topics come to occupy a substantial portion of the class time, no matter how bland or innocuous in nature, then students are being cheated. They have a right to object, and the administration has a duty to respond.

Equally important is the tone of the comments—the degree to which the professor seems to be imposing personal views on students rather than simply offering neutral and objective comments. And of course the subject matter is crucial. Religion is quite likely the most sensitive of all topics, with race not far behind. Thus even a few minutes of religion in the classroom may be cause for concern, whereas taking umbrage at similar treatment of sports or even politics would seem unreasonable. Even a single disclosure in the classroom of one's own religious beliefs may be once too many, unless the reference is central to the subject matter. When the discussion extends to the personal religious views of students, the situation is even more problematic.

This last comment brings us to another difficult issue. The AAUP policy proscribes persistent intrusion of material "which has no relation to their subject." This policy poses two problems. For one, it is not always clear when controversial material is unrelated to the course. Even sexist jokes would, for example, be germane to a course in American humor. And the use of sexually explicit posters would almost certainly be acceptable in a lecture about "troop morale during World War II" in a military history course. In fact these are relatively easy cases; the nexus becomes more difficult as one moves out from there.

There is also an intriguing conceptual issue. The greater the departure from assigned subject matter, the weaker seems the professorial claim for tolerance. Yet the potential harm to students may vary directly, rather than inversely, with proximity to the theme of the course. The political scientist who repeatedly tells students how he or she plans to vote in the presidential election (and implies they should do likewise) poses a graver risk of intimidation or coercion than the botanist or classicist who reveals comparable personal political perspectives. Yet it is the botanist or classicist who, by reason of this very attenuation, more clearly offends the established professional norms. Perhaps the best answer is that if such intrusions are "persistent" and come from the podium, they are unacceptable regardless of discipline. Familiarity does not always breed contempt, however.

The last set of issues concerns the students and the effect of such comments on them and on the learning process. There is a difference between a required course and one that is optional. There is also a clear difference between a freshman lecture and a graduate seminar. Attention must also be given to the possible risk, if any, to students who dissent or object. If grading is blind or is not done personally by the professor, the risks are reduced. Yet it is fair to ask whether such safeguards adequately protect students to whom such comments may be troubling. And in other situations—Ernest Dube's analogy between Zionism and Nazism, for example—grading systems would be irrelevant. The harm lies in the remark itself, not in whether the grading system protects the student's right to confront the professor.

The next issue is that of institutional response. One must have great sympathy with a chairman or dean suddenly confronted with such a challenge. No manual or guide offers quick and easy answers. The institution must respond, quickly and sensitively, to charges. Yet certain types of response—for example, City College's creating and advertising "shadow sections" for Levin's classes before any students had complained—would be overkill. Surely any talk of terminating a tenured appointment would be obvious excess.

The first such complaint the chairman or dean receives should result in an informal conference between the professor and the responsible academic administrator. The students could simply be mistaken. Or there may be some other reason—a vendetta against an unpopular teacher—why they are not to be trusted. Or they may have misunderstood a comment with an innocent meaning that could be clarified through the dean's or chair's mediation. If such steps yield no resolution, then the administrator may need to consider two further steps—to admonish the professor and to protect the students. It is at this stage that inviting students to transfer to other sections might be appropriate, for the critical event not yet present in Levin's case would now have occurred. There is good reason to offer alternatives to students who have taken the quite drastic step of complaining to an administrator and deserve an academically valid option.

Suppose the complaining students have left, but the professor persists in unacceptable departures or deviations. More formal sanctions may now be warranted. A chair or dean might send a letter of reprimand, which, since it goes in the faculty member's file, would almost certainly give rise to a formal hearing at which the issues could be joined and the process challenged. If such steps still yield no satisfaction, sanctions short of dismissal do exist and should be considered—sanctions such as denial or lessening of certain benefits and perquisites of academic status that do not go to the heart of a faculty appointment. Only in the most extreme cases, where such departures give unmistakable evidence of unfitness to teach and to remain a member of the academic community, could dismissal responsibly be considered.

So much for what happens in the classroom. The cases of extramural speech with which we began may in fact be harder, partly because the scope of academic freedom is less clear and partly because pressures from legislators, governors, and others outside the campus may be more intense. And the need for guidance in these cases is surely as great.

The Levin and Jeffries cases tell us much about what the institution should *not* do. No matter how provocative the professor's off-campus speech or writing may be, a single incident will rarely if ever offer a valid basis for a negative action. However outrageous or offensive, a scholar's writings in external journals would not justify a targeted investigation coupled with veiled threats against status or tenure. And students may not be offered an escape from possibly controversial professorial views before any of the students have in fact requested alternatives. That much is clear despite the eventual outcome of the Jeffries case, complicated by various legal and procedural issues.

What these cases fail to tell us is what *may* be done in such challenging situations. Some observers have despaired of near-paralysis in an era of judicial concern for such matters. "Are there any enforceable limits on academic freedom of speech?" asked an exasperated *New York Times* columnist at the height of the Jeffries affair. Of course there are, and these limits need to be more widely recognized as counterpoint to the safe-guards that courts have recently reaffirmed.

For starters, can the institution take some official note of extreme extramural statements? Surely it can. If, for example, there are several candidates under consideration for the vacant chairmanship of African studies, one of whom has made highly inflammatory and irresponsible statements at public meetings and conferences, this fact can certainly weigh in the final selection without abridging academic freedom or free speech. For the institution to close its eyes or pretend the speech had never occurred would in fact be irresponsible. There is a clear difference between taking such expression into account in choosing among potential beneficiaries and using it as the sole basis for taking away something of value or status. So, as a general rule, the fact that speech may be protected does not mean that it must be disregarded in making all institutional decisions.

Beyond this threshold, there are other levels of possible scrutiny. It is surely important whether the outspoken scholar purports to represent the institution. A simple disclaimer may not suffice to dispel an inference of attribution. Where any possibility of confusion exists, AAUP policy insists that professors must "make every effort to indicate they are not speaking for the institution." If confusion is likely and if adequate steps to avoid it have not been taken—or worse, where actual attribution is improperly claimed—important interests have been affected, and this factor surely weighs in the balance.

Central to this issue is the matter of competence. If professorial statements depart so far from universal understanding as to show a lack

of competence in the scholar's field, the institution would be irresponsible to ignore them. Thus, as AAUP associate general secretary Jordan
Kurland notes from his three decades of guiding academic freedom and
tenure cases, "A geologist who teaches that the earth is flat is not
protected by academic freedom. One cannot ignore the preponderance
of evidence." A similar standard would presumably apply to a biologist
who insisted that Darwin was wrong and Genesis was right—though the
same could not be said of a theologian (or a civil engineer).

Take the case of the Holocaust deniers. Here the speaker's academic
discipline seems pivotal to the judgment of competence. If a chemist or
(as in the actual Northwestern University case) an electrical engineer
makes such preposterous claims, they do not automatically evidence
scholarly professional incompetence. But a European historian? Can
there be any doubt that the latter ought to know better and that not
knowing better challenges the very basis on which academic freedom
rests?

Most cases do not involve demonstrated lack of competence; they
involve statements that may seem highly inappropriate, embarrassing, or
offensive but do not disqualify the speaker outright. Even when competence is not at issue, the relationship between the controversial extramural views and the person's academic field is always germane. Offhand and
off-base (or off-color) remarks about a remote subject are one thing;
similar treatment of a topic that is well within the speaker's ambit is
another. In theory, such distinctions are relatively easy. Again, though,
they are harder to apply than to formulate. The case of Professor Levin is
again instructive. Recall that Levin taught and studied philosophy. The
relationship between race and intelligence was therefore not clearly
irrelevant to his field, as it seemed in the case of William Shockley, a
distinguished chemist who expressed similar views on race. Still, Levin's
field was not as close to the subject as was Professor Arthur Jensen's;
Jensen was an educational psychologist who raised unsettling questions
about race and intelligence at the core of his area of expertise. Levin, as
a philosopher, bore some responsibility for the subject matter of his
controversial writings. Perhaps the most that can be said with confidence
is that one expects less of Shockley and more of Jensen, with Levin
somewhere between.

The forum in which the statements were made may also bear on the judgment. Levin's views were expressed in rather scholarly journals, apparently evidencing no desire to publicize or to attract attention. At no time did any of Levin's views on race and intelligence find their way into his classes. The record is somewhat less clear on Jeffries. The incendiary statements occurred during a speech delivered to a highly public (and publicized) open forum in the state capital under conditions where attention might likely be drawn and in fact was drawn, conditions for which the speaker may have been partly culpable. Context is relevant and may in fact be highly significant.

Finally, there are less tangible dimensions of tone and approach. AAUP policy again frames the inquiry, for it declares that faculty who speak or write off campus should "be accurate, . . . exercise appropriate restraint, [and] . . . show respect for the opinions of others." No precise rules can be fashioned for the application of such precepts, though they obviously suggest elements deserving of consideration in making any such judgments.

If a university can take some account of extramural statements, it is fair to ask for what purpose. We noted earlier that some decisions reflect multiple factors, of which extramural statements might well be one. But this concession does not automatically warrant major sanctions, much less dismissal or loss of tenure. It is here, in fact, that AAUP policy becomes most helpful:

> A faculty member's expression of opinion as a citizen cannot constitute grounds for dismissal unless it clearly demonstrates the faculty member's unfitness to serve. Extramural utterances rarely bear upon a faculty member's fitness for continuing service.

Cases that involve extreme extramural statements by professors are, as we noted at the start, remarkably rare. They do, however, generate intense feelings on and off campus. When such an issue arises at a public university, it may be hard to keep even the governor's office out of it. Thus it becomes critical for the institution to show that it is concerned, and to respond quickly. But the response must also be fair and evenhanded, and must avoid excessive response to an admittedly provocative catalyst.

The case of Levin once again offers insight. Concern about his published writings and their startlingly insensitive views on race and intelligence needed urgent attention. The City College administration did almost everything right but in the end made two big mistakes. One concerns the "shadow sections," born of a commendable desire to protect students. If the dean had simply been prepared to offer alternative sections to any students who came and expressed discomfort about the racial views of their instructor rather than jumping the gun and stigmatizing a teacher about whom none had complained, the policy would have been not only acceptable but in fact laudable. The other mistake had to do with the investigation ordered by President Harleston. An inquiry, as such, was not unwarranted, especially since the Faculty Senate had turned its back on an exceedingly volatile situation. What was wrong—constitutionally wrong—was the president's almost off-hand comment, "these views have no place at City College." Such a statement presaged not just a targeted inquiry but one that might lead to the dismissal of a tenured professor. If the doctrines of academic freedom and free speech have any core meaning, they protect the right of a professor to express the most unpopular views without fear of dire consequences. City College and its president learned this lesson in the most painful way.

III

FREE SPEECH AND NEW TECHNOLOGIES

To: University General Counsel
From: Vice President for Administration
Re: Computer Abuses and Other High-Tech Crises

No one ever warned us the electronic world would be anything like this. In the last three weeks, we've had dozens of complaints about the uses and abuses of campus computers. Some people have called the campus police to say they've heard our students have been using the computing system to post really vile and revolting stuff on the Internet, and they want us to stop it. In fact these complaints really run the gamut of cyberspace. Some of these issues resemble problems we have addressed in print form. Many others, however, are quite novel. What troubles me most is that we are about to enter a brand-new legal world with hardly any policies or rules that cover electronic speech. So we need to adapt old policies wherever we can and formulate new ones where the old ones don't apply—and we need to do so sooner rather than later.

Let me just give you a quick overview of the kinds of issues that we face in cyberspace—many of them on our own campus, and the rest at campuses very much like ours:

• A sociology professor was recently arrested and charged with possession of child pornography on the basis of material he accessed and downloaded on university computers.

• An art history professor has been the target of police investigation because of material he has downloaded and shared with some of his students, which is probably not legally obscene but is certainly sexually explicit. It's no worse than what you would find in some magazines sold in the campus bookstore; the question is how much of a difference derives from the use of university computers.

• A group of our students just presented us with the results of a survey they conducted on their own last semester of sexually explicit materials available from various newsgroups that can be and are accessed through the campus computer system.

• These same students also posted on their home page some of the choicest of the material they had gathered; there were so many "hits" by other students in the first few hours that a "traffic jam" resulted that almost brought the regular business of our system to a halt.

• A group of male freshmen just e-mailed to a group of female students some really tasteless—I mean truly raunchy—sexist jokes. The recipients and others are demanding prompt and firm action. Had these jokes just been sent through the mail or posted on a physical bulletin board, I doubt there is much we could or would have done. Incidentally, the United States Office for Civil Rights heard about the sexist material and is threatening to support the women students' claims—maybe even demanding that we keep such material off our campus computers (as though that were possible).

• We also have at least one electronic homophobe among our students. He recently posted some extremely inflammatory messages on a campus computer system gay and lesbian student bulletin board. The gay students accessed the messages, were deeply upset and frightened, and demanded that we take drastic action against the homophobe.

• When one of our engineering faculty was on leave last semester, a former student research assistant used the professor's password to post a barrage of deeply offensive racial slurs and other remarks. When the professor returned, he found about 500 very angry messages in his e-mail box, including several serious death threats. It took him weeks to explain to recipients of "his" offensive messages.

• Another engineering professor, who for years has written and spoken about the Holocaust—he denies it ever happened—has now gone online with his deeply abhorrent views. Jewish organizations and others who have uneasily tolerated his continued presence on the faculty now demand we cut off his access to university computers for such messages.

• The head of our computer science department was one of the first to create and use a home page on our computer system. On that page he "informs" interested colleagues about the flourishing consulting business he maintains on the side and implies that he would accept new assignments on favorable terms. (This posting is, like many noted here, in violation of no existing university policy—though of course we do forbid use of university facilities for purely private commercial gain.)

• A senior librarian was on medical leave for much of last semester. She returned to find that her supervisor, exercising general control over "university property," had found out her password and had read much of her accumulated e-mail. The librarian was outraged. She claims such action is a clear violation of her privacy. The supervisor, of course, says he was simply carrying out a routine task.

• The most volatile case came to our attention when an alumnus in Europe was surfing the net one night and discovered a really vile short story written (and posted) by one of our more creative undergraduates. It describes in fantasy terms the slow and painful torture of a named fellow student with, among other weapons, a hot curling iron. The alumnus got word to us and to the local police. The student was arrested, and a reporter's call soon after the arrest was the first the object of the curling-iron fantasy ever knew about the matter! The incident is full of irony: had this same story appeared in print, even in our quarterly literary journal, no formal action would have been taken or even contemplated.

• Finally (lest we forget) Congress early in 1996 passed the Communications Decency Act, which forbids the transmission of certain materials by computer. Unless this law is ruled invalid—it was struck down in a preliminary ruling on First Amendment grounds—many university computing directors fear they may be criminally liable for permitting the sending of "indecent" material, which could even include eminent works of art that contain nudity, or serious medical illustrations, among others. This is a frightening prospect!

These incidents share certain common qualities that begin to define the issue before us: In *medium,* they are novel because they all involve the use of electronic communication. In *content,* however, they are strikingly familiar because they all involve messages of a kind that could have been, and undoubtedly were, often communicated in print. Most campus rules are medium-bound and thus do not easily or readily adapt to such new challenges as these cases present. Meanwhile, perhaps because of the very novelty of the medium, people who have been victims of these communications often demand reprisal or protection. Yet—and here is the rub—few if any of these communications would have incurred sanctions, as a matter of free speech and press, had they occurred in print. Finally, the ability of a university and its computer system to regulate such communication is probably even lower than its capacity to regulate such messages in spoken or printed form. Thus we are entering a new world of cyberspace with few of the tools we need to address such issues.

Here, then, is the issue we need to address before our next Board of Trustees meeting: If our students, with the stroke of a key on a university terminal, can download or upload material of the kind we're seeing, may the institution not be potentially liable to someone for something? And if they can use our computer system to attack, defame, disgrace, and demean others, ought we not to take steps to put an end to such abuses? And if the university's computer system is the medium for the transmission to the world of sexually violent and dangerous material, shouldn't we be doing something about it? We have a board meeting in a few weeks, and I just know I'll be getting questions and complaints from some of our trustees, even if nothing nasty appears in the papers. And if anyone finds out that the female student who's the object of the sexual fantasy is the niece of Trustee Prufrock, you can imagine what might happen. So please tell me what we can do, if anything, to address these electronic challenges.

To: Vice President for Administration
From: Law Department
Re: Computer Uses and Restraints

Since the general counsel is on vacation this week, she asked me to reply as fully as possible to your memo. You realize these are brand-new problems, with hardly any cases yet in the courts. But we have been talking a good bit about electronic issues, expecting we might hear from you fairly soon. And of course we've been in touch with our colleagues around the country, many of whom have experienced the same sorts of problems and needs.

Let me begin, as usual, with a short answer. This one you will probably not like, but here goes. Our central point is that, as we read the First Amendment, a public university may not treat the content of electronic communications differently from print communications, except to the extent that different effects and consequences result from the very nature of the medium itself. Most of what people want done—like those who have been calling recently with complaints—is to crack down on electronic messages that would go almost unnoticed (or at least unpunished) if they appeared in a newspaper or magazine or on a physical bulletin board.

Of course there are differences between media, which we will explore more fully in a moment. For example, a message posted on the Internet is available in a fraction of a second to millions of people around the world—a magnitude of dissemination that has no counterpart in print. Even radio and television broadcasting do not approach the instantaneous scope and sweep of the Internet. The issue, however, is not simply whether electronic communication is *different*—but whether the *ways* in which it differs from print and other familiar media call for different treatment of content. Some of the contrasts we are about to explore may well warrant different approaches to content, though probably to a far more limited degree than most people would expect.

Let me state the point in another way. If the *content* of the message would be constitutionally protected in print or spoken form, then it is presumably no less protected on a computer; a different means of dissemination would not, by itself, justify a lesser standard of protection. Only if, and to the extent that, differences in medium trigger one of those very special interests that, under the First Amendment, justify restricting speech or press would there be a valid basis for suppressing the electronic message. That is, as we shall see, a rather remote prospect. Much as we appreciate your wish to deal more harshly with what you see as new and genuinely more troublesome electronic material, we must proceed with great caution and justify any policies that limit or inhibit the content of speech. We will also need to watch very closely some fast-moving developments in Congress, the courts, and state legislatures.

Let's begin with threatening communications like the "sexually violent fiction" you reported. Though I haven't seen the text, I'm willing to assume the worst. I'll also assume that if the target or object of the story had accessed and read it, she would have been terrified. In that respect it sounds a lot like the case of University of Michigan student Jake Baker, author of a story posted on the Internet about torturing his female classmate with a hot curling iron. We'll have more to say about Jake a bit later.

For now, just suppose that same student had written the same story in longhand or on his word processor and had circulated the text among friends in his dorm. Or suppose he had gone out and got the story published in one of the several off-campus underground magazines. What if the female student who was the target or object read it, knowing it was about her, and became so frightened she had to leave school for the semester or even permanently? And what then if someone suggested we bring charges against the author? The answer would be clear: we do not and cannot punish students in the 1990s for writing stories that may frighten some readers, even acutely. Someone who has been the object of such a fearsome story might have some civil remedy, like a libel suit, though even that seems doubtful.

Unless threats are uttered person to person, there is only one situation where the First Amendment permits government sanctions, and that is when someone threatens the life of the president of the United States, whether or not the president ever learns of the threat. The fact that we single out this one type of threat strongly implies the absence of similar sanctions for threatening anyone else, except in a face-to-face situation. So let's start by assuming we know what would have happened to the student for writing the same story in print form—unless he had taken some directly threatening step like shoving a copy of the text under the door or in the face of the target of his perverted fantasies.

This premise gets us right to the central issue: are there differences between electronic threats and print threats that justify a different treatment of the message? There are in fact several potentially meaningful differences, and they cut both ways. Let's look first at those factors which might seem to support more stringent content regulation. As we noted earlier, there is the incredible speed with which electronic messages may reach millions of people around the world—a scope and scale of dissemination with no counterpart in any other medium of communication. Partly for this reason, the Internet exposes its users to a vastly more diverse array of material than a print society normally generates, reflecting cultures and mores around the world.

There is also a growing concern about decorum and style that may have content significance. In the early stages of electronic discourse, the degree of candor in language and graphic material seems often to exceed the standards that govern print communication. Some observers have remarked with dismay about the lack of etiquette and civility sometimes found in e-mail. Carnegie-Mellon professor Sara Keisler, who has studied electronic interaction, offers her explanation:

> When social definitions are weak or nonexistent, communication becomes unregulated. People are less bound by convention, less influenced by status and unconcerned with making a good appearance. Their behavior becomes more extreme, impulsive, self-centered. They become, in a sense, free people.

MIT researcher Michael Schrage adds a concurrent view:

> It's a lot easier to be rude on the Net. And that's what's so intriguing about it. This medium creates new contexts for rudeness. . . . Like people who turn into maniacs when they get behind the wheel of a car, some folks just can't wait to fire up their PC's and start flame-throwing.

Such forces may be especially active and intense during what is still, for most Internet users, an early and experimental phase. Venturesome sexual fantasies, graphic and lurid images, as well as outrageous e-mail language, may in part reflect a natural human desire to test the limits of a brand new medium, especially at a time when there are few rules to constrain creativity.

There is another and quite different concern that might warrant closer scrutiny of what goes over the Internet. It is the very essence of how much is unknown in the electronic medium. A person who receives a threat by computer might well be more apprehensive than if reading the same message in print or hearing it by telephone. When we are verbally assaulted in print or by phone, we have some idea of the source and the channel, and often of the author's identity as well. Part of what makes cyberspace potentially frightening, even to fairly seasoned superhighway travelers, is its anonymity. We may or may not have any insight into the source and the pathway. The author may be halfway around the world, around the block, or even in the next room. What we do not know and may not be able to discover (at least at this early stage) about our electronic assailant could well create apprehension of a kind not normally caused by threats in more traditional media. Thus, for several reasons, electronic messages may be more worrisome; whether the differences warrant differential treatment under the law depends in part on a more complete assessment of the old and new media.

Several other differences between digital and print communications may cut the other way. The first of these is almost technical, but nonetheless critically important. Most of the special constitutional doctrines that have led courts to sustain limits on printed or spoken words do not apply to electronic messages. Take the doctrine of "fighting words," for example. Over fifty years ago the Supreme Court upheld a conviction of a New Hampshire proselytizer for spewing insults in a policeman's face on a street corner, since there was proof that physical violence might well ensue. This case has never been overruled and is occasionally still cited with approval. But it was not the angry speaker's *language* that sustained the arrest; it was the high probability that two verbal disputants would come to blows and that mayhem would follow. When the two adversaries are flailing at computer terminals, wherever the terminals may be located, what is missing is the imminent risk of violence that allows government to intercede on the street corner. By definition, protagonists at their keyboards cannot engage in "fighting words." No amount of electronic "flaming" will create the incendiary condition that alone permits an arrest for uttering epithets and insults in another person's face.

Much the same can be said of other special conditions where government may intervene to curb speech—most notably the "clear and present danger" exception that has long justified legal sanctions against a speaker. An electronic "incitement" is not inconceivable, though the risks of "imminent lawless action" (the sine qua non of intervention) seem far more remote when communication is by computer than when it comes through more personal and more proximate means. Even more clearly is this the case with respect to other recognized grounds for suppressing speech in order to maintain civility—punishing hate crimes, redressing face-to-face insults and epithets, and the like. So this first difference is one that does have constitutional dimensions: when one moves from the street corner to the keyboard and the screen, the special warrant for punishing provocative speech diminishes greatly.

One other factor appears to cut both ways: the matter of access and the risk of receiving unwelcome or intrusive electronic material. On one hand, there have been celebrated cases of parents finding that their teen and preteen children have happened upon highly explicit material available through the Internet, when such material would not have been legally available to young readers in print form. Parental control of young people's access to such material becomes harder by the month, if only because most youthful electronic thrill seekers are far more sophisticated in finding such material than are their parents in hiding it from them. Thus it may be little harder for preteens to savor the joys of cybersex than it is for them to induce an older sibling or friend to reach a copy of *Penthouse* or *Hustler* behind the high wooden barrier at the newsstand.

On the other hand, the access issue may favor protection. There is a clear contrast between active and passive communication. One who logs onto the Internet, much less accesses a particular alt.sex newsgroup, does exercise a conscious and deliberate choice; downloading sexually explicit graphics does not just happen in the manner of glancing at a newspaper or magazine, or for that matter picking up a telephone to dial a 900 number. There must be a rather complex implementation of an act of selection, presumably with some appreciation of the fare one may find at the other end. That is especially true for such specialized and focused electronic enclaves as the alt.sex newsgroups.

Even when minors are potentially at risk, parents are not wholly without means to shield their children from disturbing or inappropriate electronic material. It is true there is no exact electronic equivalent of the high shelves and partial wooden blinders that many states impose on adult book sellers. There does, however, seem to be a growing arsenal of protective weapons by which one may avoid receipt of unwelcome digital material. Apart from turning the computer off or pulling the plug, withdrawing from a newsgroup that has gotten out of hand, or even wiping out an address from one's e-mail correspondence file, the information superhighway traveler has myriad safeguards the print communicator lacks. Several of the major networks have proclaimed their ability to maintain for sensitive users the desired levels of decency and decorum. Technology seems increasingly responsive to the desire to shield electronic recipients—as through the sophisticated "cancelbots" (Norwegian electronic attack dogs that on command can wipe out a designated message from many and varied postings). Even though aggressive senders and their technologies are likely to keep pace with the blockers, the means available to shield a sensitive recipient from an unwanted digital message ought to remain well ahead of those available to the person who wishes not to be assaulted in print.

Let us take stock of the contrasting nature of old and new media. The various differences between digital and print material do not yield a clear or decisive constitutional answer. One who receives a threat by computer may indeed have greater reason for apprehension than when that same threat comes over the transom or by other low-tech means. Yet for other reasons, government may actually have less latitude in punishing or suppressing the digital threat than it would have in dealing with a similar message in a more traditional medium. The presumption should favor protection for electronic material of no lesser magnitude than exists for print material. Where specific facets of digital communication warrant stiffer sanctions or restraints than for comparable print or spoken material, there will be time enough to reflect those differences in new standards and measures. Until and unless that happens, electronic messages ought to fare no worse than the same messages in more traditional forms.

This would be a fitting point at which to introduce Jake Baker, the earliest example of an electronic assault upon collegiate civility. In mid-February 1995, Baker was arrested on federal charges of transporting threatening material across state lines. Baker, then a University of Michigan undergraduate with a penchant for creative use of the computer, admitted to having written and posted on the Internet a fictional account of the rape and torture of a fellow student. The high (or low) point of the story involved the excruciatingly painful application of a hot curling iron as the author's torture weapon of choice. Though identified by name, the object of Baker's fantasy was apparently unaware of the story until she was contacted by reporters after the author's arrest.

She was not the only one who missed the story; apparently it went unnoticed in Ann Arbor until a Michigan alumnus in Moscow, surfing the Internet one evening, came upon a tale he felt should not carry the imprimatur of his alma mater. He conveyed his displeasure to university officials, who in turn contacted law enforcement agencies. Baker was arrested on federal criminal charges and was summarily suspended from school. He was mainly charged with transmitting threats to injure or kidnap women or young girls—again not to the intended victims but to a male friend in Canada. The authorities had no trouble locating Baker. He had made no effort to hide either his identity or the nature of his material; indeed, he prefaced the main story about the curling-iron torture with his own disclaimer: "pretty sick stuff," he warned would-be readers.

When Baker's lawyer sought his release pending trial, the United States magistrate (expressing profound concern for the safety of his thirteen-year-old daughter) denied bail and ordered Baker to jail. This was, he warned, "somebody who probably should not be walking the streets." Baker was indeed off the streets (as well as out of school) for about a month, until in mid-March he was released to prepare for trial. By late June, a federal judge (who had earlier expressed little sympathy for the charges) ruled that Baker should be permanently released.

In the course of his lengthy opinion, the judge condemned what he saw as "vague" criminal charges that posed a substantial threat to free speech. Though he conceded Baker's writing was "a rather savage and tasteless piece of fiction," such qualities did not deprive it—in electronic or any other form—of First Amendment protection. Near the end of his opinion, the judge confronted and rejected the basis of the arrest:

> To infer an intention [on Baker's part] to act upon the thoughts and dreams of this language would stray far beyond the bounds of the First Amendment, and would amount to punishing Baker for his thoughts and desires.

Though the case seemed to the federal judge misplaced in his criminal court—"why the government became involved in the first place is not really explained in the record"—he was not ready to absolve Jake Baker. He felt the university had badly overreacted by invoking summary suspension, however, and "the case would have been better handled as a disciplinary matter."

Back on campus, the University of Michigan's relation to the case proved to be quite complex. Campus officials had become aware of Baker's ominous prose some weeks before they alerted the United States attorney. They urged Baker to cooperate in an internal investigation, which he did. He even agreed to undergo two psychological examinations, as a result of which he was declared no threat to himself or to others. Yet when the alumnus in Moscow called to complain and the process became formal and public a few weeks later, Baker was summarily suspended under a campus rule that gave the administration the power to protect the "health, diligence and order among its students." Such summary action is seldom taken unless the student poses a physical risk to self or others so grave that immediate removal is the only responsible course. The Joint Statement on Rights and Freedoms of Students, for example, declares that a student's status should not be altered while charges are pending "except for reasons relating to the student's physical or emotional safety and well-being, or for reasons relating to the safety and well-being of students, faculty and university property."

The use of so drastic a measure here seems puzzling in two respects. For one, the university gave no public (or apparently private) indication which of its possible interests had been jeopardized. At no time was there any threat to the physical safety of any other member of the campus community. Nor was there evidence that any fellow student even suffered emotional stress; the target of the torture fantasy knew nothing of Baker's use of her name and profile until after he was behind bars. Nor does it seem likely that "university property" was in peril; Baker's handling of the hardware he used to create and upload his material appeared to be exemplary. Thus it would be difficult to identify a university interest strong enough to warrant such extreme action. Summarily suspending Baker, in short, implied that the university could no more responsibly let him roam the campus with his keyboard than it could allow a gun-toting or knife-wielding assailant to remain on campus while charges were under review. The analogy seems strained at best, at worst outlandish.

Now to the ultimate question of university authority: apart from the suspension, was there a substantive basis for any discipline? Judge Cohn of the federal court felt there might be such a basis, just as clearly as he felt the case did not belong in court. It should be clear from information presented earlier that state universities may not punish a student for writing nasty things about a classmate in print—even threatening nasty things—unless those writings pose a direct and personal threat that would cause immediate and grave apprehension. Even then, the basis for discipline would be tenuous. Most public universities would feel they could do little more than issue a reprimand to the author and an apology to the target. If Baker's case is different, it must be either because differences in the medium give universities additional disciplinary power or because the same words in electronic form pose a risk they would not in print. Both options deserve analysis.

One obvious difference between posting sexually violent fiction on the Internet and submitting the same story to an underground magazine is that university facilities and services may have been used in the former case but probably not in the latter. This distinction may give the university a heightened stake in electronic dissemination. This stake does not, however, necessarily justify expelling one author but not the other. The outcome in such a case would depend on such issues as the applicable provisions of the university's acceptable use policy (governing its computer facilities) and the degree to which the individual student user may have violated the conditions.

Herein lies a significant challenge of drafting: even if the campus community were unanimous in condemning Baker's use of the computer system, it is far less clear how this consensus would translate into rules that a public university could constitutionally enforce. Surely material could not be banned, nor its author punished, solely because some readers might find it "threatening" (even though that is the key term in the federal law for the violation of which Baker was arrested). Nor could a valid rule be aimed at material that might cause "apprehension" or "anxiety," short of the state of mind that repeated face-to-face threats may create.

Even if such rules could in theory be written, there is no evidence that the University of Michigan invoked (or even had on the books) such rules at the time of Baker's literary excursions. Indeed, the interest invoked to justify the summary suspension—an old rule designed to protect "health, diligence and order among the students"—strongly implies the absence of any policy more precisely tailored to verbal excesses of the digital era. So the bare possibility of precise and specific rules would be irrelevant even at Michigan—a university that had already wrestled with more than its share of online content issues. If such a rule could not have been found in the Michigan handbook when Baker stepped forth, how much less likely would it be to find such rules at less seasoned institutions? So the issue at this early stage is only in part whether such rules could be written, but more whether they had already been written and, if so, whether they would fit cases like that of Baker.

Michigan's problems with student digital excess were soon to be replicated in slightly different form at two other institutions. A Virginia Tech student shocked the campus in the fall of 1995 by posting deeply offensive homophobic comments and slurs on the campus computer network. The administration felt some sanction was warranted, though it shared Michigan's dilemma of having in place no policy tailored to counter such digital assaults. A few weeks later, four Cornell freshmen drew national attention by posting on a campus electronic bulletin board a barrage of outrageously sexist jokes. Hardly anyone was amused, least of all the Cornell administration. This time, however, the absence of pertinent policy, together with sound legal advice based on print media analogies, brought a successful effort to get the offenders to apologize to the campus community. Cornell left the issue there, invoking no disciplinary sanctions and hoping the foul-mouthed freshmen had learned a valuable lesson.

While the circumstances differ, the basic issue is not new. Long before Baker went online, universities had been wrestling with different kinds of electronic content control issues. Several concerns drew attention by the late 1980s and increased in importance in the 1990s. There was, for one, a growing fear of possible criminal liability for the transmission of possibly obscene material or child pornography; what was unclear and troubling was not so much the nature of the suspect material but the conditions under which the operator of a computer system might be held liable. Specifically, institutions were becoming concerned about whether liability might flow from simply permitting members of the campus community to access (and share with others) sexually explicit and graphic material of a kind that is readily available through the Internet.

Meanwhile, there had been growing concern about possible civil liability for electronic transmission of libel or otherwise civilly actionable material. And some campuses had felt pressures (both internal and external) to curb the use of their computing systems or networks to transmit or store racially and ethnically offensive material. Each of these areas of potential risk has caused much concern to university officials, who have done their best to respond with virtually no guidance yet available from the courts.

The obscenity prospect illustrates the problem. If the campus bookstore or the university press is charged with disseminating obscene material, the state of the law is reasonably clear (even if juries may apply it unevenly). But the digital world presents a legal *tabula rasa*. Starting in 1994, computer bulletin board operators began to be charged under obscenity and child pornography laws. The first case of this sort brought the conviction, early in 1995, of a California couple named Thomas who operated a small bulletin board on which they had posted arguably obscene material. A federal postal inspector in Memphis joined the bulletin board under an assumed name, accessed the material, found it obscene, and saw to it that criminal charges were filed. The Thomases were convicted on all counts; the federal judge treated their digital materials no differently from the X-rated videos they had sent to Memphis.

A federal appeals court, upholding the conviction early in 1996, refused to differentiate for First Amendment purposes between electronic and print obscenity, despite several obvious and critical differences. In the appeal, the Thomases asserted vital differences between physical and electronic transmission of explicit material. Apart from the fact that no federal law specifically banned nonmailed obscene communications, there were other major differences. Obscenity has been denied First Amendment protection largely because its dissemination may offend—and its impact is to be judged by—the "community standards" of a physical community like Memphis. When the material is digital and presents no greater risk that it will be seen or viewed or that people will be exposed to it in Memphis than in Moscow or Madrid, the controlling interests—the fundamental concept of "community"—change dramatically. Courts are just on the verge of determining what "standards" are appropriate to electronic obscenity charges.

Another intermedium contrast is far more than merely technical. Unlike magazines, books, and such, digital transmissions from one computer to another are not intelligible material but symbols that require conscious actions (and possibly even complex decoding) on the recipient's end before the content can be judged by any standards. Thus issues that have become familiar to courts reviewing traditional obscenity charges simply do not apply, or at least apply in a profoundly different way, when the material originates and is transmitted in electronic form.

As these issues begin to emerge in court, anxiety within academic computer centers is understandable. The early cases could well be resolved by treating the bulletin board operator as something other than a publisher. What has happened in libel or defamation may be instructive. The two earliest computer libel cases offered quite variant views of the new medium. The first case absolved CompuServe as though it were a bookseller or newsdealer; the other case, several years later, held Prodigy to the far more rigorous libel standards imposed on a publisher. There were factual differences, to be sure, but far deeper philosophical differences between the first two courts to apply libel law to digital messages. Many more cases will be needed to give any clear guidance. However the courts resolve such issues off campus, the early decisions may offer limited guidance and even less solace to the university information technology director. The role of the typical campus system or network is far more complex than the Thomas's home-based bulletin board. Judgments that might define the legal status of such a simple facility could also have downside implications for the campus system that both disseminates material to and accesses material from the Internet and at the same time provides a vast local electronic highway system for thousands of daily intracampus messages and images.

Meanwhile, the courts are not the sole source of such concerns. Legislation also poses a worrisome prospect. Congress studied the issue for several years. The Senate adopted highly restrictive language, proposed by Senator Exon, barring "indecent" material from the Internet and providing criminal penalties for those who disseminate such material. The House adopted a much milder version, pressured by Speaker Newt Gingrich's view that privacy was at stake. The conference eventually adopted language much closer to the Senate version, making computer transmission of obscene and indecent material a federal offense. Earlier drafts of the telecommunications law amendment would have punished computer system operators who uploaded or downloaded or internally transmitted suspect material. Such a measure would have placed campus computer system operators at grave risk, and the prospect of such action evoked pervasive anxiety. When Congress finally approved the bill and the president signed it in February 1996, the sanctions fell only on the creator or author of the offending material and not on passive transmitters. The academic community breathed a momentary sigh of relief. A federal court promptly enjoined enforcement of these provisions pending extensive review of their constitutionality. Even so, the amendment served to criminalize speech that would be constitutionally protected in virtually all other medias.

The Communications Decency Act did not fare well when the court reached its merits. In mid-May 1996, three federal judges in Philadelphia unanimously invalidated its key provisions on First Amendment grounds. The court first ruled that speech on the Internet was as fully protected by the Constitution as speech in more traditional forms. Accordingly, such prohibitions in the act as those against "indecent" electronic speech and the communication to minors of "patently offensive" displays of sexually explicit material could not stand. Despite various exceptions and exemptions in the law (some of which might have protected university computing networks), the court was deeply troubled by "a criminal statute that hovers over each content provider like the proverbial sword of Damocles."

The judges also rejected what seemed to have been a central assumption of Congress—that senders of digital messages could (with the exception of individually addressed e-mail) so target their communication as to keep material designed for adult audiences out of reach of all minors. Such selectivity simply was not feasible, and it provided a deeply flawed premise for government policy. Thus the three-judge federal court not only gave electronic communication a clearly protected status; the court also warned that regulation of Internet messages must meet First Amendment standards. It seemed almost certain that these issues would reach the Supreme Court.

Meanwhile, state lawmakers have not ignored the Internet controversy. By the summer of 1996, at least eight states had enacted restrictive measures aimed at electronic material. Ten other states were actively considering such laws. Washington State's computer-obscenity law, passed by the legislature in its 1995 session, was vetoed by the governor because of its feared impact on business activity. The New York measure, passed in July 1996, attracted particular interest. Its declared target was pedophiles who use computers to gain the trust of young people, then lead them into increasingly explicit discussion of sexual topics. The law makes it criminal to transmit "indecent" material to minors, defining such material as that which depicts actual or simulated nudity or sexual conduct and which is "harmful to minors." The law contains limited exemptions for online service providers but would not exempt material with serious value (such as AIDS information or serious literary works). New York lawmakers learned of the Communications Decency Act judgment late in their session but adopted the bill nonetheless just before adjournment. This law and others enacted at the state level seem to pose First Amendment problems comparable to those raised by the federal law and undoubtedly will be challenged on similar grounds.

Some of these state laws failed to distinguish with any precision between the originators of suspect material and the operators of systems or networks used to transmit the material. The threat is therefore quite real that such laws might be invoked by zealous prosecutors against university computer systems, whatever the probable outcome of a full court test. Thus administrators understandably remain apprehensive, and may well seek means of protecting themselves and their systems against such liability—or at least of persuading a judge or a lawmaker that they had done what they reasonably could to reduce the risk of unlawful activity in a new and bewildering electronic age. Such efforts would be by no means the earliest precautions.

Concerned about several possible abuses of computer communication, universities began in the early 1990s to adopt two types of protective measures—acceptable use policies, including content provisions, and restrictions on certain types of access. The most celebrated such initiative was that taken by Carnegie-Mellon University in the late fall of 1994. Though it had been the nation's earliest fully wired campus, CMU felt the need to restrict use of its computer system (named "Andrew" to honor both its patrons) to access certain material readily available on the Internet. The university's concern was triggered by a widely publicized study, conducted by two of its own undergraduates, of salacious Internet content. While the accuracy of the study was later challenged, the results apparently left administrators uneasy about the range of sexually explicit material within easy reach of Andrew's terminals. Thus the university announced that it would no longer make available through its system access to the alt.sex newsgroups. This was not quite the first such ban; Stanford had announced such a step in 1989 but almost immediately reversed itself and made no subsequent attempts to control electronic content.

The Carnegie-Mellon user community was indignant. Responding at once to intense criticism on and off campus, the administration modified its decree. The alt.sex pictorial or graphic newsgroups would still be off-limits, but access to text material would be unaffected. A campus committee was soon created to study the whole issue and recommend a comprehensive access policy. The vice provost in charge of information systems at CMU explained that this revision was a "good faith effort to comply with the law, but also to recognize academic freedom and freedom of speech." "Somehow," he added, "we're going to have to navigate between the shoals." The committee did report the following year. It proposed that "in cases where the university has decided that carrying a newsgroup is illegal . . . carrying of this newsgroup on computer equipment owned and operated by the university is prohibited." The policy would apparently preclude Andrew from carrying or retaining newsgroups under two conditions—where "the stated purpose and content violate the law" and where "the newsgroup consistently violates over a reasonable trial period legal canons, regardless of the stated purpose of the group." The Faculty Senate soon met to discuss these proposals. During the debate there emerged an ingenious alternative—designate Andrew as a "library," since Pennsylvania law (like that of many states) exempts libraries from criminal liability for storing data and information that might be found legally obscene. This proposal reflected at least the virtue of ingenuity in adapting old rules to new media. It remains to be seen how viable such creative alternatives may prove. It is also unclear whether such a solution would be responsive to the twin concerns that had impelled CMU officials in the first place—"that local servers carrying newsgroups may make the university complicit in the provision of illegal materials to . . . members of the CMU community" and that as part of a global network, "university servers provide feeds to servers at other locations."

These are hardly trivial concerns. They are distinctive to electronic material and the way it is accessed and disseminated. Old rules and policies prove to be of quite limited help. The fears expressed by Carnegie-Mellon administrators are hardly idle or disingenuous. Indeed, what is perhaps most surprising is how calm most computer center directors have been during this unsettling period. Yet the legal status of such restrictions deserves early attention. For a public university governed by the First Amendment, adopting content-based access limits would almost certainly abridge both free speech and academic freedom. While private universities are not constrained in the same way by the Constitution, most would be loath to deny free expression in ways their public peers could not. Carnegie-Mellon's claim that most of the target material could be obtained through other channels is rather like saying that if CMU's library banned certain books, they could be ordered on interlibrary loan from Pitt or Penn State. Such an option seems no more persuasive here than the Supreme Court found it in the analogous context of public school libraries; the justices some years ago dismissed a school board's defense that students could easily obtain a banned book at the public library or a bookstore. Given the rapidly growing importance to scholarship and inquiry of university-sponsored and maintained computer networks, there should be a strong presumption that free speech includes unfettered access to all electronic material that does not clearly violate the criminal law.

Two other features of the off-campus context deserve attention. Along with fears about obscenity charges, some computer system operators have also become increasingly uneasy about being sued for libel by people whose reputations suffered from statements carried on the campus network. Here too the legal boundaries are in the early stages of being forged in the courts. There are two early cases, and (as briefly noted earlier) they take seemingly conflicting approaches to the new media. In 1991 a federal court in New York absolved a major commercial computer network (CompuServe) of liability for defamatory statements. The circumstances were unusual, however, and limited the potential force of the judgment. The allegedly libelous statements had been made within a discussion group that was managed and moderated by another organization, to whom CompuServe had effectively turned over responsibility; this fact seemed to mitigate the likelihood that CompuServe knew or could have known what was being said. Under these conditions, the court found no greater basis for holding the network liable than it would in a libel suit against a bookseller or newsdealer, who could not be expected to read every word of the vast array of print materials passing over the counter or through the shelves. This analogy initially gave some comfort to electronic communication media.

Four years later, a New York state court offered a much less generous view of a libel suit by a Long Island investment firm against the Prodigy network. In holding that the network might have to pay damages for libelous statements made by one of its users which it had carried, this court stressed several factors not present in the CompuServe case. For one, Prodigy had proclaimed itself the "family-oriented" network and had at one time screened all new messages posted on its bulletin boards (though such screening had stopped a year before the statements that led to the suit). For another, the person who managed the forum ("Money Talk") where the offending statements appeared was deemed an agent of Prodigy and was thus quite different from the outsider who managed the CompuServe forum. This court accepted the notion that a computer network more closely resembled a bookstore or a library than a publisher. This analogy did not, however, persuade the court that Prodigy could avoid all liability for carrying defamatory material, even though it had no direct knowledge of the contents. Late in the year the case was settled, leaving many difficult issues of electronic liability open for another day.

Network operators and others—university system directors, for example—may now face an acute dilemma. On one hand, the prospect of civil or criminal liability may cause them to exercise tighter control over the material they carry. Yet the very fact they engage in such oversight may in turn strengthen the case against them, along lines marked out by the Prodigy court in citing the greater care with which the network had monitored material it carried. Only time, more cases, and more experience can give adequate guidance on steering between those shoals. For now the situation is both fluid and uncomfortable.

One factor remains—the practical issue of how far digital content could be controlled, whatever the law may require or anticipate. This problem is well illustrated by one other recent campus episode. In the summer of 1994, the Federal Office for Civil Rights (OCR) received and acted on a complaint by two women students at Santa Rosa Junior College in California. The complainants were deeply offended by certain sexist comments that male students had posted on a men-only campus computer bulletin board. They characterized the comments as "anatomically explicit and derogatory." The women brought suit against the college, charging unlawful sex discrimination, and OCR joined them in federal court. The college soon settled with the complaining students. But the Office for Civil Rights refused to drop its claims.

During negotiations that both sides hoped might yield a settlement, OCR proposed (under federal laws barring sex discrimination) that the college agree to ban the posting of computer comments that "harass, denigrate or show hostility toward a person or group on the basis of sex, race, or color." Such a ban would include slurs, negative stereotypes, jokes, and pranks. The college refused to accept such a condition. Not only did it believe it should not be in the business of monitoring its students' computer comments, but it also harbored grave doubts about the enforceability of any such ban, even on a relatively small campus with a fairly basic computer network.

The practical problems of imposing any such ban would be immense for a small and technically modest institution. For a large research university the practical problems of such oversight are inconceivable. The volume of traffic on the information superhighway may, ironically, both compound the problem and complicate the solution. Take the case of Texas A & M professor Grady Blunt, who was on leave for several months in 1994 and returned to campus to find that someone had used his computer password to post a series of racist messages that were received around the world and understandably, though erroneously, attributed to Blunt. In his e-mailbox he found no fewer than 500 replies with threats of one sort or another, including several death threats. Such an episode poses the problem quite starkly. It should never have happened in the first place; tighter security for passwords would have prevented the unauthorized access that set the events in motion. The case does, however, remind us of several of the novel and distinctive features of electronic communication. E-mail can do harm to a degree far beyond the potential hazards of print communication. Yet the very scope and speed of problems like this one also attest to the virtual impossibility of monitoring or of devising any protective device (other than password security).

While awaiting more extensive guidance from the courts, what steps should a conscientious institution take to adapt and update its policies? Several principles may be helpful in this early and uncertain environment.

First, every college and university should adopt, promulgate, and require all users to sign a comprehensive acceptable use policy as a condition of system access. Such a policy mainly addresses matters of time and place—who can use the system, at what hours and for what purposes, and what happens if a password is improperly used—but may include a few content provisions not likely to be controversial. As a nonprofit institution, a university might well bar all commercial advertising from its computer system. It might also forbid direct solicitation or inducement to criminal activity. And a university might declare that its system may not be used for the transmission of material that would violate the state's obscenity or child pornography laws. Additional content provisions—dealing with such real and troublesome matters as access to sexually explicit but not obscene material—are certain to be problematic.

Second, a basic policy premise ought to be that the content of electronic speech may be curtailed only in ways that oral or written expression may be regulated. Thus a constitutionally valid policy which bans verbal sexual or racial harassment in face-to-face situations might be applied to the electronic equivalent of such harassment, presumably in the form of individually addressed e-mail. But the current legal context affords no basis for going further, as the Office for Civil Rights has sought to require Santa Rosa Junior College to do, by barring offensive electronic messages that could not be proscribed if they were spoken or written. For just this reason, a university faced with demands to curb the electronic excesses of a professor (such as the pronouncements of Northwestern's Holocaust-denier Arthur Butz) should be as firm in defending academic freedom online as it has been in protecting more traditional forms of professorial speech. There is nothing about the medium that changes the basic scope of free speech or academic freedom; the indisputable fact that electronic messages travel farther and faster and may thus do greater damage does not, by itself, dilute the fundamental freedom that is central to discourse within an academic community.

Third, universities may find that existing policies will serve the new needs of the electronic world better than they might have expected. Take the case of the homophobic student at Virginia Tech, for example. What this student did was to intrude his highly offensive comments into a gay and lesbian computer discussion group. Had the student physically broken up a closed meeting of a gay and lesbian organization in the student union, sanctions would have been in order, and not because of any words the intruder might have used. By analogy, the homophobic intrusion at Virginia Tech might be punishable on conduct grounds rather than on speech grounds. Similarly, the case of the four sexist Cornell freshmen might have involved some punishable conduct, though the administration wisely preferred to wring an apology from the offenders. The point is one that needs to be more fully explored across the electronic landscape: before framing new rules to deal with digital transgressions, consider the potential of existing conduct rules that may prove more flexible than would initially appear. The advantages of being able to address new problems with tried and tested policies should be obvious.

Fourth, the prospect remains that higher or different standards might eventually be justified by some special or unique feature of electronic media. If a particular message became more dangerous simply because it passed over wires in digital form, then such a claim should receive close scrutiny and might find its way into the equation. Unleashing a computer virus designed to destroy valuable files, regardless of the message or motive that accompanies the infection, is a type of harm unique to electronic communication. Other special interests and circumstances may emerge through further experience. In this regard, there is one obvious difference between media that will probably turn out to be without legal import but needs further study. A university may often learn of the content of certain messages passing over its computer system that would never come to light or attract attention if they passed by telephone or campus mail. This difference should not, however, enlarge the scope of a university's authority over the message itself; computer "flaming" may be more visible and potentially more embarrassing, but it is not for this reason alone more regulable. The key to defining the scope of institutional control should for most purposes be the message itself, not the medium or characteristics of the medium.

Fifth, policies on the content of digital communication should be the same for all users. Thus an art historian or a sociologist or a professor of ob-gyn should not enjoy a greater right to transmit material like that found in the alt.sex newsgroups than would faculty (or students) in other fields. Of course some access differences might simply reflect the different priorities and needs of scholars on one hand and browsers on the other—quality of equipment, online time, costs, downloading capability, and so forth. But the basic test of what types of material a member of the campus community can and cannot access electronically should not be a product of the user's status, any more than the library's one copy of *Penthouse* or *Hustler* can be kept from the hands of casual readers in deference to serious students of sociology or art. Whatever differences may separate the senior art historian or the sociologist from the merely curious graduate student should not shape the basic conditions or standards of access.

Finally, recent special legislation at the federal and state levels poses novel and troubling prospects. Until the new laws are declared inapplicable or unconstitutional, they are of course binding on the university (unless specific exemptions blunt their force). Here the directors of computing centers need expert guidance from their university attorneys—who in turn are increasingly dependent for guidance on a small but growing group of experts in the field of electronic expression and its regulation. Perhaps all that is clear now is that the law will evolve rapidly, change continually, and keep the academic community of electronic communicators guessing for some years to come.

IV

THE CONSTITUTION AND THE
OFF-CAMPUS SPEAKER

To: University General Counsel
From: Vice President for Student Affairs

Help! Here's a crisis we never expected—but maybe that's the definition of crisis in our business. The Black Student Alliance has invited Khalid Abdul Muhammad to campus next fall as part of an African American awareness program. They've filled out all the right forms and provided the necessary information. The auditorium is (I'm sorry to report) free on that evening. The question of the hour is whether we have to provide a forum on our campus for someone we know will surely spew hate against almost every group in sight.

In case you have forgotten, let me refresh your recollection about Mr. Muhammad. He first hit the speaking trail in the fall of 1993. After Thanksgiving, he spoke at Kean College in New Jersey. Apparently this was the first time anyone had been able to tape his remarks; he usually barred all reporters and recorders, and thus kept himself and his views out of the news. By January the text of the Kean College speech had come to the attention of the Anti-Defamation League of B'nai B'rith. Its members were so outraged by Muhammad's extreme anti-Semitism they took out a full-page ad in the *New York Times,* on the eve of Martin Luther King's birthday, to reprint some of the most offensive portions of the speech.

The speaker spared hardly any group in society. While Muhammad aimed his most venomous attacks against Jews—calling them "bloodsuckers" and worse—he lambasted Catholics, gays, and many others as well. There was something in the speech to offend or outrage just about everyone. Of course there weren't many members of the target groups in the audience. The occasion was a closed meeting of a black student organization, to which others had not been invited and were not likely to come. But when the text appeared in the *Times,* Muhammad suddenly became a household name. He also became a prominent figure on the college lecture circuit that spring. Most of these later events went peacefully, with a couple of exceptions I'll mention. Along the way Muhammad's mentor, Nation of Islam minister Louis Farrakhan, distanced himself from the provocative language of his protégé but made no apology for the "truths he spoke" about such matters as the alleged role of Jews in promoting the slave trade.

Three incidents that give us pause happened in different times and places. The most publicized of Muhammad's appearances was at Howard University, the historically black institution in Washington, D.C. There in late April he addressed a crowd of some 1,500, who (in the words of a *New York Times* reporter) "cheered wildly" his repeated anti-Semitic attacks and other diatribes. The aftermath was painful for Howard, though apparently no more than fifty of those in the audience were Howard students.

A distinguished Jewish historian from Yale either withdrew from a speaking engagement at Howard or had the invitation canceled; the facts remained in dispute for many months. Howard's image took a beating in the white academic community, even among liberals who would normally have urged toleration and understanding. So the Howard episode is one that any other institution would view with grave apprehension. In fact, the next fall Howard did cancel a rally that would have featured another Muhammad appearance, citing a "moratorium" on the use of campus facilities for such events pending revision of the applicable rules.

Then there was the experience of the University of California–Riverside, apparently Muhammad's last scheduled stop of the spring speaking tour. The lecture itself, held at a campus gym in late May 1994, was actually more temperate than many of the others. The trouble came immediately after the program. Without warning, Muhammad disregarded a carefully worked out security plan. He continued to answer audience questions outside the gym rather than departing at once, as campus security and his own bodyguards had expected. Moments into the questioning, he was shot and seriously wounded in the leg. The assailant turned out to be a disgruntled member of the Nation of Islam who had been expelled three years earlier and had been biding his time for revenge. Both he and Muhammad were taken at once to a hospital, where both remained in serious condition for days.

The third incident came after months of quiet on the campus speaker circuit. Muhammad had been invited by students to address a Black Solidarity Day program at York University in New York City in November 1995. Given the speaker's track record elsewhere, the administration at first balked. The college's head, an African American named Thomas Minter, warned that "a college president cannot condone someone who is a messenger of hate speaking on a campus." He expressed his doubts whether the college could provide adequate security. The student sponsors, however, took umbrage at what they saw as a threat to Black Solidarity Day.

After hours of tense confrontation, the administration eventually yielded and allowed Muhammad to speak. The event was heavily guarded by campus police in riot gear. The text was classic Muhammad, with vicious attacks on whites, on Jews, and on York's own senior black administrators (whom he termed "plantation Negroes that the master [City College's white chancellor] had sent to the gate"). Of the previous weekend's assassination of Israeli prime minister Yitzhak Rabin, Muhammad quipped, "What goes around comes around." He termed the slaying "not a case of the chickens coming home to roost, but of the chickens coming home to roast." Apropos of the recent acquittal of O. J. Simpson, Muhammad asked his audience: "If you believe that blondes have more fun, ask Nicole Brown Simpson." Mercifully, the event concluded without mayhem or injury; only one student was arrested, and that for seeking unlawful entry. In short, it could have been much worse.

Such volatile events point toward one other risk. You can imagine the sort of media exposure that accompanies a visit by such a virulent speaker. It may take years for a place like Kean to recover. Howard's reputation suffered badly; though of course there were other unsettling events, the Muhammad speech probably did the worst damage. In the spring of 1994, the United Negro College Fund reported a spate of protest letters and actual cancellations from past contributors who expressed anguish at what they saw as complicity or weakness toward Muhammad on the part of black college administrators. (Ironically, very few of the campus appearances by Nation of Islam leaders—only three of fifty-five, according to the Anti-Defamation League—occurred at black colleges.) So among other dimensions of the controversial speaker quandary are some very serious public relations problems.

Now, we need your advice on a series of issues. First and foremost, can we cancel or withdraw the invitation for next fall or tell the Black Student Alliance it must do so? May we not point to the venom that Muhammad spews everywhere he goes—the trail of hatred and even bloodshed he has left across the country? Can't we take into account the public relations disaster such an appearance would create for us, especially among our Jewish and Catholic alumni and legislators? If we had to do it, I think it would even be worth canceling all off-campus speakers for next year, although that would be a painful solution and would create other public relations and alumni support problems for us.

If we have no choice but to permit Muhammad to speak, then we need guidance on several subsidiary issues. For example, can we demand to see a text of his speech in advance, and can we insist he stick to it? Can we require that he avoid certain subjects or phrases of the kind that have so inflamed other campuses? Can we arrange to have a semiofficial "response" delivered right after the lecture by some respected person at the same time and place? Or if not on the same stage, can we arrange a "counter" event elsewhere on campus right after the Muhammad lecture? Could we insist that Muhammad respond to questions after he speaks? Can we insist the event be open to all members of the campus community, even if he would like it closed? How about security—can we demand that he leave all that to our campus police and insist he use his own bodyguards only under the police's direction? And speaking of security, can we charge any of the special costs—heavy police protection and overtime pay, for example—to the sponsoring student organization? And what should be easiest of all, can we take out ads in the student paper and the local daily the next morning denouncing what he has said—or, actually, what we are quite certain he will be saying?

Well, these are the key questions. We need your answers as fast as possible, since we have a meeting with the black student leaders a few days from now—and we know they'll be pressing us for details on the Muhammad visit. Please give us as much leeway as possible!

• • •

To: Student Affairs Staff
From: University General Counsel

Well, you certainly know how to make life tough for your lawyers. We haven't had an off-campus speaker question in many years. Most of us college attorneys were in grade school the last time the courts handled such a case. So while the Muhammad issue as such is new, the legal materials on which the courts would rely have much earlier antecedents.

Maybe a little of that early history would be helpful. Then I'd like to review some of the policy considerations—the pros and cons of speaker bans, if you will—before giving you our best judgment about the current state of the law. Of course we will advise on options you may have short of barring a speaker—something which, in all candor, I doubt very much we as a public college can or should do. But that's getting ahead of the story. There was a time, not so very long ago, when barring certain speakers was assumed to be both necessary and permissible, even at some quite prestigious universities.

A. Origins of—and Reasons for—Campus Speaker Bans

Soon after World War II, during the McCarthy era, many campuses found it increasingly difficult to explain or defend visits by controversial speakers, especially by speakers who were (or were thought to be) Communists. Even much less visibly radical visitors ran afoul of the politics of those perilous times. A noted pacifist was denied permission to speak at Ohio State University. Dr. Robert Oppenheimer, the eminent physicist who was the father of the atomic bomb, was barred from addressing a scientific conference at the University of Washington because of his liberal political views. Yale University once revoked a student invitation to Alabama governor George Wallace, though it eventually relented and let the governor speak. Even conservative columnist and *National Review* editor William Buckley was barred from speaking at New York City's Hunter College.

One must recall the temper of those bleak days to appreciate why so many universities, both public and private, felt compelled to question or restrict appearances by certain outside speakers. First and foremost, there was intense political (and sometimes alumni and donor) pressure against providing a campus podium for "radical" speakers. During the late 1940s and well into the 1950s, there was a genuine hysteria about the message Communists and others might convey to "impressionable" students. While the study of different and competing economic systems might be tolerated in the classroom (though in a few celebrated instances even the role of communism in the curriculum was questioned), what happened in the central plaza or on the steps of Old Main was a different matter.

Speakers of several types drew the brunt of these bans. Actual or suspected Communists or "fellow travelers" were the prime targets. There was also a growing concern about people who, regardless of their own politics, had invoked the Fifth Amendment's privilege against self-incrimination when called to testify about others before congressional or state legislative committees looking into subversive activities. There were some vaguer and broader bans against—to use the words of an Illinois law that wound up in court—representatives of "any subversive, seditious, and un-American organization."

Still other policies (for example, that of Auburn University) proscribed campus visits by "persons who could reasonably be expected to advocate breaking a law," while the University of Tennessee decreed that an outside speaker could be approved only if "there is no reason to believe that he might speak in a libelous, scurrilous or defamatory manner. . . ." Still others, like the regulation that governed Mississippi's public campuses, barred anyone who might advocate not only the violent overthrow of the government but also "the wilful damage or destruction . . . of the institution's buildings" or "the forcible disruption or impairment" of classes and other scheduled campus events and activities. The list of proscribed speakers and forbidden themes went on, more detailed in some states than others, reaching much of the material that controversial speakers might bring to the college campus.

Several other factors, apart from genuine aversion to the message, helps to explain the speaker-ban mania. While public parks and streets have always been viewed as suitable sites for expressive activity, the same view never applied to the college campus. In fact, the locations where speakers might command an academic audience—the central campus plaza at noon, the largest lecture hall or auditorium in late afternoons and evenings—are extremely valuable resources that must often be rationed carefully among competing claimants.

Moreover, members of the campus community do and should have first claim on such speaking sites. Given the scarcity of attractive forums on the typical campus and the need for their rationing, the adoption of some standards was hardly surprising. Nor was it surprising that some institutions, in the course of allocating their scarce space, might favor "good" or "positive" messages rather than negative or hostile themes. Thus many trustees who banned communists and other "radical" or "disloyal" visitors in the McCarthy era saw themselves as doing no more than setting appropriate priorities for the allocation of a valuable and desirable resource.

Some speaker bans may even have reflected (or at least asserted) a genuinely educational concern. If the mission of a college or university is ultimately to educate and if this mission transcends the classroom and the laboratory, one might find a basis for faculty concern about the quality, the accuracy, and the integrity of information that reaches students within the learning environment. Communists, at least, were widely believed to distort, misuse, and pervert truth in ways that could seriously mislead "impressionable" students. On essentially this basis, the Administrative Council of New York's Queens College justified its 1961 decision to bar Communist speaker Benjamin Davis from the campus:

> The faculties and administrative officers are . . . charged with making certain that the time of students is properly spent in the examination of the various facets of human experience which can give the greatest educational value. There can be no assumption that a commitment to free expression and discussion relieves the professional staff of its duty to discriminate and choose among the welter of ideas, positions, convictions, facts and theories which present themselves for consideration.

However specious or disingenuous such reasoning may strike us today, it had some credibility in the 1960s. An administration that felt it had to bar certain speakers and their messages, whatever the real rationale for doing so, might console itself that such a policy protected immature minds from exploitation by intellectually dishonest subversives. We should give the educational rationale its due, noting the nature of the times.

Some speaker bans reflected a plausible concern about the appearance or image of institutional "sponsorship." No listener believes that a city endorses the views of an orator it allows to declaim from a soapbox in the park on Sunday afternoon. When a permit is issued to a labor union or a civil rights group to hold a march or rally on public property, few observers infer governmental sanction for the views that are expressed. The high profile of a speaker on a university campus may, however, create a different inference. The Hunter College administrator who barred William Buckley in 1960 tried to explain what worried him about publicity that might follow reports of the conservative columnist's appearance on his campus:

> Academic institutions of a public character must avoid giving the appearance or creating the suspicion that they favor particular movements or groups over other groups opposed to their positions or their points of view.

The arrival of the visible and controversial speaker may more readily imply a sort of institutional endorsement not likely to be found in any other setting. Several forces may lead to such a result. The scarcity of campus podiums and the concomitant need for rationing might imply that the institution had made some choice among competing users and their messages. News reports of the event will routinely cite the college or university at which the speech occurred, whether or not the institution did more than open the gates. The routine disclaimer—"the views of the speaker are not necessarily those of . . ."—that seems to work well enough in airports and other settings may be less effective in the campus context, especially in allaying the concerns of skeptical legislators, alumni, and others who believe that the administration could, if it chose, bar a particular speaker or viewpoint. So an inference of sponsorship or endorsement does distinguish the appearance of the campus speaker from the obviously unsponsored user of the streets and public parks— though it is a factor that cuts both ways.

So much for the "why" of speaker bans. It is time to look more closely at the forms they took, before tracing their denouement. Speaker bans took effect in several ways. In some states, the legislature imposed a ban, as did Illinois through its infamous Clabaugh Act of 1947, which provided that

> no trustee or official, instructor or other employee of the University of Illinois shall extend to any subversive, seditious, and un-American organization, or to its representatives, the use of any facilities of the university

for the purpose of carrying on, advertising or publicizing the activities of such organization.

Such language left campus officials minimal latitude. In the case that brought this particular statute into court, administrators insisted that an invited Communist speaker provide the university written assurances that he would not "publicize the subversive and seditious activities of the Communist Party"—assurances neither the speaker nor his sponsor was willing to submit.

North Carolina's 1963 speaker-ban law cut an even broader swath. It effectively compelled officials at all the state's public campuses to deny platforms not only to Communists but also to any person who was likely to call for the overthrow of the government or had invoked the Fifth Amendment when interrogated about Communist or subversive activities. Similar proscriptions could be found in laws of a dozen other states from the 1940s through the 1960s.

Speaker bans had quite disparate sources. Many were the products of state legislation. Others were creatures of the university's own governing board, sometimes framed in terms even more sweeping and less precise than the statutes. There were also a host of speaker policies that simply appeared in student handbooks or other compendia of campus rules, sometimes framed by an apprehensive administration without formal board imprimatur.

B. Concerns about Speaker Bans: Public Policy

Lest one assume that no voice of concern greeted such policies, we should note that speaker bans were controversial even in the McCarthy days. Some administrators who were charged with enforcing these policies recognized the futility and hazard of their task. The "sponsorship" issue, in fact, emerged early as one of the traps. University of Oregon president Arthur Flemming, who had served as secretary of health, education and welfare in the Eisenhower cabinet, warned on this very point:

> The first time a university bars a speaker it will put itself in a position of either endorsing future speakers, or at least saying they are not as bad as the one who is barred. The only way in which a university can avoid putting its stamp of approval on an outside speaker is to follow the policy

of permitting a faculty or accredited student group to invite anyone they desire to hear.

Thus banning the first radical speaker might be justified by a desire to avoid the appearance of endorsing the speaker's message or political affiliation, but such an approach would work only once. The next time a controversial speaker loomed, and every time thereafter, the institution would face an impossible dilemma: either ban all other speakers, including some you would genuinely like to have on campus, or risk creating the impression that you have given an official imprimatur to the views of every speaker who is not rejected. This quandary soon became apparent. The wisdom of Flemming's counsel caused some states to modify or repeal speaker bans and persuaded others simply never to adopt them in the first place.

Apart from the double bind of "sponsorship," there were even more basic policy concerns about speaker bans. The key operative terms in most such policies were so broad and so vague as to be almost meaningless—even those that were limited to members or suspected members of the Communist Party, and much more clearly those that barred persons who might bring to the campus loosely specified unwelcome or unsettling messages. The task of differentiating in advance between those speakers whose themes would prove acceptable and those who would offend or insult or incite was really never feasible.

Most basic was a deeply educational concern about speaker bans and their effect. California governor Edmund G. "Pat" Brown courageously answered on essentially educational grounds a citizen demand that a noted liberal be barred from campuses in his state: "As long as I'm Governor of this state, the students can invite anyone they please to speak on the Berkeley campus." One of the preeminent university leaders of the 1950s, University of Minnesota president O. Meredith Wilson, put it best in explaining to skeptical state officials why he had allowed Communist Benjamin Davis to speak on campus in response to a student group's invitation:

> We believe it would be a disservice to our students and an insult to our nation's maturity if we were to deny Mr. Davis an opportunity to speak. Over-protected students might at once assume that Davis had something to say which was too strong for our reason and our convictions. The University is the product of a free society. It is neither afraid of freedom,

nor can it serve society well if it casts doubts on the ability of our free institutions to meet the challenge of doctrines foreign to our own.

Such statements as these, regrettably rare though they were in the heyday of speaker bans, brought home to the college campus the most basic values of free expression. From John Milton on, the core case for free speech derives from a belief that society is better served by permitting than by suppressing those viewpoints it finds hateful or unsettling. From the early Supreme Court cases, the eloquent views of Justices Holmes and Brandeis invoked these values to justify tolerance for abhorrent speech and dangerous speakers. It was only in the desperate days of Senator McCarthy that even the courts had their doubts; people could be jailed as dangerous conspirators, Justices Black and Douglas warned in dissenting opinions, not because they fomented a revolution but because they wrote, taught, even read "subversive" material. It is thus easy to understand, in retrospect, why so few academic leaders were willing to take the bold position of Minnesota's president Wilson and to refute the central premise of the speaker bans.

C. Speaker Bans in the Courts

Whatever the level of misgiving about their wisdom and efficacy, speaker bans were not to disappear easily once they were on the books. Repeal efforts often proved unpopular and dangerous, even in states where speaker bans had been enacted with little popular demand. The courts thus became the most, sometimes the only, viable avenue of redress. Test cases were not only predictable, in some states they were actually welcomed by boards and administrators who had no heart for speaker laws they wished to escape but could not avoid. These cases, the last of which is now a quarter-century old, yield virtually all the legal guidance we have in addressing such current and vital questions as those raised by Khalid Muhammad's travels on the academic circuit.

Curiously, the first major case presented the issue in reverse. A group of New York State taxpayers sued the Trustees of the State University to force withdrawal of an invitation that had been extended to Communist Party official and editor Herbert Aptheker. This time, alone among the cases, it was the governing board that argued for expression and academic freedom. Just as curiously, it was the trial judge (holding in the taxpayers' favor) who imposed a speaker ban where the university and its board had refused to do so. By taking this course, requiring the university to bar the speaker, the judge disregarded the interests of Aptheker's potential listeners; it was enough for him that Communists (at least according to FBI director J. Edgar Hoover) had regularly advocated violent overthrow of the government and thus were properly denied access to college campuses where they might ensnare unwitting disciples.

Such a judgment was not likely to survive appeal, and this one did not. New York's appellate courts deferred to the trustees and allowed Aptheker to speak. This outcome, of course, said little about the legality of legislative or institutional speaker bans; this issue would reach the courts in a more familiar form.

The test cases that soon followed posed a novel set of free speech issues. In the late 1950s and early 1960s, the general body of law defining freedom of expression was very much in flux. The same Supreme Court that struck down many New Deal laws in the late 1930s was surprisingly protective of free speech, even in several cases that involved Communist speakers and organizers. These precedents, though never quite overruled, had been sharply qualified and narrowed in the McCarthy period. Moreover, the rights of government beneficiaries like public employees had reached a low ebb; the Supreme Court could say as late as 1952 that people who objected to signing a broad disclaimer loyalty oath in order to get or keep a government job were "at liberty to take their beliefs and associations and go elsewhere" if they preferred. Thus the general body of free speech law that awaited the first speaker-ban cases offered little comfort to controversial speakers. Even off campus, this was not a good time to press free speech claims—much less in the special and yet untested campus environment.

Moreover, the college campus, even the public campus, was obviously different from streets and parks in ways that might limit or modify the scope of general free speech law. Since speaking sites on most campuses are in high demand, reservation procedures are standard. The allocation of scarce campus space must also respect the academic mission of the institution. There is also a lingering concern about apparent sponsorship. So at the very least there are differences in fact between the public park and the college campus.

There has always been one other intriguing difference. The free speech claims in the early campus access cases often went beyond those of the speaker and included the interests of would-be listeners as well. Indeed, occasionally the speaker was not even a plaintiff, leaving to the would-be audience the full burden of litigation. Much as with challenges to book censorship that readers brought to court, the right to receive information was coming to play a significant role.

The two earliest court tests of speaker bans—the Buckley case in New York and the Aptheker case in North Carolina—reached results that were at least superficially similar. Both courts found the challenged bans to violate free speech rights of speakers and/or listeners. Central to both judgments was the vagueness and lack of precision in the ban's operative language. The key terms not only created genuine doubt on the part of those who were charged with their enforcement. Such vagueness also invited arbitrary or discriminatory administrative action in a field fraught with First Amendment implications.

Beyond such specific and familiar grounds of decision, both courts were troubled by the notion of government policies that allowed an institution of higher learning to limit ideas and viewpoints. "I would have thought," observed the New York trial judge, "that one of the aims of a college worthy of the name was to stimulate thought and provoke intellectual controversy." He continued:

> a college should, to my mind, pursue a policy of fostering discussion and the exchange of opinion by providing an open forum for it to all who want to be heard. A college should generate intellectual excitement, it should attempt to awaken the public mind from the torpor and quiescence of accepted and conventional opinion.

Other courts shared this skeptical view of imprecise language or loosely (if at all) defined terms and struck down speaker bans of the early variety. Yet there were a few judges, like the one who initially barred Aptheker from speaking in New York, who deferred to real or imagined institutional needs, such as the protection of campus property that might be put at risk by the visit of an inflammatory speaker. Several courts that struck down imprecise bans hinted that speaker access might still be curtailed by using more precise terminology. For example, the federal judge in North Carolina who invalidated the state's ban in the Aptheker case at Chapel Hill expressed ambivalence about the precedent he felt obliged to create:

> University students should not be insulated from the ideas of extremists, but there is a danger that the voices of reason, throughout the broad spectrum they cover, will remain unheard if the clamor of extremists is disproportionately amplified on university platforms.

Such a caution is easy enough for a court to offer in dictum. Yet for the administrator who must act in real situations, guidance of this sort is far from self-executing. If some ideas are "safe" for college students while others are not, who is to draw such lines and on what basis? Such distinctions surely could not depend, at a public institution, on the viewpoint or the organizational affiliation of the speaker. There was no basis for a judgment, even in those uneasy and fearful times, that the needs of the public campus were so different from those of the outside world as to warrant a different First Amendment approach to the speaker's message or affiliation.

There were, however, other interests to which courts might give greater deference on than off campus. The treatment of a speaker's past conduct offers a useful illustration. One court upheld a college's edict against the return to campus of a political group that had done extensive damage during earlier visits. Of those visits and their legal significance the court observed:

> Plaintiffs or others, at their instigation, deliberately returned to the campus time and again, marching, clapping, singing and hurling obsceni-ties at school officials and highway patrolmen. . . . Eventually, college students were aroused to such a pitch that buildings were burned and equipment wantonly damaged.

Such reasoning would not have justified curbing free speech in the outside community. Prior conduct would not, for example, warrant barring a group that had previously shown bad manners (or worse) from taking to the streets or holding a rally in the park. Off campus, those who destroy property may be made to reimburse the owner, but that is the proper sanction. Added police protection may be required for future events involving the same group. Conceivably the size of the gathering or the time at which it occurs may be regulated. Even a trail of violence will not justify denying a forum to a group that would otherwise be entitled to use the site for expressive purposes.

When the same issue arises on the public college campus, there is a persistent suggestion that a higher deference to institutional needs may warrant different treatment. The underlying issue is this: to what degree (if any) is the public college campus legally different, for speech purposes, from the park or the streets? Courts have seldom addressed this issue directly; they have either assumed that different treatment was warranted, without saying why, or more often (and more recently) have assumed that any factual differences between conditions on campus and in the park are without constitutional significance. We need to face the issue, even if we are convinced of the latter view.

There are at least two obvious threshold differences. First, campus speakers (unlike soapbox orators) need to be invited to speak. There has never been a serious claim that a speaker no one wants to hear has any right to claim a campus platform. The applicable policy of the American Association of University Professors, for example, declares only that "students should be allowed to invite and hear any person of their own choosing." The court cases have all involved speakers who were invited to campus by a student or faculty group. While one might posit a challenge from a speaker for whom there was no prospective campus audience, the free speech claim would be attenuated. A recent federal appeals court decision strongly implies the validity of neutral campus rules requiring some modicum of sponsorship. In this sense, then, the campus setting is already different from the street or the park, where the speaker needs no invitation before claiming a right to speak.

There is a second and deeper difference. A university campus is simply not a communal thoroughfare or gathering place. It is, in contrast, a place uniquely dedicated to learning. Many parts of the college campus are entitled to special protection; demonstration and protest may well be incompatible with the primary functions of such areas. Speech throughout the academic community may occasionally yield to the institution's academic mission. It is not simply that all speech in the classroom is regulated by the professor or that loud speech is unacceptable in the library stacks or reading room. The need to study, to learn, to read, to take examinations, may more broadly constrain campus speech in deference to the academic mission.

To some degree the campus is in this regard analogous to parts of the larger community; quiet is of course enforced in library reading rooms, courtrooms, hospital operating rooms, and other special-purpose sites.

But there is something different and distinctive about the academic setting that might argue for a narrower concept of public forum and expressive activity than is appropriate for society at large.

Thus the ultimate question is whether the open and public spaces on the state university campus partake of a different character for expressive purposes than do streets and parks in the larger community. One constitutional scholar has made a thoughtful case for a distinctive type of forum analysis. Professor William Van Alstyne, an early and ardent critic of speaker bans, wrote some time ago that "a college campus is constitutionally distinguishable from a public park in which no form of prior restraint of political assemblies is sustainable." One of the very few recent speaker cases reinforced the distinctive character of the public campus:

> A university differs in significant respects from public forums such as streets or parks or even municipal theaters. A university's mission is education, and [courts recognize] . . . a university's authority to impose reasonable regulations compatible with that mission upon the use of its campus and facilities.

A federal appeals court judgment at the end of 1995 reinforced this difference, holding that an itinerant preacher had no blanket constitutional right to speak at the site of his choice on a state university campus; "other policies," said the court, "must determine the particular campus site most appropriate for his presentation."

Such statements bring us to further, related questions: Are there aspects of the public university's unique mission that may affect speaker access beyond the need to ensure that learning can occur, that students can study and faculty can teach and pursue research? Might such interests extend even to the plaza, the stadium, even to the auditorium when it is not in academic use? Such an extension may be appealing, but is ultimately risky. The danger of invoking such broadly protective interests is that their application might prove too much and could even lead back to something akin to speaker bans. Of course there are places on a campus where speaker access may be restricted to a greater degree, and for different reasons, than at comparable off-campus sites. Yet for those parts of the campus that have historically been used for speech and expressive activity—the plaza, the forum, the central square, etc.—no special academic interests seem to warrant a cordon against outside speakers in general, much less against speakers who bring abhorrent or unsettling messages.

What, then, of the implausible public campus that claims it never created a forum, having never made space available for outside speakers, and is therefore under no duty to provide a platform for a particular speaker? There will be few enough such institutions in the real world, but let us assume one does exist. Might it be able to remain speaker free? Or is there an overriding reason to require the creation of a forum for those outside speakers who have been invited by campus groups? If the institution ever had speakers in the past, that should end the matter; you cannot uncreate a public campus forum that has once been created, even if such a forum may not have been constitutionally required in the first place. Even if there is no such precedent, the case seems less than compelling for insulating a campus community uniquely from the flow of ideas and views that buffet the rest of the academic world. Moreover, the essence of the educational process argues for access and openness; a college or university campus, least of all the sites in our society, should be permitted to shield itself from ideas and viewpoints of the kind that controversial outside speakers bring to it and its students.

This analysis brings us back to the specific dilemma posed by Khalid Muhammad. Whatever may be said about speakers in general, such principles are uniquely tested by a visitor who spews venom and hate at all groups and needs a legion of police in riot gear just to deliver his speech. Is there no special basis on which, as York's Thomas Minter pleaded in resisting Muhammad's visit, "a college president cannot condone someone who is a messenger of hate speaking on campus"?

As a matter of educational policy, the answer must be negative. As a matter of law, the answer is almost certainly negative as well. Such a speaker would be barred expressly on the basis of message or view-point—and at that, on the basis of presumed or anticipated viewpoint or message extrapolated from past appearances. This is a process that decades of unhappy experience with speaker bans taught us to eschew at all costs. However clearly we may think we can draw lines between Muhammad and other speakers who may be controversial but are not "intolerable," we know the grave risks of inviting others to use this same process for less benign ends.

None of the asserted contrary interests—appearance of sponsorship, effect on public relations and support, internal harmony, even preservation of personal safety and property—no such interest would suffice to bar an invited speaker. Perhaps this result is not all bad—at least if one believes that a central goal of education, like that of free expression itself, is to create an environment in which all ideas are welcome, no matter how hateful, and in which students will best reach sound conclusions by having before them the broadest range of views.

D. Beyond Access: Policies and Options

There seems no way to avoid the conclusion that if a recognized campus group wants Muhammad to come and speak, he will come and he will speak. This prospect does not, however, end the inquiry. It only shifts the focus to several other issues that would face an institution which cannot (or decides not to) bar a controversial speaker. We might briefly review a series of such questions.

First, to restate one conclusion we have already reached: no outside speaker may demand a campus podium without having been invited. Many institutions require that the invitation come from a recognized student or faculty group. Such a requirement seems reasonable as a way of ensuring accountability, unless the recognition process is used to stifle or inhibit viewpoints. Unlike the street or park, the university setting means that a probable audience—or at least an expression of interest from some group on campus—is a valid prerequisite. (Here we put aside a rather technical issue of legal procedure—what happens when the speaker is not in the lawsuit? Can the would-be listeners carry the case alone? The issue is one of legal "standing"; it concerns procedure in court and not the merits of the case.)

Second, there are numerous "time, place, and manner" rules which, if consistently invoked, can surely be applied to controversial speakers. Groups are typically required to sign up for space a substantial time ahead and to provide certain information with the application. The nature of the facility may limit the size of the audience. The decibel level of sound amplification equipment may be regulated, and the university may require the use of its sound equipment, even that it be operated by a university employee. Announcements about the event may have to meet certain university rules. The sponsoring group may be asked to pay a modest charge to defray specific costs if the room needs to be set up specially or rearranged after the event. Each organization may be limited in the frequency with which it uses a given facility. These and myriad other procedural rules may be imposed so long as the application is uniform and so long as the rule itself does not become a subtle means of viewpoint suppression.

Beyond time, place, and manner lies a set of more troublesome issues. There may be categories of expressive activity the institution wishes to bar altogether, regardless of viewpoint. Selling commercial products may be the clearest example. Though commercial speech now enjoys partial protection under the First Amendment, the Supreme Court has made it clear that public universities may, for example, restrict "Tupperware parties" and similar commercial ventures, not only to protect the privacy of dormitory residents but also to avoid having the campus become an extended commercial bazaar.

More difficult is the status of partisan political speech and campaign activity. On one hand, political expression is at the core of what the First Amendment protects. On the other hand, a public university has a unique interest in not being used, or seeming to be used, for partisan purposes by one political group. This interest may warrant certain limits on extreme forms of political activity, such as hard-core electioneering. It is less clear, though, that even this need would justify barring speakers solely because they hold or are seeking public office or because they support people who hold or seek office. Political expression is fully protected, while advertising is not. Where an incumbent or candidate for office has been properly invited, it would be extremely difficult to frame a rule that would justify canceling an event because of the speaker's partisan role or probable message. There is one possible exception—the acutely delicate case in which a candidate proposes to use a campus forum and a clearly recognizable backdrop to launch a campaign, raising the risk that voters would infer some institutional complicity from photographs or news clips of such an event.

Suppose the institution would like to know in advance what the speaker will say. May it demand a copy of the text? There seems to be no harm in asking. Many institutions do so, if only to help prepare press releases that will do the speaker justice. But there is little else that such a policy could accomplish. It seems clear that a refusal to comply, much less the insertion of controversial material not in the draft, would not justify adverse action on the university's part.

Nor could a speaker be asked in advance—as some of the old speaker policies contemplated—to avoid discussion of particular subject matter, even if the subject matter were unlawful. Of course a speaker who comes to campus and violates the law from the podium may be held accountable. One who incites the audience to riot can presumably be charged and punished under the general criminal law. A speaker who slanders another in the course of a lecture is no better off for having defamed on the college podium than having done so in the local newspaper. Indeed, the potential availability of such postspeech recourse offers the best answer to any doubts about the invalidity of prior restraint.

Several other issues of format deserve attention. There may be differences between speaker and institution on such issues as press coverage, security arrangements, even audience eligibility. Here the balance tips strongly in the institution's favor. A public college or university may surely insist that an event in a campus facility be open to all persons regardless of any restriction the speaker or the sponsoring group might wish to impose. The speaker's freedom to speak does not extend to barring blacks, whites, Jews, Catholics from the auditorium. When it comes to the sensitive issue of security, the institution bears the burden and thus must be able to make and enforce the rules. As the shooting of Khalid Muhammad after his appearance on a California campus reminds us, the need for security is ever present. Thus while personal bodyguards might remain with the speaker for immediate personal security, even they must function under the direction of the campus police or other university officer in charge of security for the event.

The question of press coverage may be even more difficult. Unfettered media access could, and probably should, be made a basic condition of all public campus events. In extreme cases, a speaker might be permitted to limit photographic coverage and perhaps also to bar the use of tape recorders to protect the intellectual property in the lecture and even in responses to questions. Other restrictions should be resisted. In the event of a legal showdown, the institution's position on such issues would almost certainly prevail—unless, of course, such rules had been selectively imposed in ways that belied a content or viewpoint bias.

We turn finally to what may be the most sensitive of format issues. The institution might well wish to have the speaker respond to questions after the lecture and might even insist on a question period. The success of a speaker's challenge to such a demand would depend on a balance of contending claims. On the speaker's part, one might ask first about the rationale for refusing to take questions. Some reasons for such reticence might bear directly on the right to speak freely—in the case, for example, of a speaker who fears that any departure from a carefully prepared text could distort or risk misunderstanding of a precisely articulated position on a delicate issue.

On the other side, one should ask why the institution cares so much about having a question period and whether such a rule is consistently imposed. Forcing the speaker to submit to questions might genuinely enhance the vitality of the forum and the quest for understanding. Students may learn far more from such events if they have an opportunity to confront and interrogate the speaker. A question-period rule premised on such values as these would at least be entitled to some deference if challenged in court.

A similar analysis would presumably apply to a university's demand for a pro-and-con debate. Here, however, consistency of application would seem highly unlikely. Most campus speakers appear without instant refutation, and many would probably be offended if confronted by a "shadow" adversary. They might refuse to take part in a debate if they had been invited for a solo lecture. Such a refusal on the speaker's part would quite likely be sustained by a court in the event of a formal legal challenge. Thus there would be a fairly strong presumption against a debate-requirement policy, at least in the absence of heavily compelling interests behind it.

There may also be serious issues in the institution's relationship with the sponsoring organization. Making sure the students who extended the invitation are aware of the consequences seems perfectly proper—even to the point of suggesting, without coercion, that they reconsider. Beyond this step, temptations abound to take action that would not be acceptable—for example, requiring the sponsors to bear part of the special security costs because their chosen speaker might be more controversial than others. Here, as in many other sensitive areas, the key is consistency; rules and policies that are imposed on all groups and events are far more defensible than those that come into being or are brought out and dusted off selectively to deal with special events or controversial groups and speakers.

Of course mere consistency may not be enough if the policy is simply not compatible with free expression, as our basic discussion of speaker bans should make clear. Free speech, on campus as anywhere else, demands more than simply uniformity of treatment. In matters of process, however, the standard should be clear—if a policy is to be imposed upon or applied in the case of an especially controversial speaker, this policy must not only be on the books before the controversy arises but must also have been uniformly and consistently applied regardless of message or viewpoint or prior appearances. A public university, of all institutions, should both demand and practice such fairness and consistency.

Ultimate solutions to the volatile speaker problem may best come from within. A poignant story offers valuable guidance. At the close of Khalid Muhammad's vitriolic address at Kean College, a single African American student named Todd stood up and told the speaker that he found the theme to be "something out of Hitler's Third Reich." Muhammad retorted angrily: "No cracker at this university had the nerve to come in here and challenge me, but you wanna be the one they will recognize as a good nigger. It makes you look like a damned Tom to stand up in here and defend white folks. Don't stand up in here and defend them." Todd refused to recant or temporize. But, as *Washington Post* editorial writer Colbert King later observed, "Todd, abused by Khalid and ridiculed by some in the audience, did not back down. But that night in New Jersey, Todd stood alone." In a column headed "Who Would Stand with Todd?" King went on to ask his readers: "Where would we have been that night? Standing with Todd? Or would we have been cringing in our seats hoping not to be noticed—or worse yet, part of the fawning crowd, pretending to be one of them? What do any of us do these days, when bigots show their hands?"

V.

GAYS, GREEKS, AND OTHERS

To: The Board of Trustees
From: Carlton Caper, President

I had hoped not to intrude on your summer, but we seem to have a crisis on our hands. There's a group of students on campus called Gays and Lesbians Organized for Action (the acronym for which is GLOA). They have chapters at a number of other colleges and universities across the country, and they now seek recognition here for the first time. This would be a tough issue for us, as you can appreciate. The GLOA members among our students claim their goal is to "raise awareness" on gay and lesbian issues by providing information and sponsoring programs. That sounds harmless enough. The problem is what this group has done at some other campuses. We've had reports that GLOA chapters have held gay awareness rallies at which homosexuality was openly practiced. These groups have passed out fliers urging students to join off-campus same-sex groups. They have urged active support of gay and lesbian causes, including the use of forceful protest if necessary. Any group coming onto our campus with that sort of agenda could create lots of problems for us.

Now, let me clarify my view. It's not that I personally have anything against homosexuality. Some of my friends are gay. But we've got more than a few alumni and legislators in this conservative state who just wouldn't understand. I am certain they would make life very hard for us if we voluntarily invited in a gay and lesbian group. We may not have that kind of luxury to make the choice. GLOA representatives have told us they'll file suit if we deny them recognition. Such a threat seems to have worked at some other places, because student organizations have won a good many similar disputes over the years.

There is more to it, I'm sorry to say. If recognized as a student organization, GLOA would at once be eligible for support from our mandatory student activities fee. The student council allocates the fee, and we make no decisions about who gets what. Like some other groups, GLOA considers anyone who pays a fee as a "member"—and that would mean all students would become members the moment they paid the fee.

Lest you think all our problems are on one side, now enter a conservative student group, Rush for Freedom (followers and admirers of radio talk show host Rush Limbaugh). The Rush people have heard about GLOA and the possibility of recognition and funding. If this does come to pass, they've said they will go to court to block our whole mandatory student fee structure—the one we worked out so carefully two years ago with input from that wonderful faculty-student commit-tee. Rush for Freedom would claim in such a suit that students are being unconstitutionally required to "support" through their fees organizations and causes they abhor and fervently wish to avoid. That's a suit I would hate to face—not only because it might upset our whole fee system and hurt all the other organizations but also because it would compound the bad publicity we'd expect over the GLOA recognition issue.

There is a third part to the puzzle. I haven't told you much about some incipient and very worrisome gay-bashing on campus. Late last spring, during GLOA's organizing drive, one of our fraternities—Lambda Gam-ma Lambda—produced a tasteless skit with really dreadful homophobic jokes, ridiculing gay and lesbian lifestyles. A few of the brothers dressed in crude drag, holding hands and kissing on stage, speaking in mock gay voices, and doing other things that not only the few gay students but many of the straight students in the audience found extremely offensive. The student council has now demanded we put this fraternity out of business, at least suspending it for a year, and maybe something more drastic. But our dean of students (who tends to be soft on fraternities and sororities) tells us that even Greek organizations have free speech rights. He warns that we might face yet another lawsuit if we do come down hard on the fraternity—anything more than a slap on the wrist to a bunch of "bad boys."

As you can tell, we feel we're caught right in the middle on each of these issues. Politics, and sometimes policy, tell us to do one thing. But the law seems to be saying we can't do those things. To get our meeting next week started, I'm sending along a copy of a detailed background memo our general counsel prepared, with some help from our dean of students. It will tell you as much as we know about the legal aspects of these very difficult and complex issues. They're not likely to go away, and we need to be ready to face them quite soon.

• • •

To: Board of Trustees
From: University General Counsel

We might begin by looking at the basic legal status of student organizations. That may seem a difficult task, given the vast range and variety of purposes for which students get together in a large university. But as we will see, there are certain themes that cut across everything from the mountain climbers to the philosophy society to the butterfly collectors to the people pushing for legalization of marijuana. It might be most helpful to start with the issue of recognition, since that's one we do face in dealing with the GLOA group.

I. Recognition of Student Organizations

Can a public college or university deny recognition to a student organization because the group's goals or actions clash with the values of the institution? The short answer appears to be no, and for several reasons. For one, organizations as well as individuals have rights of free expression that government must respect. Moreover, recognition is essential for a student group to achieve a meaningful place in a college community; without recognition, little can be done. Finally, a denial of recognition based on administrators' or trustees' views of the organization's goal or mission would almost certainly involve an adverse judgment about content—something the First Amendment generally forbids government from doing. So let's start by assuming that throwing a student group off campus, or not allowing them to come on campus, because of what they espouse or advocate would almost certainly be unlawful censorship.

That's the easy part. Like most short answers, it has had a fairly tortuous history, and even today contains some qualifications. We need to review the history and examine a few highly significant cases. First, though, it might be worth asking why universities are concerned about recognition of student groups in the first place. Should not every group that wants to exist simply declare itself a student organization? In the real world, things are not quite so simple. There are several reasons why recognition is not and should not be automatic. Institutional recognition typically entitles an organization to access scarce and valuable university resources such as facilities, computer time, funding, and the like. Since the institution cannot provide such resources to the world at large, it may reasonably give priority to its own students, and thus needs to know which groups are proper claimants.

Second, the university ought to know who it can hold accountable if the organization destroys property, fails to clean up as promised, or transgresses in some other way. In this connection, it also needs to know which organizations' off-campus activities may cause outsiders to look to the university and maybe even bring suit against the university for harm done by student groups—whether or not the institution can in fact be held liable, which is quite another matter. People outside the academic community quite naturally assume that if the university chartered a student group, the institution is accountable for whatever the group does anywhere in the world. Finally, granting recognition to a student organization gives the group ready access to the student body and imparts at least some measure of credibility and stature. Thus for various reasons, the institution may well care about the implications of recognition.

It was inevitable that the issue of recognition would get to court; indeed, the wonder is that a real test did not occur until the 1970s. At the height of the Vietnam War era, a local chapter of Students for a Democratic Society (SDS) sought recognition at Southern Connecticut State College. The administration, having heard reports of violence that SDS chapters had caused on other campuses, denied recognition, claiming that the SDS "philosophy was antithetical to the school's policies." The would-be chapter's founders went to federal court, asserting their rights of free speech. The lower courts sustained the administration, finding no actionable violation of First Amendment rights. But the students pressed on. They got a more receptive hearing in the Supreme Court, which unanimously held in their favor.

Early in the opinion the justices addressed the two issues with which we began—the nature of a student group's rights and the effect on these rights of denial of college or university recognition. The relevant constitutional interest was freedom of association. Though the language of the

First Amendment makes no mention of such a right—it guarantees "speech," "press," "assembly," and "petition"—such an associational interest was first recognized by the Supreme Court in the late 1950s. This interest has been consistently applied since then for the benefit of myriad political groups and causes. Because SDS was clearly a political organization, it could claim protection under this branch of free expression. That was the easy part of the case—one the college had never really disputed.

The more difficult question was whether the freedom of association had been abridged by denial of recognition. The court observed that, lacking recognition, a student group could not "remain a viable entity" and could not "participate in the intellectual give and take of campus debate"—dimensions which the First Amendment clearly protected. Thus the justices readily found a close link between recognition and protected expression:

> There can be no doubt that denial of official recognition, without justification, to college organizations burdens or abridges that associational right. The primary impediment to free association flowing from nonrecognition is the denial of use of campus facilities for meetings and other appropriate purposes. . . . [SDS'] associational interests were also circumscribed by the denial of the use of campus bulletin boards and the school newspaper.

In fact, the record in the case provided the clearest proof of how denial of recognition could have such an effect. The SDS organizers sought to hold an introductory meeting on the Southern Connecticut campus but found their unrecognized status disabling. Such, observed the Court, was the "practical effect" of the limbo in which the students had been placed by the administration's quarantine. So whatever theoretical inference one might draw from unrecognized status, the circumstances of the case convinced the justices that the harm was real and of proper concern to a court.

Such conclusions did not end the case, however. The college administration had argued that this was no routine organization but one to which higher standards might properly apply at the recognition stage. While its members had not yet broken any Southern Connecticut rules, their mission, their record, and their behavior at other campuses alarmed the administration. Cited in support of the denial of recognition were the chapter's ties to a national SDS that by now had a long record of disruption and violence on other campuses, the chapter's apparent espousal of a national agenda that had produced a trail of violence elsewhere, a reasonable prospect that a local chapter would become a "disruptive influence" at Southern Connecticut, and the alleged dissonance between SDS's goals and the values of the college. For these reasons, the college had refused recognition—apparently the only group it had ever treated this way.

The Supreme Court was unimpressed. The justices recognized that in extreme cases there might be some "justification" for such adverse actions. But no such justification could be found here, despite the unsettling evidence the administration had cited. State colleges could not infer a penchant for violence on one campus from activities of a national group or of other chapters, especially when (as was the case here) the local group insisted it would eschew the bloody trail of national SDS. Drawing such an inference would be akin to "guilt by association," presuming that all SDS chapters were equally prone to disorder and disruption:

> The mere disagreement of the [college] President with the group's philosophy affords no reason to deny it recognition. . . . The College, acting here as an instrumentality of the State, may not restrict speech or association simply because it finds the views expressed by any group to be abhorrent.

This rejection of the asserted basis for denial of recognition formally ended the case. But the court did leave open a few options. The case would have been different, for example, if the college's concerns about SDS had not been so clearly speculative. If, to illustrate, "there were an evidential base to support the conclusion that CCSC-SDS posed a substantial threat of material disruption . . . [the denial of recognition] should be affirmed." The court cited one other potentially important source of college authority in dealing with potentially unruly student groups:

> A college administration may impose a requirement . . . that a group seeking official recognition affirm in advance its willingness to adhere to reasonable campus law. Such a requirement does not impose an impermissible condition on the students' associational rights. . . . It merely constitutes an agreement to conform with reasonable standards respecting conduct.

The court thus left at least two possible grounds on which recognition might be denied—direct evidence of a serious threat to the stability and order of the institution, and refusal to be bound by "reasonable" campus rules.

In the years since the Southern Connecticut case, many issues have remained untested. The nature of the organization and its mission posed several questions: How far beyond "political" groups does the First Amendment protection of the court's judgment extend—to purely social or other nonpolitical groups? What would a court say if a student political organization lost recognition because it refused to agree to a campus rule it deemed "unreasonable" or unduly restrictive of free speech? And if recognition were refused because the organization seeking it had behaved badly on the campus in question, how much "disruption" would be required; would courts impose the high standard appropriate to dismissal or expulsion of an individual student for disruptive speech? And might a group with a violent past or some other cause for concern be granted a probationary recognition, subject to full recognition following a period of good behavior?

Light may be shed on these and other questions by returning to the most vexatious of issues, that of the gay and lesbian student organization. It is there that the abstract principles have met the harshest test. Whatever the Supreme Court said about politics, institutions have had trouble with sexual orientation. Logically this issue ought not to be any harder than recognition of any other kind of student group; emotionally and politically, though, there are inescapable differences. Thus it is hardly surprising that several notable refusals to recognize gay and lesbian groups have ended up in court.

Four cases, spanning a quarter century, are helpful. The earliest followed the Southern Connecticut case by less than a year. Though the gay and lesbian group had been formally recognized by the University of New Hampshire, its status was in jeopardy when the governor attacked plans for a dance and other social events. When the students went to court, a federal judge saw the Southern Connecticut precedent as controlling. The university was told to treat this group no less favorably than any other student organization on the campus.

The next case involved recognition as such. The issue was the status of a group at Texas A & M University called Gay Student Services. The administration had denied recognition on two grounds that were not readily reconcilable—first, that the group (most logically defined as a "fraternal" organization) did not fit the campus criteria for such groups; and second, that the group was not qualified to fulfill its stated goal of informing the community about gay issues. The student organizers took the administration to court, challenging the validity of both desiderata.

The federal courts first found the group to be political as well as social in nature, ensuring that the issue of recognition would be governed by the Southern Connecticut ruling. Accordingly, neither of the university's extenuations was legally even relevant, much less dispositive. Both the asserted grounds for denial reflected administrative judgments about the viewpoint, message, values, or virtues of the organization. Such considerations were simply not acceptable—no more so in regard to sexual orientation than in regard to radical politics.

The Texas A & M court did, however, enter one intriguing caution, somewhat akin to the Supreme Court's "actual disruption" exception. Had the university refused recognition because of demonstrated concern about public health, linked to overt homosexuality, the court hinted the outcome might have been different. The point played no part in this case, because the administration had cited no health concerns about a gay lifestyle. But the court raised on its own the possibility that a felt need "to discourage this public health risk might be a sufficient basis for denial of recognition" of such a group.

That comment predated public awareness of AIDS and its special threat to the health of the gay community. Such a basis for adverse action today might strike a court as even more plausible; the practical question, of course, is whether a responsible university administration would ever feel comfortable raising such a concern. For if such a claim were advanced and if the supporting evidence struck a court as credible, an institution might conceivably deny recognition to such a group unless it agreed never to encourage gay student social gatherings. This conclusion may, to be sure, reflect an overreading of the dictum in the Texas A & M case. For such a judgment would seem potentially at variance with the Supreme Court's standards in the Southern Connecticut case.

The third recent case arose at the University of Arkansas. The Gay and Lesbian Student Association there had been officially recognized. The dispute involved funding for the presentation of a film and a panel discussion. Both the administration (under strong political pressure) and the Student Senate balked at providing such funds. The senate in fact resolved not to fund "any group organized around sexual preference." The GLSA then went to court, seeking both vindication and funding. The federal appeals court set aside a district court judgment in the university's favor, finding clear evidence of forbidden "viewpoint discrimination." While the motives of the student government may have been mixed, "some student senators freely admitted they voted against the group because of its views." Moreover, the unambiguous focus of the funding ban revealed its rationale. Meanwhile, the treatment of GLSA was unique; no other qualified student organization had been denied funding for such activities. Thus the appeals court concluded that

> the First Amendment violation is apparent. . . . Government may not discriminate against people because it dislikes their ideas, not even when the ideas include advocating that certain conduct now criminal be legalized.

The closing comment deserves elaboration and offers a useful addendum. The university advanced as a further reason for denial of funding that GLSA had advocated sodomy, or at least had lobbied for changes in the state laws on homosexual conduct. The group denied it had such a mission, and the court accepted its denial. Even if changing the sodomy laws had been on the group's agenda, that would not have altered the outcome; "its speech about an illegal activity would still be protected by the First Amendment. People may extol the virtues of arson or even cannibalism. They simply may not commit the acts." Thus advocacy of unlawful conduct—be it sodomy or marijuana use or draft law violation—would not justify differential treatment of an otherwise eligible student organization.

The issue returned to the courts in the winter of 1996. Two developments in Alabama brought about a solid constitutional judgment. Recognition had been denied to a gay and lesbian student group at the University of South Alabama, and the state attorney general had sought to bar an annual gay and lesbian student conference at the University of Alabama at Tuscaloosa. The claimed basis for both actions was a 1975 statute which forbade state colleges and universities to use public funds or facilities to "directly or indirectly sanction, recognize, or support the activities or existence of any organization or group, that fosters or promotes a lifestyle or actions prohibited by the sodomy and sexual misconduct laws." The statute also prohibited "any group permitting or encouraging its members or others to engage in or provide materials on how to engage in the lifestyle or actions."

On the eve of the scheduled conference, a federal judge (relying heavily on the Supreme Court ruling in the Southern Connecticut case) struck down the law as a clear violation of the First Amendment. Such a law, he ruled, imposed clear discrimination against a viewpoint or message; indeed, it sought to impose on anyone using state funds or facilities an official state viewpoint on such matters and "further attempts to dictate the information, and even the actual words, that may not be used to convey an idea or belief." The challenged law also "attempts to draw within its reach even a 'lifestyle' which in some instances could require little more than a frame of mind." None of the asserted state interests came close to validating so sweeping a constraint on expressive activity. The conference at Tuscaloosa apparently proceeded as planned, despite the attorney general's request for a stay of the federal court decree during the conference period.

With such helpful guidance as the courts have now given, we return at length to the most difficult and persistent question about student organizations: Are there any substantive grounds on which a group might be denied recognition—purposes or activities so clearly unlawful that the Supreme Court doctrine in the Southern Connecticut case would not apply? The court seemed to leave this possibility open in the abstract while foreclosing it in the particular case. Meanwhile, lower courts have consistently refused to find such justification in a wide range of student programs and activities. But it may be that the limits have never been fully tested.

To probe that possibility, one might look to the most closely analogous off-campus context, the body of law that developed a half-century ago in connection with the status of the Communist Party. Curiously, the ultimate issue—whether the party could be outlawed—never did get to court, but enough related issues reached the Supreme Court to afford some guidance. Drawing upon cases dealing with employment, investigations, loyalty oaths, and the like, it seems clear that even the Communist Party could have been outlawed only upon proof that all its members were actively pursuing unlawful goals (such as the violent overthrow of the government) with full knowledge of so clearly illegal an agenda. If any members were inactive or remained in the party to pursue lawful ends such as civil rights, fair housing, or peaceful redistribution of wealth, then the party as such could not have been outlawed. Given this standard, the Communist Party's survival as an entity becomes more readily understandable. At no time could the conditions for the party's demise ever have been met.

What spared the Communist Party should also protect student organizations on state college campuses. Presumably something similar to the Communist Party standard would limit administrative policy toward student groups. Only if the organization and all its members knowingly engaged in exclusively unlawful activity or willfully and consistently refused to accept valid rules and regulations could recognition be refused or other campus sanctions be imposed. The Supreme Court's safeguards are surely no longer confined to groups we would classify as traditionally "political." In fact, it would be difficult to envision a type of organized student activity to which these safeguards did not apply, whether the group's mission be literary, artistic, recreational, or simply social. A constitutional doctrine forged at a time of intense political activity on the nation's college campuses survives to a more tranquil time and reaches far beyond politics.

B. Student Fees—Mandatory and Inevitable?

The other side of the coin is the relationship between students and their organizations. Not all students are joiners; much less are they equally anxious to have their mandatory activities fees (which most colleges simply bill along with tuition) go to all groups on the eligible list. The courts have wrestled over the past quarter century with the issue of whether, and in what ways and for what reasons, students may resist supporting particular causes or groups through their fees. The objections run the gamut—from newspapers and magazines, to political organizations, to gay and lesbian groups, to just about any group that might find disfavor with some part of the student body.

The issue typically arises after the university has collected the fee from all students and delegated its allocation to student government. Obviously, the allocation process is itself subject to the First Amendment; student government can no more play favorites among recipients than can the college administration. While there is seldom enough money to meet all requests, so that priorities must be established and some categories foreclosed, the decisions that result must of course be content neutral and not based upon content or viewpoint or message. Judges have from time to time had to remind student fee allocators that they may not cut off funding for the campus daily because they took umbrage at a critical editorial or an unflattering news account of a senate meeting. On the other hand, policies may be established that rule out a whole category or type of organization, regardless of message or viewpoint, or that encourage fledgling groups, or that differentiate in other ways which import no judgment about content and mission.

Before examining specific issues that arise within the fee allocation process, it might be useful to understand why a university would assess a mandatory activities fee in the first place. There are several interests— different for the most part from those of any other entity in society that requires such support from its "members." As one author notes,

> By using fees to fund student groups, the university ensures that a variety of groups will participate in the overall exchange of ideas. In creating this marketplace, the university fulfills its duty "to provide that atmosphere which is most conducive to speculation, experiment and creation."

This interest is fundamentally educational. It reflects the view that a full range and variety of student groups and activities may contribute almost as much to the student's total educational experience as academic curriculum—or at least that a campus without such an array of co-curricular options leaves students much the poorer.

Some interests that underlie a mandatory fee system also relate closely to the university's goal of facilitating or enhancing expression. One court found such fee support a valuable way of promoting "uninhibited and vigorous discussion on matters of campus concern," warning that without the fee-assisted groups, "college would be a very quiet, intellectually diminished and ultimately irrelevant place." Moreover, as a practical matter, in contrast to the world outside the campus, many small and marginal student political groups simply could not survive without some fee support. Student preferences may change dramatically as one class graduates and another takes its place; such changes create an unusual need for continuity and stability in funding.

Finally, there are few if any good alternatives to the mandatory activities fee. The university could conceivably provide direct subvention to student groups—but only by creating risks of control and attribution, and (since student tuition would likely be part of the resource base) without avoiding the problem. The more plausible option would be to leave student groups to their own devices, expecting that each would garner its own support directly from students and outside donors. This approach has the virtue of simplicity, and on the surface ensures parity. But such an impression may be quite misleading.

In practice, the effect of a self-help system would likely be major inequality among organizations; those with off-campus "angels" would fare well, while those that must look solely to the shallow pockets of fellow students would atrophy. Thus a major rationale for the mandatory fee approach is to ensure a common source against which all groups may make some claim—granting that no group is guaranteed support in a given year, much less that all its needs will be met.

Given so cogent a case for mandatory activities fees, who could object? The dollar amount involved is usually trivial, even for students—maybe a fraction of one percent of tuition and general fees. Yet some students do object strenuously, sometimes enough to take the issue to court, where the arguments against a mandatory fee have emerged.

Such plaintiffs have brought to court concerns of both principle and practical application. Some students simply object to being forced to pay a fee any part of which may go to support causes with which they disagree. They often quote the seemingly apposite view of Thomas Jefferson that "to compel a man to furnish contributions of money for the propagation of opinions which he disbelieves, is sinful and tyrannical."

Objectors also point out that in a series of constitutional cases involving required labor union dues, the courts have been solicitous in protecting dissenters from having their money used for extraneous purposes and activities. Such cases involve so-called agency shop agreements, which do not force a worker to join the union but do compel everyone to support financially those union activities from which all workers benefit. Through a long series of complex Supreme Court cases, lines have been drawn that permit an objecting worker to recover (or avoid paying) that portion of union dues assigned to activities other than direct bargaining service. Thus advocacy of social issues or even general union positions on certain labor matters must be excluded from the mandatory dues base.

The most recent such case involved professors at a state college in Michigan who successfully forced the union to relieve them of the costs of certain union activity and advocacy that did not contribute directly to their economic welfare. Students who object to mandatory activities fees point to this case, arguing that what is good for the professor ought to be equally good for the student.

There have also been student objections to particular expenditures. In the mid-1980s a group of University of North Carolina–Chapel Hill students went to court to challenge the use of their activities fees to support publication in the *Daily Tar Heel* of views and positions they found objectionable. By that time there had been several previous cases, the results of which were in conflict. State courts in Nebraska and Vermont had rejected such challenges, distinguishing the labor union dues cases; these courts were not persuaded that students (unlike dissenting union members) had made out a sufficient claim of coerced speech, partly because they could advance their own viewpoints through other campus media. The Washington State Supreme Court reached a somewhat different view, however, in the mid-1970s. While the case was not conclusive on the validity of the particular fee, the court warned that mandatory fees were vulnerable:

> There is no room in the First Amendment for such absolute compulsory support, advocation and representation. We recognize that First Amendment rights are not absolute, but the university presents no arguments or facts to justify any exception, narrow as it would have to be, which might exist if a compelling state interest were presented.

The federal courts have also split on the analogy between dissenting union members and student fee objectors. Another North Carolina case had rejected challenges to the use of mandatory fees to support a student paper at a different UNC campus. Meanwhile, two federal appeals courts upheld policies that institutions had adopted in an effort to remove the dilemma. One involved the narrow issue of whether the University of Maryland could bar the state's Public Interest Research Group from using student fee money to support litigation; in upholding the restriction, the court did not address the broader issue of mandatory fee support as such.

The other case did reach the broader question, and resolved it differently from the North Carolina case. The challenge was brought by Rutgers University students who objected to the use of activities fees to support the program of the New Jersey Public Interest Research Group (PIRG). Even though the Rutgers fee system ensured a pro-rata refund to objectors, the federal appeals court twice ruled that collecting a specific fee for the support of an off-campus advocacy group violated dissenting students' rights. But the focus of the holding was quite limited—a special fee earmarked for an essentially off-campus group whose educational benefits could be found through other on-campus programs.

The court took care to distinguish (and thus implied the validity of) the more common mandatory student activities fee programs, especially those with a pro-rata refund option for students who objected to particular expenditures. Such mandatory fee pools reflected the view that "a university will strive for balance and afford adequate opportunity for offering opposing viewpoints." The educational value of some, if not all, the groups entitled to share in the fee pool could readily be shown. Thus the negative implication of the Rutgers case was crucial: while the PIRG-specific fee could be invalidated, most other fee arrangements would be valid. And in the view of the dissenting judges, even the PIRG fee should have been sustained:

> Outlets for effective speech or association on campus cost money, some of which may and often does come from students' tuition or fees. Ofttimes a conflict between speakers and objectors arises. Unless a veto is to be granted to all objectors to "political" speech, we must consider the competing interest, and seek an appropriate balance. Here the availability of a refund further protects the rights of objectors. Only in rare cases should the balance be struck by excluding political speech.

It was in this confused setting that the federal courts faced the *Daily Tar Heel* challenge. The Carolina students claimed the Supreme Court had grown tougher in recent years on other mandatory fees arrangements, such as dues for union agency shops and integrated state bars. But the courts now upheld the University of North Carolina fee, even though some part of it went to support editorials and other views that offended some students. The court conceded that an individual student had no choice, being "required to contribute financially to the *Daily Tar Heel* as a condition of enrollment at a public university." But the key to the decision was the university's emphasis on the educational nature of the purposes for which the fees were used:

> The University's academic judgment is that the paper is a vital part of the University's educational mission, and that financing it is germane to the University's duties as an educational institution. The *Daily Tar Heel's* financial need for mandatory fee support is established by undisputed testimony. . . . It would appear, therefore, that funding by mandatory student fees is the least restrictive means of accomplishing an important part of the University's central purpose, the education of students.

Distinguishing the union dues cases (where subsidies for political advocacy had been vulnerable), the appeals court added:

> In contrast, the *Daily Tar Heel* increases the overall exchange of information, ideas and opinions on the campus.

And it conceded that dissenting students' rights were to some degree impaired by the fee requirement:

> Government may abridge incidentally individual rights of free speech and association when engaged in furthering the constitutional goal of "uninhibited, robust and wide-open" expression.

The mandatory fee issue, which had been dormant after these cases of a decade ago, acquired new life in the 1990s with two major decisions. That they reached sharply divergent conclusions should surprise few observers. Nor should anyone assume the last word has been written on the subject of mandatory student activities fees.

Let us go first to New York, then conclude in California. The State University of New York had recognized many chapters of the New York Public Interest Research Group in ways that made NYPIRG eligible for student fee support. Conscious that this was an off-campus advocacy group and quite sensitive to the recent New Jersey litigation, SUNY officials imposed an unusual condition on NYPIRG: the organization must devote to on-campus activities a dollar amount equal to the amount it received through student fees from the campus. This arrangement was challenged by objectors on both sides.

The provision did, however, satisfy a federal appeals court. The court began by acknowledging that mandatory fees involved an element of coercion and that "the freedom to keep silent as well as to speak is . . . the product of our view of personhood. . . ." The court also noted that because of the mandatory fee, a student's unavoidable contribution to NYPIRG "is forced association and speech." There were, however, powerful countervailing forces. The mandatory fee served to "expand campus speech by facilitating the activities of a wide variety of speakers." One of its central values was to stimulate "uninhibited and vigorous discussion on matters of campus . . . concern." Without NYPIRG, "students would cease to be linked by a common bond to the tolerant support of all points of view." Since no alternative form of subvention was likely to meet these laudable goals, the federal appeals court found that the SUNY fee structure and NYPIRG's share of it constituted the least restrictive path to a constitutionally valid end.

Just when the New York case seemed to offer the last word, the action shifted to California. With the support of the Pacific Legal Foundation, University of California students had gone to state court seeking to enjoin the mandatory fee system. A lawsuit that had its roots in the late 1970s finally reached the state supreme court in 1993. A judgment in favor of the student claims provided the most sweeping victory to date for dissenters. The basis of the student claim was that mandatory fees collected by the university and allocated by student government went in part to support various abhorrent political and ideological positions. Both the lower courts rejected such claims and upheld the mandatory fee.

The California Supreme Court, with only two dissents, took a quite different view. The majority found more apposite than had any other court the union and state bar dues cases. Indeed, it found the burden on students' free speech rights even greater than the constraints on agency shop workers or integrated bar lawyers. The California majority also thought it had a way of reconciling its judgment with the seemingly different views of other courts, including the recent judgment of the New York federal court (because of New York's insistence that only "educational" activities could benefit). In the end, however, the California court offered a significantly different view on the merits of the issue:

> To fund a [political or ideological] group through mandatory fees will usually entail more of a burden on dissenting students' speech than is necessary to achieve any significant educational goal. The University can

teach civics in other ways that involve a lesser burden on those rights, or no burden at all.

Later, in a similar vein:

> To fund such a group may still provide some educational benefits, but the incidental benefit to education will not usually justify the burden on the dissenting students' constitutional rights.

Despite these unkind cuts, the California Supreme Court did not quite dismantle the fee system. Rather, it sent the case back with a clear directive to the university's regents to "identify any groups that are ineligible for mandatory funding" under the standards of the union and bar dues cases and "offer students the option of deducting a corresponding amount from the mandatory fee." The case contains more than a hint that a fee system apportioned in this way would pass constitutional muster:

> A university may, in general, support student groups through mandatory contributions because that use of funds can be germane to the university's educational mission.

The harder question beyond legal validity is whether, as a practical matter, such a system could survive. It was such doubts that caused the California dissenters to warn that "the Regents' practical options are limited, and none of them is appealing." At the very least, such changes as the court had required would alter the way in which University of California students would support activities and organizations. These changes might well cause the demise of some groups that had depended heavily on activities fee funding in the past but would be disabled by substantial ineligible political and ideological components. The number of such groups remains uncertain, though even the plaintiffs had questioned the eligibility of only fourteen of over 150 registered and currently funded organizations.

Moreover, the practical effect of the decision will vary with the degree to which students avail themselves of the option it affords; the court made clear that "the Regents must provide a refund only to those students who object. . . ." Such questions of impact will take some time to assess—if not quite the fourteen years the litigation took on its way through the California courts.

Returning to the immediate issue before us, what would courts do with a mandatory fee challenged on the basis of the inclusion of a gay-lesbian advocacy group? Two principles emerge from the cases. First, the validity of such a fee may depend on how convinced the court is of educational values in the program as a whole and among the organizations that benefit from it. Second, a refund option of some kind seems essential. No fee system containing such an option has yet been invalidated. The basis for the refund would be the proportion of each group's activity that is ineligible because it entails political or ideological advocacy of a kind that would be excluded from mandatory union or bar association dues. Even in California, a fee system that incorporated both elements would almost certainly have survived. In this regard as in many others, what works in California should work elsewhere.

C. Fraternities and Free Expression

It is now time to address a third, quite different free speech facet of how students organize—the tension between fraternity and sorority expression and other university policies. We began with deep concern about a homophobic skit put on by a Greek group. Such an event would evoke intense pressure from the campus community to do something fairly major to the fraternity—something like canceling its registered status. There is a central issue to pose at the start of our analysis: whether such primarily social organizations enjoy constitutional rights similar to those of political groups or whether they may be treated quite differently.

Greek-letter fraternities and sororities have been around for a century and a half, during which time they have been objects of adulation by some and of obloquy by others—and for many, simply of indifference. Yet the legal status of the Greek-letter groups has not been fully resolved. On the basic issue of where Greek-letter groups fit in the constitutional equation, there are strong arguments on both sides.

Let us look first at the case for withholding First Amendment protection from fraternities and sororities. It is obvious that the "speech" in which they engage or the "association" that brings members together is of a very different nature from the views and values that bind adherents to political groups. While we were ready to assume that First Amendment safeguards extend to a gay and lesbian advocacy group (styled by one court as "primarily political and social"), the typical fraternity is seldom more than a social group. Moreover, the link between individual student speech and the status of the fraternity is attenuated. Even if the organization is muzzled, its members remain free as individuals to express controversial views on race or sexual orientation or any other topic. Silencing the organization is quite different as a First Amendment matter from silencing the individual member—unless the former has the practical effect of the former.

Those who take a restrictive view of free speech would question whether a group organized for mainly social purposes really has any business raising First Amendment issues anyway. To some degree the Supreme Court has fostered such doubt, recently sustaining civil rights and public accommodation laws against the associational freedom claims of members of social clubs and even service groups who say they wish to interact only with other white males.

There is a substantial body of law dealing with Greek-letter organizations in the college context, but surprisingly little of this law relates to the central issue that engages us here—how far the university can go in limiting the expressive activity of fraternities and their members. The courts offer us very modest guidance, to which we now turn.

Many years ago, judges were asked to intervene on behalf of fraternities that faced abolition or at least disaffiliation from a national or parent organization. In the one such case to reach the Supreme Court, the justices showed little sympathy for the asserted rights of Greek organizations or their members. In upholding the power of states to abolish such organizations, the court simply deferred to the legislative or governing board judgment that students and the institution would be better served without such social gathering places. Similarly, a federal district court in New York said of the State University's 1950 ban on fraternities:

> A state may adopt such measures, including the outlawing of certain social organizations, as it deems necessary to its duty of supervision and control of its educational institutions.

The courts continued for many years to offer minimal sympathy to fraternity rights claims and consistently upheld state bans on fraternities linked to national bodies that still had racially discriminatory membership clauses. One such policy, enacted by the University of Colorado regents in the late 1950s, was the subject of a federal court test. A three-judge court found no occasion to question the continuing validity of the old cases. The precise issue before the court seemed easier in two respects—first, because the university goal was ensuring equal opportunity, and second, because the sanction—required disaffiliation from a racially discriminatory national—was much milder than the total prohibition that earlier decisions had sustained.

The Colorado federal court showed minimal concern about freedom of association. The Supreme Court had found in the guarantees of the First Amendment an implicit liberty of persons of like views to associate for political ends without government intrusion. Freedom of association claims had been raised in this case against the University of Colorado ban. The Colorado judges made short shrift of these claims without even deciding how far freedom might extend to primarily social and nonpolitical associations. It was enough that freedom of association "is a relative" interest and that "the particular relationship before us renders [fraternity members] susceptible to regulation of the kind here questioned."

The issue of free expression and fraternities remained dormant for many years. Then the 1990s brought to court a quite different perspective. In the major case, the Sigma Chi chapter at George Mason University in Virginia found itself on the wrong end of a set of sanctions and sued for redress. The trouble traced to the annual Sigma Chi Derby Days, a campus fund-raising event during which Greek-letter groups sought to outdo each other by way of caricature. One year a Sigma Chi brother appeared on stage, as the court later recounted,

> dressed as an offensive caricature of a black woman. He was painted black and wore stringy, black hair decorated with curlers, and his outfit was stuffed with pillows to exaggerate a woman's breasts and buttocks. He spoke in slang to parody African-Americans.

Many students, black and white, were outraged by the skit. The dean of students suspended Sigma Chi for the rest of the semester and put the chapter on a two-year probation, allowing only a handful of events for which approval had already been given. The fraternity was also required to plan and implement an educational program that would address cultural differences and campus diversity.

The brothers did not accept these sanctions quietly. They filed suit in federal court, claiming a denial of their First Amendment rights. The case was one of first impression on the specific issues, and the first in many years to revisit the tension between fraternity status and university authority. When the courts last spoke on that subject, back in the 1950s, they had left the university with virtually unfettered authority over social organizations. Much had happened since then, however, and a reassessment was in order.

Even so, the trial judge's vindication of Sigma Chi's First Amendment claims was rather startling. Even more surprising was the affirmance by the appeals court. At the outset, the reviewing court characterized the fraternity skit (however offensive many may have found it) as clearly protected speech. Even viewed as "a crude attempt at entertainment . . . [of] an obvious sophomoric nature," it was well within the First Amendment. Less elegant forms of entertainment—"even crude street skits"— had recently been found to be protected speech. Moreover, the skit qualified as "expressive conduct" under the Supreme Court's recent flag-desecration cases. The dean's sanction letter evinced an unmistakable focus on the message or viewpoint of the skit; it was not even all skits dealing with race that seemed problematic but only ones which "perpetuated derogatory racial and sexual stereotypes." Given that some, at least, of the live audience saw the skit's message as one of "satire and humor," the sanctions clearly targeted a particular viewpoint or message the administration found distasteful and divisive. What the dean had done was to punish a whole group because a few of its members had publicly expressed a message of which the administration disapproved.

The university sought in vain to press several countervailing interests—promoting racial harmony, protecting the status of minorities, and maintaining an educational environment free of race or gender bias. The appeals court was unimpressed. Such interests simply did not warrant sanctions here any more than they would have justified refusing recognition to a radical political organization. Whatever may have been the institution's valid concerns about the skit,

> The University should have accomplished its goals in some fashion other than silencing speech on the basis of its viewpoint.

A concurring judge was not prepared to go quite that far. He joined the majority because the university had actually given its blessing to the skit in advance and in his view could not now revoke permission because of something in the skit it disliked. In the concurring judge's view, however, "the University does have greater authority to regulate expressive conduct within its confines as a result of the unique nature of the educational forum." Pursuant to its central interest in maintaining a sound learning environment for students of all backgrounds, he ventured,

> the University must have some leeway to regulate conduct which counters that interest, and thereby infringes upon the rights of other students to learn.

Under other conditions—if, for example, the university had not expressly approved the event in advance—"forbidding the skit or requiring substantial amendment was not beyond its power." Even the concurring judge cautioned, however, against any inference "that a university has the unrestricted power to silence entirely certain perspectives."

Clearly the Sigma Chi case charts new ground. What would once have been viewed as routine administrative regulation of unruly student groups must now be judged by standards that limit government's power to curb protected speech on matters of public interest and value. For if a fraternity brother donning a mop wig, blackface, and pillows conveys a constitutionally protected message, then relatively little expressive activity in which a student group might engage would fall outside the First Amendment.

Fraternities can still be banished or suspended for drunken orgies, of course, even though speech at loud volume may constitute part of the offense. And all sorts of campus rules, some general and others fraternity-specific, can be imposed on an organization and its members without abridging protected speech. Yet the virtually limitless range of options the university once had with regard to fraternities and sororities has now been sharply limited. The only remaining question is whether a social group such as a fraternity can be treated any differently than a student political club. Where expressive activity is concerned and where it is the message that evokes official disapproval, that seems unlikely. Even the noblest of institutional interests will not justify suppressing the content of student expression. A racist caricature by a Greek-letter group now claims protection comparable to a discussion of the role of race in public life by the Young Republicans or Young Democrats. The only basis for differential treatment would be a judgment that the offending behavior is simply not expressive. Otherwise, college authorities must now treat symbolic, and certainly verbal, expression as presumptively protected. That seems to be the lesson that George Mason's administration learned the hard way.

VI.

FREE PRESS ON THE COLLEGE CAMPUS

To: University Attorney
From: Paul Penn, Dean of Journalism School

You may recall that I serve as faculty adviser to the *Daily Campus* as well as J School dean and professor. The two roles seem to have come into conflict recently. In my professorial role I try to impart values of free expression to future journalists, editors, and publishers. But in my adviser role I have begun to wonder whether the press—especially the student press—really can handle all the freedom we give them. The last few weeks have been especially taxing. Let me share with you a few horror stories. The editors of the *Daily Campus* have been on an "investigative reporting" crusade about the academic performance of minority students. They have gathered some data they think prove our special admissions program lets in a lot of kids who just can't make it in college, and don't make it. The editors think they have a sure winner and plan to publish a five-part exposé next week. I've seen a few rough drafts, so I know what their theory is. (There is a superficial validity to their theory, but the data tell only half the story; if one follows these students through five or six years, they actually fare quite well academically.) So the thesis of the series is plausible and alarming—but wrong. If they do publish, it will not only damage the minority students and the university (making future minority recruitment virtually impossible) but will also do irreparable harm to the paper itself. I would also fear some counteraction by the Black Student Alliance; at other campuses groups of students have seized and burned the entire press run containing articles they found offensive. That could happen here. If I can't persuade the editors to back off, is there no way we can prevent them from doing themselves in? And if we can't flatly prevent them from publishing these stories, could we at least force them to run an op-ed or letter from the president that will set the record straight? I can't abide censorship, but there must be some way to stop this disaster.

As if that weren't enough, the editors are about to shoot themselves in the other foot. There's a group going around the country trying to get student papers to run full-page advertisements that claim the Holocaust never happened—that six million Jews in Europe got sick or committed suicide between 1935 and 1945. The editors are determined to reject the ad even though the sponsors would pay the full rate to run it. The text of the ad is outlandish and would outrage all thoughtful people, Jewish or not. But it seems clear to me that editors of a newspaper supported in large part (about 70 percent in our case) with student fee money can't impose their own beliefs or values or tastes on ad copy in this way. That would be a kind of censorship we ought not to tolerate at a great state university, whatever may be our individual views.

While I've got your attention, let me mention one other related problem. Those nice people who authored the Holocaust-denial ad have also funded an underground student weekly called the *Clarion* which prints really vicious articles and editorials. The coverage is not limited to Holocaust denial but also attacks the competence of some of our most visible minority and female faculty members (including two of my Journalism School colleagues). Now I realize we have to tolerate circulation of such a paper on campus, since it's privately financed. But if the editors run into trouble—for example, if all their papers are seized and destroyed—do we have to do anything to help? Tell me freedom of the press doesn't go *that* far!

My problem, as you can see, is how to balance against the stark reality of what's happening on this campus today all the nice things I've always taught my journalism students about the vitality of a free press. The law must have some useful answers. I need them soon.

• • •

To: Dean Penn, Journalism School
From: Office of the University Attorney

Well, we can help, but you're not going to like what we have to say. In fact, for starters, we would say you are zero for three on the steps you propose to take. In summary, there is probably nothing you or anyone else can do to the *Campus Daily* to prevent publication of the inaccurate story about minority student performance. On the other hand (and for some of the same reasons), the editors probably could reject the Holocaust-denial ad—or at least no court would force them to run it against their judgment. And finally, if the *Clarion* is a recognized student publication, we may well be obligated to protect it by going after people who seize and destroy copies of even so hateful a journal. So, if I infer where you would have come out on each of these issues, that makes you 0 for 3. But each of the issues is really much more complex, and you'll find some solace in the details and qualifications.

Let's look first at the potentially very damaging (and apparently inaccurate or misleading) *Campus Daily* series about minority student performance. Censorship of college student papers is an issue whose time came and went a good many years ago, at least as far as the courts are concerned. There has not been a reported case of this sort since the mid-1970s. But the legal principles shaped at that time still serve us well and presumably account for the paucity of recent censorship attempts.

We should have some sense of why a college administration would even think about restraining student editors in ways one might like to treat an off-campus daily but would never attempt to do. There are several special factors that distinguish the college press. Student fee support is a major difference; only a handful of campus newspapers are truly "independent" in the sense that they receive no fee subsidy—and even some of them benefit in other forms such as office space, mailing privileges, telephone lines, etc. Those papers that operate wholly at arm's length to the university they serve could be counted on one hand. All the others, in greater or lesser degree, receive some subsidy, directly or indirectly, from student fees and thus arguably incur a duty to serve the entire student body in ways that do not apply to the general off-campus media. Moreover, most campus papers are seen as speaking for or representing the campus community, even though the editors and the administration may both vigorously deny any such role. Where the name of the institution appears (as it usually does) in the paper's name, such a link is inescapable. Even where the name is generic (as with our *Campus Daily*) the nexus is present in a more muted form, since virtually anyone reading the paper knows or will soon find out whence it comes. So whether or not that is the intent, an inference of representation arises with respect to most campus papers. In virtually all cases, the impact of the student newspaper is much enhanced by its exclusivity—except at the University of Wisconsin–Madison, the University of Virginia, and a handful of other campuses with viable and frequently published "alternative" papers, the campus daily or biweekly is the only such medium of communication. Even in a large city, where students have myriad other information sources, most news about the campus comes through the student paper. Only the most major stories will find their way to the general media, and the student paper remains the only outlet with the time, interest, and inclination to do in-depth coverage of campus issues. Finally, and for the same reasons, views or reports appearing in the student paper carry a high degree of credibility off campus; these are the people who know, who are closest to the scene.

Thus when the student daily mishandles or distorts a sensitive story, it is not hard to see why people on campus may take umbrage and seek whatever recourse exists. Take the minority student academic performance issue. The minority students themselves may be most deeply aggrieved; it is, after all, in part their student fees that made this calumny possible. And the *Daily's* misleading account of their achievements will have high credibility off campus, since it comes from so seemingly expert a source.

The administration shares the student concerns but has added worries of its own. Since the source of the stories is a paper published in part with university imprimatur and supported by fees the university collects from its students and reallocates, the official stake is clear. And most people off campus—legislators, even trustees—assume the administration has a far higher degree of control over the paper and what it prints than has in fact been true for a good many years. If the paper does violate the law—infringing a copyright, publishing state secrets, or libeling a prominent citizen—the trustees and administration are likely to be sued, even though they may later convince a court they are not culpable. Finally, and perhaps most pertinent to the case we are facing here, what appears in the campus paper may directly and profoundly shape what occurs on the campus for some time. If the paper publishes a story that misleadingly disparages the academic performance and potential of minority students, trouble will not be far behind. Thus the nature of official campus concern over such a matter is quite understandable. The only question is how far a concerned administration may act on this concern.

The answer the courts have given is "not very far." In a series of cases that went through the federal courts starting in the late 1960s, the courts have set high standards for state colleges seeking to stifle student newspapers or their editors. In fact, courts have been strikingly solicitous of the college student press. The cases arose in various parts of the country and involved different kinds of publications. The sources of administrative concern also varied—offensive language in some instances, criticism of campus officials or trustees in others, volatile comment on off-campus issues in still others. But from these cases emerged a clear principle: that any suppression of the campus press "must be necessary to preserve order and discipline." Other courts have demanded an "overriding state interest." We have little sense of conditions or circumstances that would trigger such standards. No court seems to have found a sufficient threat to "order and discipline" or an "overriding interest" that would warrant even punishment of an editor after the fact, much less prior restraint. Thus, while courts and commentators have recognized that the campus press may not be as free in all respects as the general media, student editors do enjoy substantial latitude.

Evidence of the reach of this protection comes from one later case involving the subtler administrative sanction of shifting the funding source of a student publication. The *Minnesota Daily,* the student newspaper on the Twin Cities campus, published at the end of the 1979 academic year a humor issue, complete with cartoons, ads, and articles, some of which deeply offended Catholics, evangelical Christians, and other groups. The Minnesota legislature, responding to citizen outrage, held hearings on the issue in both houses. The Board of Regents, finding the humor issue "flagrantly offensive," changed the funding mechanism. In place of a mandatory fee charged to all students, in effect since 1920, the regents substituted a refundable fee. This change was attributed to the regents' solicitude for students who might object to "buying" a newspaper they did not wish to receive.

A group of student editors and the Board of Student Publications promptly challenged the regents' action in federal court. The trial judge dismissed, finding no violation of the First Amendment. But the court of appeals took a quite different view, finding against the regents despite the apparently mixed motives behind the funding change. Reserving the possibility that a state university "could certainly choose not to own or support any newspapers, so long as its motive is permissible," the court found here a highly suspect motive. The appeals court noted, for example, that no comparable funding change had been made at the university's other, smaller campuses—a lack of that consistency one might have expected from an abstract regental concern for unwilling student readers. The state of the student press at the other campuses had not even been a subject of regental study.

The appeals court stated its central premise:

> it is clear that the First Amendment prohibits the Regents from taking adverse action against the *Daily* because the contents of the paper are occasionally blasphemous or vulgar.

While the governing board might have been driven in part by valid concerns, "evidence of the Regents' improper motivation was clearly brought out in the testimony," including the board resolution "deploring" the humor issue and calling for administrative action. Thus the appeals court had no hesitation in reversing the dismissal of the student editors' complaint and sending the case back for "appropriate injunctive relief."

There matters came to rest, except for two later developments that have at least peripheral bearing. The year after the *Minnesota Daily* case, Colorado's Supreme Court reviewed a junior college student senate's action that removed student fee funding from the campus newspaper on what were unmistakably content grounds. The suit had been brought by a journalism instructor who was the paper's faculty adviser. She asserted First Amendment interests of her own, in using the paper as a teaching vehicle, which the court rejected. She also argued the free press claims of the student editors, who were not involved in the suit. The state's high court found the instructor a proper person to press such claims and accorded her legal "standing" to do so. This finding, of course, begged the issue on the merits. Several years later the trial court where the case had begun did decide the merits, finding that the student senate had legally valid reasons for taking funding away from the paper—a finding which made the First Amendment claims moot.

The other late development is far more ominous to the campus press. The United States Supreme Court took its first direct look at student newspapers in 1988. The immediate concern was the Hazelwood, Missouri, high school paper, which had been censored by the faculty adviser on the principal's orders. The Supreme Court majority upheld such censorship, partly because the school had lent "its name and resources" through the name and support of the newspaper and partly because the adviser had "acted reasonably" in an emergency situation (even though the most potentially damaging statements had already been removed before the order was given to excise the offending story). This judgment sharply qualified the "disruption" standard which had governed regulation of high school student speech and which supplied the First Amendment test that lower courts had consistently applied to college newspaper cases. The immediate concern was whether this substantially lower standard would now find its way onto the college campus as well—a question the courts have not yet faced, but which clearly deserves attention. There are more than superficial similarities— especially in regard to the "sponsorship" the court found in the Hazelwood paper's use of the school name and its resources. Yet the justices also stressed the degree to which the paper was "part of the school's curriculum"—a factor which would affect some, but by no means all, fee-funded college dailies. While in other free expression areas the courts have carefully avoided letting high school cases limit the speech of university students and faculty, the newspaper area is unusual; the earlier college cases derived their broad protection for the student press largely from the Supreme Court's once-sweeping (and now more limited) protection for precollege student speech. So it remains to be seen whether that same Court would sustain state university curbs on campus papers that meet the Hazelwood criteria of sponsorship—use of the school name and funds and incorporation in a journalism curriculum. Such a result seems unlikely, but the seeds of caution have been planted and should be watched.

Let us accept that censorship of the campus paper would violate the First Amendment, even in a subtle form like making a mandatory fee refundable. Are there, however, other options open to the administration that faces a grave threat of the kind with which this inquiry began? Suppose the student editors consistently covered only one side of major campus issues, then hid in the sand—refusing to print letters to the editor or guest columns on the other side or even to list phone numbers at which indignant readers could reach them. Would such intransigence be protected by freedom of the press? For a private newspaper off campus, of course it would. Such practices might be thought unprofessional, but any governmental attempt to interfere would be unconstitutional. (A decade ago Florida passed a law that required newspapers to print responses from people who had been attacked in its editorial or news columns. A unanimous Supreme Court struck down the law, finding it so clear a violation of the First Amendment that little more need be said.)

The situation might, however, be different with a student newspaper. There are no cases that come even close to addressing these issues, so one can only speculate. What if, for example, an administration adopted a policy requiring that any student activity that received fee support must list the names and phone numbers of its officers in its publications and applied this rule to the campus newspaper? Such a uniform requirement would not seem to intrude unduly on press freedom, even if the editors wished to remain inaccessible. More difficult would be a requirement that fee-funded media, including the campus daily, accept and (reserving the right to select and edit) print letters to the editor. Such control of format alone, with no element of content, would seem to be a tolerable time, place, and manner regulation in the subsidized campus newspaper setting.

Suppose the university feels compelled to take one further step—requiring some modicum of balance (e.g., through guest columns, op-ed pieces, and the like) on volatile issues such as race relations on campus. Here the situation with the outside media remains mixed. Newspapers and magazines are of course free of any such requirements; they can be as biased as they wish and still distribute on city streets and enjoy all other benefits available to any publication. But licensed radio and television broadcasters may be forced to provide balanced treatment of controversial issues on grounds that might possibly apply by analogy to the campus press—that the airwaves represent a valuable and scarce government-owned resource, that the number of frequencies is quite limited, and that each licensee therefore enjoys a kind of publicly created monopoly in the communication process.

Whether or not these assumptions remain sound in a time of hundred-channel cable systems, the reasoning that validated the fairness doctrine as applied to licensed broadcasters might have some bearing on the typical campus newspaper. Especially if the paper receives fee support and uses the university name in its banner (as most do), government may have a stake in the way the media monopoly is in fact used to inform the campus community. Even so, there are genuine and serious concerns about any regulation that would constrain the content of the campus press. At the least, any such policy must be uniform and consistent in its application and must not be the product of a particular controversy; a selective or issue-generated rule would fare as badly in the courts as did the Minnesota regents' funding shift imposed on a single student publication in direct response to an offensive issue. A genuinely comprehensive and viewpoint-neutral "fairness" or "balance" policy might at least be worth exploring, conscious of the perils and pitfalls and hopeful that less-intrusive measures could be found.

One other option remains for consideration—the paid publication of an administration statement or position paper on a volatile issue such as minority student academic performance. Suppose such a statement is prepared and submitted but the student editors refuse to run it, even at regular advertising rates? Does the administration have any recourse? This question brings us to the issue of the Holocaust-denial ad, which tormented a number of campus newspapers in the early 1990s. When the ad first appeared in advertising offices in late 1991 and early 1992, editors found themselves facing a cruel dilemma. The ad was submitted on behalf of the Committee for Open Debate on the Holocaust to a number of major student dailies around the country. The content of the ad (presented as though it were a news story) was almost universally abhorrent; it claimed that the Holocaust never really happened and that the deaths of millions of Jews had either been greatly exaggerated in number or could be traced to causes other than Nazi extermination. Editors responded in quite different ways. Harvard's *Crimson,* the *Daily Californian,* and others flatly rejected the ad, giving no reason or citing the inflammatory content or the doubtful veracity of its central claims. Many more editors reluctantly agreed to run the ad, sometimes without comment and at other times with an accompanying editorial explanation. Concurrent columns gave editors a chance to justify a decision they knew would be unpopular with many on and off campus. As the editor of the *Michigan Daily* explained to his readers,

> Hiding the ideas of the Holocaust revisionists won't make them go away. The best way to make them go away is to bring them out in the open and explain why they're wrong.

The *Daily's* editorial page editor added his concurrence:

> Misinformation is subjective. Instead of letting newspaper editors decide what is right and what is wrong, allow the reader to decide. Oppression must never be thwarted by using the tools of the oppressor. I'd rather win this war in the marketplace of ideas.

The editor of Michigan State's *Daily News* added her similar view in support of the same outcome:

> Personally, I want to know what people are thinking, even if it hurts me. . . . Should the First Amendment give people the right to hurt others? Unfortunately, yes, it can.

The timing of the ad complicated the issue. On one hand, the opening in Washington, D.C., of the United States Holocaust Memorial Museum reinforced other sources of information that seemed to raise awareness of that dark period in European history. On the other hand, polls seemed to show rising skepticism about the Holocaust as the numbers of Americans with any personal recollection dwindled. Holocaust denial, in fact, had become a sufficiently important subject to generate three major book-length studies in the early 1990s—studies suggesting that the crude Holocaust-denial ad was but the tip of an ugly and dangerous iceberg.

Though some state university papers did refuse to run the ad, no one ever took them to court. Had the legal issue been raised, answers would have been less clear than in many other areas we have examined. The issue of abhorrent or troublesome advertisements has been through the courts several times, with varied results. In the late 1960s the editors of the student paper at Wisconsin State University–Whitewater rejected two ads, noting the antiwar message of one and the antidiscrimination appeal of the other. The rejection letter observed that such material might normally be deemed "public service," but "your ad . . . deals with political issues, and is therefore not a public service." The sponsors of the ad went to federal court and prevailed on appeal. Elsewhere, courts had insisted that "a state public body which disseminates paid advertising of a commercial type may not reject other paid advertising on the basis that it is editorial in character." Citing the recent cases that had rebuffed administrative efforts to suppress the college student press, the appeals court found equally applicable to advertising policy the First Amendment rule that only "disruption" of campus activities would warrant rejection. Nothing approaching "disruption" had even been suggested by the student editors. That was the end of the case, and for a time it was the last word on controversial advertising.

The mid-1970s brought a major reexamination of the issue by another federal appeals court. Student editors of Mississippi State University's *Reflector* had rejected paid advertising copy submitted by the Mississippi Gay Alliance. The same message was also rejected for publication in the paper's "Briefs" announcement section. The Gay Alliance then sought the aid of the federal courts, claiming the paper had a legal duty not to discriminate on content or viewpoint grounds. Both trial and appeals courts sustained the student editors' plea that any such intervention would threaten freedom of the press. Under the First Amendment and given the state laws against sodomy, said the higher court, "the editor of the *Reflector* had a right to take the position that the newspaper would not be involved, even peripherally, with this off-campus homosexual activity."

One judge dissented, and wrote at length. He stressed the importance of the medium and its means of support:

> The *Reflector* is the official newspaper of MSU, a state supported and controlled institution. . . . The major portion of the *Reflector*'s financing comes from the Student Activities Fund, which is collected by MSU and disbursed to the *Reflector* [which] is printed on MSU facilities and is an organ of MSU.

The dissenter also rejected the majority's suggestion that the ad was unprotected because it incited unlawful conduct. Though the ad's content appeared nowhere in the record, its message was apparently innocuous and informational—an attempt to apprise gay and lesbian students of services of potential interest and benefit. At no time did the student editors claim the ad urged violation of sodomy or other state laws. Thus the Gay Alliance could take advantage of a brand-new legal doctrine. Just months earlier, the U.S. Supreme Court had conferred limited First Amendment protection upon nondeceptive commercial advertising that proposed a lawful transaction; such protection had been available for at least the previous decade for "editorial advertisements" of a noncommercial character. Given this protection, the dissenting judge argued that the Gay Alliance and its ad had asserted a First Amendment right of access to what was, for other purposes, a public forum. Such access could not, he went on, be denied on the basis of content or viewpoint. Reasonable rules might, he conceded, limit the time, place, and manner of access; he left open such questions as whether advertising space could be limited to MSU students and faculty. The frequency of any one group's use of the ad and notice columns might also be limited to keep the forum open for all messages. But there was no doubt here that the *Reflector*'s editors had acted solely on the basis of content. For the dissenting judge, the case was legally indistinguishable from the earlier Wisconsin-Whitewater case, in which another federal appeals court had compelled access to campus paper advertising space. The Mississippi State case also seemed to him no different from a city's refusal to allow a Gay Alliance speaker to use a "speaker's corner" in a public park. Whatever free press interests the editors may have asserted were, for the dissenter, clearly subordinate to the interests of the Gay Alliance in gaining access to this valuable campus forum.

There matters remained until 1987, when a third federal appeals court weighed in. The *Daily Nebraskan,* another major state university student paper bearing the institution's name, refused to print ads seeking gay or lesbian roommates. The trial judge ruled that the paper could not be required to print such ads—or any ads for that matter—and the appeals court agreed. The reason was not, however, the same as the basis for a similar outcome in the Mississippi State case. Both courts did note that "where student publications of state-supported universities are concerned, editorial freedom of expression has consistently triumphed over attempts at censorship." But that was not the root of the judgment. This time the basis for upholding the ads' rejection was more technical than substantive. The claims asserted by the would-be Nebraska advertisers ran only against government action and not (with very narrow exceptions) against action by private persons. So the question here was whether the *Daily Nebraskan* and its student editors were government actors. Both courts responded in the negative, relying heavily on the safeguards the university had created to shield the student editors. On that basis the Wisconsin-Whitewater case could be distinguished; there the appeals court had found close ties between the campus paper and the governing board—ties that lacked analogues at the University of Nebraska. The source of the challenged action was not the regents or the administration but "discretion exercised by an editor chosen by the student body." The court might have stopped there, resting the judgment quite narrowly on procedural or jurisdictional grounds. But the judges wanted to remind readers that they were, after all, talking about a newspaper. Thus the factors they cited led them to conclude that "the First Amendment interdicts judicial interference with the editorial decision." In the only separate opinion, a concurring judge restated this phrase and added:

> Had the editors decided to publish the ads, and had that publication been prohibited by university authorities, we would have another case and a reversal would be required.

The Nebraska case nonetheless leaves at large several intriguing issues. We do not know how the appeals court would have ruled if, for example, the board or administration had directed the editors not to accept such ads and the advertisers had challenged this action; such a case could not have avoided the merits on the ground there was insufficient governmental involvement in the challenged action. Nor do we know what this court would have said about the same student-generated rejection if the ties between paper and administration had been as close as they were at Whitewater and (apparently) at Mississippi State. One way of reconciling the several cases is to say that rejecting controversial ads is permissible only if the judgment of independent student editors causes the rejection—but not when either the administration demands rejection or the student editors who seem to be acting on their own are so closely tied to the administration or board that their apparent independence in such matters is illusory.

Well, what about the Holocaust-denial ad? Clearly, if the editors of a semiautonomous daily like that at Nebraska reject the copy, even if the only reason for so doing is their abhorrence of what the ad says, it is unlikely that any court would countermand their judgment. The basis for upholding rejections would continue to vary as they have in the few cases to date. Some courts might refuse to intervene on technical grounds—like the absence of governmental action—while others would invoke the measure of editorial discretion the First Amendment accords to the college student press. Presumably such reasoning would apply even if the ad and the message were more appealing than denying the Holocaust or seeking gay and lesbian roommates—closer to the messages the Seventh Circuit upheld in the Whitewater case. Yet the picture remains muddled and incomplete, with many important situations and issues not yet addressed by the courts. Before we can speak with certainty about rejecting Holocaust-denial ads or any others for content reasons, we need a bit more guidance from the law.

Now we come to our third set of issues, those involving "underground" student newspapers. If you think the *Campus Daily* is bad, you haven't been reading the *Clarion!* This new entry into our campus culture came on the scene a few months ago, apparently with the financial (and spiritual) backing of an ultraconservative group, including even a few of our own prominent alumni. The supporters and the student editors they helped get this rag started are against just about everything that's gone on here for the last ten years or so—affirmative action, minority student programs, diversity, cultural sensitivity, you name it. The *Clarion* selects a new topic each month and runs it into the ground. This month they've gone after the "competence" of several of our senior African American faculty.

The *Clarion* is very much like the notorious *Dartmouth Review* of the late 1980s. In fact, we suspect our students look to the *Review* as their model. It caused no end of trouble up in New Hampshire, especially when the editors caricatured a black music professor (and then got into a fist fight with him) and printed anti-Semitic cartoons and other attacks on the college's Jewish president. Dartmouth did crack down in the end and drove the *Review* further underground, if not out of business. The student editors did bring suit, and lost—but of course Dartmouth is a private college, where such matters get very different treatment from the courts.

The issue for us is whether we can do anything to the *Clarion,* however bad its copy and its cartoons get. The Black Student Alliance leaders apparently haven't seen the latest issue yet—but when they do, I'm certain they'll renew their demands from last spring that we banish the *Clarion* and its editors. And if we don't act, some students will almost certainly take matters into their own hands by stealing as much of the current issue as they can find—the sort of thing that happened not long ago at Penn, Penn State, Maryland, and a half-dozen other campuses. I doubt we're any readier for that sort of standoff than our sister institutions proved to be. So we need urgently to know two things. First, whether there is anything we can do to the *Clarion* or its editors, even if their issues foment a riot on campus. Second, we need to know whether we have to take any steps to help the *Clarion* if other students take matters into their own hands and steal most of the next issue.

The short answer to both questions, as you might expect, is no. But they are very different questions, and we should address them separately. Let's start with the status of the "underground" newspaper. I mentioned earlier that Dartmouth had successfully taken steps against some of the *Review*'s editors. But there were two special circumstances. One was that the basis of the college's suspension of the students was not what they had written but a physical tussle with the black music professor they had caricatured in the *Review*. So their attempt to get freedom of the press into the case met little sympathy from a court that had no occasion to look beyond a physical assault. But the court made pretty clear that even if the students had been suspended for what they wrote in the *Review*, federal judges would not be of much help anyway because Dartmouth is a private institution not engaged in governmental action that federal courts can review. The students did press one further argument that a federal judge could have heard—that since they were white and the object of their attack was black, they were victims of race discrimination. They also argued that black students who had recently broken campus rules were treated leniently. But the tie between the editors' suspensions and their race was tenuous at best; though the dispute had clearly racial roots and there may have been some differences in treatment, they could hardly be deemed victims of a racial animus on the part of college officials. Thus the *Dartmouth Review* case, factually relevant and interesting though it is, in the end tells us very little of what we need to know about how a public university can deal with a student journal of this type.

The remainder of the cases, and there are not very many, deal with off-campus papers. But they are helpful in an obvious and immediate way; whatever a public institution may not do to an outside publication, surely it may not do to one brought forth by its own students. Thus there is valuable guidance for us in the consistency with which courts—in cases from Arizona, Texas, Ohio, and Illinois—have said that off-campus papers may not be barred because of their content. The element that triggered official concern varied among these journals—religious pros-elytizing in one case, radical political advocacy in another, excessive commercialism in a third. But the response of the courts has been quite uniform across this varied landscape.

The most recent case, a 1992 federal appeals court judgment about a Texas state college, says it all. The administration had sought to bar distribution on campus of an outside newspaper, the *Guardian,* that featured "environmental, peace, and social justice issues." The paper was free, supported by donations and advertising. The college sharply lim-ited the channels for distribution of publications containing commercial material. An off-campus paper that contained any advertising had to receive student group sponsorship before any student could disseminate copies on campus. The regular student paper (the *Star*) was exempt from this and other regulations to which the *Guardian* was subject. A group of students wishing to distribute the *Guardian* brought suit in federal court, claiming abridgment of free press and denial of equality. The trial judge dismissed the suit, but the appeals court found in favor of the *Guardian.*

The campus in question, like virtually all state colleges and universi-ties, was legally a "public forum" of the kind that is generally open to expressive activity. Moreover, the college freely allowed circulation of the official student paper, a publication not obviously different from the proscribed *Guardian.* To focus on the "commercial" element in the latter "was an anomalous departure from the general policy of protecting speech such as the political reportage and commentary in the *Guardian."* Even if the college's anticommercial policy did not amount to content-based discrimination—an assumption the court was willing to make—the restriction failed the First Amendment test because it was broader than necessary to serve the college's valid interest in curbing purely commercial "solicitation." And if the administration was concerned about excessive litter or congestion at crowded areas, it could frame much narrower rules that would serve such practical needs.

Finally, the college claimed such rules were needed to sustain an "academic environment." Unlimited distribution of newspapers and pamphlets, it argued, "would create a circus atmosphere, destroying the unique quality of the University campus." But the argument did not, in the appeals court's view, fit the facts. Such reasoning might warrant curbs on purely commercial hawking but did not apply to the free dissemination of a newspaper devoted in substantial part to "speech about matters of highest public concern—political and economic reform and the local and international environment."

Thus ended the case, a nearly complete victory for the *Guardian* and its would-be student distributors. The student plaintiffs pressed their luck one step too far. They had argued that university funding of the official *Star,* containing views different from those of the *Guardian* and its supporters, abridged their freedom of speech. Clearly not so, replied the court of appeals; a state university may use student fee funds to support a newspaper that does not reflect the views of all students. There is no duty either to exempt those students who do not agree or to subsidize counterspeech in the form of alternative journals. The remedy in such a case is precisely the one this court affirmed: to give students with contrasting views maximum and unfettered access to the campus forum, but not necessarily to subsidize that access or spare dissenters from supporting the official student press.

Are there, then, any measures that might be taken against the truly outrageous underground student paper? Almost certainly not. Surely the *Clarion,* an unofficial student journal, is no more reachable than an off-campus, nonstudent publication like the *Guardian.* Unless the institution is ready to take the highly improbable step of sealing itself off from all publications—claiming it is thus no longer a "public forum" for any purposes—there seems no basis on which one student paper could be barred while others are tolerated.

Only one option remains, and it is a personal rather than an institutional one. A recent encounter at Virginia Tech may illustrate. A ranking student affairs officer understandably bridled when a student newspaper characterized her as "Director of Butt Licking." This was no mere epithet; in her view, the term used in the paper effectively charged her with committing sodomy, which remains a crime in Virginia. She realized no reprisal was possible against the paper or its editors, so she opted for the one remaining course and filed a libel suit in state court. Such recourse is, indeed, about the only viable option—and never an easy one at that. If the person is a public official (like a college administrator) or a "public figure" (like a renowned scholar or a star student athlete), then more than factual error and harm to reputation must be proved in order to recover. And libel suits are long and painful, even when one is suing a wealthy publisher; when the object of the suit is a student editor or a publishing board, the prospects of redress are even more remote. But the possibility does at least exist, and several successful libel suits against student newspapers remind us that freedom of the campus press, like that of the general media, has at least this one limitation. And, it goes without saying—though hardly of much help here—student papers can also be held accountable under obscenity and child pornography laws. But freedom of the student press is now substantially parallel to freedom of the commercial, off-campus press in all respects that matter.

Our final question asks if the student press may in one respect be even more fully protected. If the entire run of a daily newspaper is stolen for whatever reason, the publisher's recourse is presumably the same as that of any other victim of larceny. We have no special laws that make stealing newspapers or magazines different from stealing cars or jewels. (If someone pirates the contents of a copyrighted newspaper story without permission, that is a special crime. But that is a quite different situation from the one we envision here.)

The case of the student newspaper may, however, be different. Campus papers are uniquely vulnerable to theft for several reasons that reflect both content and manner of distribution. The semimonopoly and campus subsidy most such papers enjoy make them and the views they espouse more visible targets of self-help and other recourse. The lesser susceptibility of such papers to either subscriber or advertiser pressure compounds the problem. And the manner of distribution, often through large piles placed early each morning at central campus locations, makes them exceptionally vulnerable to theft. Indeed, there is even some question whether taking multiple copies from an open bin is even theft at all. If, for example, a person wants extra copies of an issue containing an important story, the paper is usually pleased by such demand. It is only when the motive changes and the interested group helps itself so liberally as to deny other readers any access to the issue that we even talk of "theft."

Yet without doubt there have been exponentially more such cases in the early 1990s, and they have rightly caused concern to guardians of the student press. During the spring of 1993, the Student Press Law Center in Washington reported that "more than a dozen college newspapers have lost thousands of copies of their publications to thieves who objected to the publications' content." Perhaps most widely noted was the seizure in April of virtually the entire run of one issue of the *Daily Pennsylvanian*. The focus was apparently the paper's carrying of a conservative columnist whose views were abhorrent to minority and other student groups. The incident claimed national prominence partly because the university's president, Sheldon Hackney, had just been nominated to be chairman of the National Endowment for the Humanities. Though he issued a strongly condemnatory statement, some critics felt he should have been bolder in his espousal of press freedom and should have threatened harsher sanctions against the thieves—despite the unlikelihood that individual offenders could or would be identified. Similar incidents occurred that spring across the country at a remarkably eclectic array of campuses—Penn State, North Carolina State, California Polytechnic, Northern Illinois, Yale, Central Arkansas, Georgia, Wisconsin-Stout, Southeastern Louisiana, a Kansas community college, and, not surprisingly, back at the *Dartmouth Review*. By the summer of 1994, the Student Press Law Center noted no fewer than thirty-six such incidents of theft, a dramatic rise from what had for years been three or four each semester.

The administrative response also varied. Only at the University of Maryland–College Park, it appears, were student thieves actually charged with violating campus disciplinary standards. In the late winter of 1994, two students accused of seizing a substantial portion of one issue of the *Diamondback,* the campus daily, were found guilty of theft. They were placed on probation for a year and ordered to perform sixteen hours of community service. They were also directed to write essays analyzing recent United States Supreme Court decisions defining freedom of the press.

Elsewhere, the Student Press Law Center lamented, "many school officials have treated newspaper theft as an insignificant prank if they reacted to it at all." Penn, for example, agonized over the issue for some weeks and eventually (after President Hackney had been confirmed and had taken over at the NEH) declined to prosecute several black students identified as having taken most of one day's issue of the campus daily. In fact, the center's director, Mark Goodman, laid blame for the rapid rise in campus paper thefts at the feet of administrators who were slow to condemn such acts and "law enforcement officials who refuse to arrest and prosecute the thieves as criminals." In fairness, there were two distinguishing features: one, the difficulty of apprehending the thieves—the Maryland case was unusual in the ready identification of those responsible for the seizure—and two, the uncertainty of the line between larceny and liberally helping oneself to newspapers offered without charge in bins and boxes.

When charges have been brought, results both on and off campus have been mixed. In a contentious and complex case, Duke University's undergraduate Judicial Board acquitted a student who had taken many copies of the ultraconservative *Duke Review*—not because the facts were in doubt but because the expanded definition of "theft" on which the conviction turned was found violative of due process. Courts have had no easier time of it. A Louisiana judge early in 1994 acquitted one student charged with newspaper theft, finding insufficient evidence of the requisite intent. The judge called the incident "a college prank" that "should have been addressed by normal school disciplinary proceedings."

The Maryland legislature, however, vowed to take the matter more seriously after the *Diamondback* seizure, even though campus discipline had been imposed at College Park. In action aimed at (but not in terms limited to) the college press, Maryland's lawmakers in the spring of 1994 became the first to make it criminal to take "one or more newspapers with the intent to destroy the newspapers or prevent other individuals from reading the newspapers." A *Washington Post* editorial, after conceding ambivalence on the merits of the issue, offered what seems to be the latest word on the subject:

> It can be argued . . . that scooping up copies of publications—whether to send a message or protest one—may in itself be a form of free speech. But you don't even need to get to that point to conclude that trying to

draft, enact and enforce regulations criminalizing the removal of free newspapers is neither an easy nor worthy pursuit.

That comment may put to rest the final question we face: does the First Amendment require specific measures to guard against or prevent theft of campus newspapers? If there are reasonable steps that could be taken to make the distribution safer or to secure copies once they are on display, a plausible case can be made that the institution should take these steps. Perhaps it should also consider whether rules could be framed that would at least discourage, if not necessarily criminalize, newspaper theft. Beyond that, little can be done. Surely the First Amendment does not compel the impossible, even for the best of causes.

VII.

ARTISTIC FREEDOM ON CAMPUS

The third week of May 1994 was a stressful one for the arts on northern California campuses. Stanford University barred four members of its Pac 10 champion men's baseball players from taking part in the imminent NCAA playoffs. Their offense? Using locker-room benches to bash a recently installed campus sculpture entitled "Gay Liberation," which tastefully portrayed gay relationships. The wooden bench had been forcibly rammed between two of the sculpture's figures. Black paint had been splattered over several of the figures. The attack was not unprecedented; this was at least the third time the sculpture had been defiled during the year but the first time an assailant was identified.

Things were even tenser up the peninsula at San Francisco State University. Early in the week a ten-foot-square mural was unveiled on the side of a university building. The mural had been commissioned by university officials, though it had not been reviewed or formally approved before the unveiling. What appeared on the mural when the curtain went up shocked many members of the university community. The scene caused special anguish for many Jewish students. The mural's central focus was a portrait of Malcolm X, made public on what would have been the slain black leader's sixty-ninth birthday. The portrait was, however, bordered by a United States flag, several dollar signs, a Star of David, and a skull and crossbones with the words "African blood."

The first person to voice concern was Professor Lois Lyles, an African American faculty member, who tried to write "Stop Fascism" next to the mural, protesting what seemed to her its anti-Semitic theme. After a scuffle with some of the mural's supporters, Lyles was arrested for vandalism. In response to early protests, the artist, Semay Dennis, insisted he had meant no offense to Jews or to anyone else. He was only seeking, he declared, to create a graphic image that would recall Malcolm X's outspoken anti-Zionism. The president of the Pan African Student Union added, "our intention was not to hurt anyone; all art is open to interpretation."

University president Robert Corrigan appealed to the student government, hoping it would mediate the rapidly rising tensions. Despite three attempts, the student senate could not muster a quorum and thus took no action. Meanwhile, the administration ordered the mural obliterated by being painted over. Mural sympathizers twice removed the paint cover, each time reopening the controversy. Students with contending views demonstrated for and against the mural. At the end of an explosive week, President Corrigan finally ordered the wall sandblasted in a way that left no trace of the offending mural.

In a statement explaining his action, the president insisted free expression was not involved. He cited several factors to justify administrative intervention: the mural had originally been commissioned by the university; it was created on school property; and its contents had never been finally approved. In further extenuation, the president added:

> This University absolutely will not tolerate expressions of hate. . . . Intolerance and prejudice are abhorrent to our deepest values as individuals and as a community.

As the week ended, Corrigan acknowledged the experience had been painful but added his firm belief that "inaction would have been more painful and morally insupportable."

San Francisco State is no stranger to controversy. Even before free speech protests surfaced at Berkeley in the 1960s, there had been much student political activity at this smaller institution across the bay. This was the campus which became nationally renowned in the late 1960s for two events—the violent death of a student protester in the act of carrying a homemade bomb to a target building and the shutting down of a campus rally by university president (later U.S. senator) S. I. Hayakawa's ripping of amplifier wires from a public address system.

Yet the 1994 controversy over the mural differed in important ways that illustrate the special nature of artistic freedom on the public college campus. For one, the capacity of vivid art to offend, insult, and inflame transcends the potential of even the most volatile of words. The emotive force of visual display is inevitably more powerful. Suppose the Pan African Student Union had invited to San Francisco State a speaker known for strongly anti-Semitic views. Jewish students would probably have been upset and might have asked that the invitation be withdrawn. But the degree of potential trauma caused by words alone would have been of a different order. The depth and intensity of the reaction that ethnically offensive art evokes may go well beyond the feelings likely to be aroused by even the most offensive of slurs, epithets, and other verbal invective.

There is a second vital difference between verbal and visual assaults. A major premise of our national commitment to free speech is that the opportunity always exists for response and refutation—the belief that (in Thomas Jefferson's words) truth will combat error if given the chance. Thus we insist on broad latitude for unsettling words except where the threat is so grave and so immediate that the impact of the words cannot be allayed by counterspeech.

The creative arts, however, do not easily fit this equation. Consider the illogic of using "counterspeech" to allay the trauma created by the Malcolm X mural. Would anything be gained, for example, by placing alongside the mural a painting or photo of the slain black leader with his arm around a man wearing a yarmulke? In this sense, then, artistic expression is at least different from, if not less protected than, verbal expression.

A third difference between offending words and visual images lies in the state of applicable law. The courts have dealt with provocative speech in countless cases, arising from myriad settings. Controversial works of visual art have produced surprisingly few court tests. Those who must decide how to handle such art works face a largely uncharted legal terrain. There are few cases in point, on or off campus. Constitutional experts can and do disagree on the issues within a broad range of options with few legal guidelines.

Thus First Amendment experts were all over the lot on the propriety of San Francisco State's action against the Malcolm X mural. Professor Thomas Grey of the Stanford Law School (the chief architect of his university's speech code) insisted "there's no First Amendment issue [at San Francisco State]," adding:

> You might not like the fact that they [university officials] edited your message, but they have the legal right to decide what picture of the university they want to project.

The executive director of the Northern California American Civil Liberties Union, Dorothy Ehrlich, concurred cautiously, though she added her belief that "simply painting over the offending remarks in the dead of night is not good enough." Under such conditions, she urged, the institution should have done more to address what was clearly "a great deal of tension and intolerance on campus." Others, on and off the campus, insisted that for a public university to obliterate a mural because some people find its theme offensive is clear censorship that violates both the artist's and potential viewers' First Amendment rights. There was respectable support for claims on both sides.

While no court decisions give direct answers about an offensive or demeaning mural, a few cases yield limited guidance. One might begin with the most recent of the cases, since it has obvious relevance to the San Francisco State incident. It arose at the Art Institute of Chicago—a place that is also no stranger to controversy, having just before this case weathered public outcry over a student exhibit that required viewers to trample on a U.S. flag if they sought proper perspective on the artwork. Art Institute student David Nelson submitted a singularly provocative entry for the annual display of original student work: a full-length frontal portrait of the late Harold Washington, Chicago's first black mayor, clad only in a white bra, G-string, garter belt, and stockings. This unusual attire apparently reflected an unconfirmed rumor that when the dying mayor arrived at the hospital, he was wearing female underwear beneath his business suit.

Though the student exhibit containing Nelson's work was not open to the general public, news of the content of the portrait, tantalizingly entitled "Mirth and Girth," quickly spread across the city. When Art Institute officials asked Nelson to remove the painting, he refused. The City Council then ordered that the work be removed, under threat to terminate city funding for certain institute programs if the display persisted.

When the institute's president declined to intervene, three Chicago aldermen took matters into their own hands. They marched into the gallery, removed the painting from the wall, and were about to carry it out of the building when they were detained by a guard. By the time the rescued painting reached the president's office, it had suffered a foot-long gash. The work was not destined to remain there long, however, for a city policeman was directed to take the painting into city custody. There it remained until, late the following day, it was released to the artist.

Nelson soon filed suit in federal court against the aldermen and other city officials, seeking damages for abridgment of his civil rights because of the destruction and removal of the painting he had created. The case languished in trial court for over five years, bogged down by such issues as the city officials' immunity, when the court of appeals insisted the district judge reach the central issues. Judge Richard Posner, who has had much to say over the years about law and the arts, took this occasion to express his sympathy with the artist's claims.

The aldermen argued that but for their bold and timely intervention, the painting might have set off a riot approaching the level of urban unrest right after the assassination of Reverend Martin Luther King, Jr. (to whom Mayor Washington's admirers often compared him). Judge Posner recognized that such events might conceivably pose a "clear and present danger" of disorder so great as to warrant government action against a creative person. But the appeals court could not on this basis absolve Chicago officials of defacing the painting:

> [Where] an artist's intentions are innocent, at least of any desire to cause a riot, but his work so inflames the community as to cause a riot in which people are killed and injured . . . First Amendment rights are not subject to the heckler's veto. . . . The rioters are the culpable parties, not the artist whose work unintentionally provoked them to violence. . . . [Cited cases do not hold] that police and other public officials can seek to protect the populace at the expense of the artist, by "arresting" the offensive painting rather than the violent rioters.

Judge Posner also doubted whether such disorder was ever an imminent threat: "Burn down Chicago over a painting?" he mused. "Paris, maybe, but Americans have never taken culture *that* seriously."

Posner's insight is illuminating and helpful, even to one who may be less sanguine that Americans do not take their culture so seriously as to riot over a painting. In fact, on this count—perhaps only on this count— one has modest sympathy with the aldermen. However unacceptable may have been their invasion of the gallery and removal of the painting, the law can appropriately condemn the *means* without necessarily disparaging the *motive*. We could better address the underlying issues of artistic freedom and free speech if we were willing to assume—as Judge Posner apparently was not—that some Americans are indeed as ready as Parisians to take to the streets in protest against the message or theme of a volatile painting.

Depicting a nearly naked likeness of the city's first black mayor in nothing but lingerie is undeniably provocative, just as it was to embellish a portrait of Malcolm X with a Star of David and crude dollar signs. Art, more than words, may have the capacity to trigger a violent physical reaction to unsettling images. But this prospect does not make any easier the resolution of hard cases, at the Art Institute of Chicago, the San Francisco State University campus, or elsewhere.

The Chicago case is also novel in the way it presented the issue of artistic freedom. Instead of the more familiar contest between an artist and an institution that seeks to curb artistic expression, here the institute and its student were not only on the same side; they were equally aggrieved by the intrusion of an external force in the person of the indignant aldermen. Yet the claim of artistic freedom may prove more elusive in such a case, as Judge Posner recognized in giving guidance to a trial judge who had yet to address the merits.

The arts were seldom the focus of campus controversy in the era of campus unrest triggered by the Vietnam War. There was, however, one artistic freedom case—really the first of its kind to reach the courts—at the University of Massachusetts–Amherst. The walls of a corridor in the student union had often been used, apparently without incident, for the display of original art by members of the campus community. Charles Close, a young art instructor, was invited to exhibit some of his works on this corridor. His paintings contained some nude figures, with explicit and detailed genitalia. The display soon attracted considerable attention and evoked scattered protest.

The administration ordered the materials removed, calling them simply "inappropriate." Close sued the university in federal court, claiming a violation of his First Amendment rights. The artist's claim was a novel one, to which the district judge was sympathetic from the start. The nature of the site seemed to him to support Close's plea; because of recurrent use of the corridor for art displays, the site had become a "public forum" where speech could not be restricted because some people found distasteful the content of a particular display. Yet that was precisely what the administration had done; calling the display "inappropriate" reflected an adverse view of artistic content or message that was simply incompatible with the First Amendment. There was no question about the artist's compliance with content-neutral rules dealing with the "time, place, and manner" of expression; he had been invited to display his work in just that place. Thus the district judge found the university to have acted wrongfully by abridging the artist's freedom of speech and held that it must restore the exhibit.

The university appealed and found a more sympathetic tribunal. The appeals court, in this very first campus art case, gave Close's claims remarkably short shrift. The appellate judges took a markedly more deferential view of administrative edicts about what was or was not "appropriate" in the student union. The reviewing court seemed to have been heavily influenced by the nature of the display area—"a passageway regularly used by the public, including children," where depiction of nudes and genitalia seemed especially "inappropriate."

The higher court was also far more sensitive to the public nature of the site, remarking upon the sensitivities of passersby who might be assaulted by Close's work:

> Where there was, in effect, a captive audience, [the university administration] had a right to afford protection against "assault upon individual privacy" short of legal obscenity.

There was at least one other factor at work here, perhaps even more clearly adverse to the artist's claims. While the district judge had found substantial merit in Close's work, the appeals court expressed only disdain for the quality of the artistic material, offering doubts whether it even deserved constitutional protection. The opinion began with a strikingly disparaging comment:

> There is no suggestion, unless in its cheap titles, that plaintiff's art was seeking to express political or social thought. . . . [Speaker ban cases] involve a medium and subject matter entitled to greater protection than plaintiff's art. . . . We consider plaintiff's constitutional interest minimal.

The implication was unmistakably clear: words—any words, even words of marginal merit—have a higher claim on First Amendment protection than does most art, especially art that does not embody "political or social thought." While the court stopped short of holding that unconventional or avant-garde art is simply not protected speech, the opinion contained more than a hint of such a disparaging view of visual expression.

In fact, doubt has persisted to the present, in surprising measure, on the degree to which the First Amendment fully protects art as "speech."

Even though art often conveys a message or viewpoint (though it need not) and though the First Amendment's framers presumably saw art as "speech," thoughtful constitutional scholars have questioned on several grounds the basis for full constitutional protection. They note that the core of free speech—and the clearest rationale for its protection—is political expression. While art occasionally treats political themes, that is more the exception than the rule; any constitutional standard tied to politics would be of little value. Thus a narrow view of free speech—one that would confine protection to the historic core—easily excludes most artistic expression from its scope.

There is a second troubling element. The classic case in support of free speech reflects a belief, best stated by Justice Brandeis, that

> if there be time to expose through discussion the falsehood and fallacies, to avert the evil by the processes of education, the remedy to be applied is more speech, not enforce silence. Only an emergency can justify repression.

All well and good when counterspeech is meaningful and likely to prevail. But artistic expression offers no comfortable analogue, as the case of the Harold Washington shows. How consoling to indignant admirers of the late mayor would have been the placement nearby of a conventional portrait of the subject in a business suit—even if accompanied by a statement such as "this is the real Harold Washington, as he should be remembered"? Whatever damage the offending caricature might do to Washington admirers could hardly be erased by a laudatory portrait. Or for Jewish students at San Francisco State, how reassuring would be a Malcolm X portrait without a Star of David—or, for that matter, an adjacent Star of David with no Malcolm X? In neither case would such an accompanying portrayal do much, if anything, to offset the damage done by the offending work. "Counterspeech" simply does not operate in the same way or to the same degree in regard to artistic expression.

That difference, however, should not place art beyond the First Amendment, but should sensitize us to a greater analytic challenge. The hostile and benighted view of judges such as those on the appeals court in the University of Massachusetts case deserves some understanding. The basis for First Amendment protection for the creative arts demands further probing and analysis.

The case for comparable constitutional protection of works of art rests on solid, if slightly different, ground. All art contains an indisputably expressive element, whether or not a conventional message can be discerned. The framers of the First Amendment, most of them learned patrons of the arts, would surely have given some signal if they wished artistic expression alone to fall outside the constitutional ambit. Thus courts have from time to time conferred protection on specific art forms, more often musical than visual, while stopping short of blanket protection for all forms of artistic expression.

These courts' judgments have also produced a more welcome climate in cases involving the status of the arts on the college and university campus. Only a few years after the University of Massachusetts litigation, California courts wrestled with an art controversy of a very different sort. William Spater, a graduate student in art at California State University– Long Beach, submitted ten life-size nude figures of plaster and wax as the core of his master's degree project. Some of the figures depicted sexual and erotic acts. The critical issue soon became one of public display, which was the normal (if not universal) final step in the degree process.

The dean of fine arts informed Spater that "due to the frankly sexual subject matter of the project and its realistic depiction, it would be inappropriate for there to be an exhibit of . . . [the] . . . project on campus." The artist, initially ambivalent and disinclined to fight, now demanded a chance to display his work. A growing number of fellow students protested in support of his claim. The art faculty also backed Spater's wish to display the work. The dean then decided to permit the exhibit, and the president of the college upheld the decision. But within days the issue reached the capitol in Sacramento, where it became the focus of a legislative hearing. Under apparent political pressure, the chancellor of the statewide system reversed the campus head and canceled the exhibit.

Spater and a group of fellow students now filed suit in state court, claiming violation of rights that were both contractual and constitutional. The trial judge was not the least bit sympathetic to the work or to its champions. The sculpture, he declared, was "about an inch away from an act of perversion." The judge rejected all the claims, leaving the plaintiffs only the recourse of taking an appeal, which they promptly did.

The higher court was only slightly more accommodating. It affirmed the trial judge on mainly procedural grounds, finding in Spater's ambiguous conduct a waiver of whatever rights he might otherwise have preserved. The constitutional issue was relegated to a footnote, which barely hinted what the court might have said of a properly preserved free speech claim. On one hand, it cited a California Supreme Court case holding that public transit systems could not refuse display space for messages they found distasteful. But the court also cited the University of Massachusetts case and invoked, in support of a skeptical view, a recent federal decision that state university law journal editors had substantial discretion to reject articles submitted by outsiders. As the footnote revealed, California courts had fashioned principles of free expression that might have some bearing on campus art disputes; the tortuous way this case arose, however, kept them on the shelf.

One other case involving campus visual arts is more helpful and brings back on stage the informed views of Richard Posner, the judge in the Chicago Art Institute case. Albert Piarowski, chairman of the art department at an Illinois junior college, contributed several stained glass panels to the annual faculty exhibit. The display site was a highly visible area, adjacent to the central mall of the college's main building. The gallery bordered the area through which students and visitors passed enroute to classrooms, offices, and meeting rooms on the upper floors. Three of the panels immediately drew critical attention. The court described their content as follows:

> One depicts the naked rump of a brown woman, and sticking out from (or into) it a white cylinder that resembles a finger but on careful inspection is seen to be a jet of gas. Another window shows a brown woman from the back, standing naked except for stockings, and apparently masturbating. In the third window another brown woman, also naked except for stockings and also seen from the rear, is crouching in a posture of veneration before a robed white male whose most prominent feature is a grotesquely outsized phallus (erect penis) that the woman is embracing.

The exhibit evoked extensive complaint from students, custodial personnel, and African American clergy. Though the college had no specific rules governing art displays and did not claim the panels to be legally obscene, administrators nonetheless told Piarowski he must relocate his work. An alternate site near the art department's fourth-floor offices was suggested. When the artist refused to relocate his windows, the administration stepped in and had them removed. When the issue reached federal court, the college insisted it had wanted only to relocate the offending display and took the more drastic step of removal only when Piarowski defiantly refused the milder sanction.

The trial judge dismissed the artist's suit in a brief, unreported opinion. When the case reached the appeals court, though, Judge Posner sensed an occasion for careful analysis of the constitutional status of campus art, a subject that, even by the mid-1980s, was largely untested except for the University of Massachusetts case. This appeals court could thus write on a relatively clean slate. The threshold question was whether art was protected speech. This much the court was ready to assume, noting that other courts had held "the First Amendment . . . to embrace purely artistic as well as political expression" except for what was legally obscene. Moreover, cautioned Judge Posner:

> If the college had opened up the gallery to the public as a place for expression it could not have regulated that expression any way it pleased just because the gallery was its property . . . or because the artist happened to be a member of the college's faculty.

Piarowski's case did not, however, test the limits of free speech for campus artists. This dispute could be resolved more narrowly. Several factors led the court to uphold the college's action. First, the display site was not a "public forum" where outsiders were regularly invited to offer their art; though noncollege artists' works were occasionally displayed there, the gallery was generally limited to college student and faculty use.

Second, there was serious concern over what the court termed "image." The administration had expressed deep fear about the effect such a display might have on its ability to recruit and retain students, especially women and students from underrepresented minority groups. (Among the early complainants had been a group of African American clergy, who argued that some black visitors to the campus might find the portrayals to be racially offensive or demeaning.) On this point, the court added, "if we hold that the college was forbidden to take the action that it took to protect its image, we limit the freedom of the academy to manage its affairs as it chooses."

Third, there was the fundamental issue of location. The initial exhibit site was a prominent and visible area near the center of campus activity;

"the offending windows could be seen by people not actually in the gallery." This prospect justified a higher standard of taste than would have been warranted if the exhibit never ventured beyond a remote fourth-floor gallery. Moreover, the college never insisted on banishing the work entirely; its proposed solution left the artist a means (which he rejected) of keeping the exhibit on display on campus, even if off the main artery and apart from the rest of the faculty show. Indeed, Piarowski's lawyer conceded the college might reasonably have installed some device like venetian blinds to shield the gallery from users of the mall. It was only a small leap from using such a shield to the actual relocation that had been ordered. The court offered a consoling comment about the context within which the college's removal occurred:

> A decision as to where within a public forum to display sexually explicit art is less menacing to artistic freedom than a decision to exclude it altogether. . . . If Piarowski had given to the man's face in his pastiche of "Adoration of the Penis" the unmistakable likeness of the chairman of the college's board of trustees, we doubt that we would be hearing the argument that the First Amendment prevents any tampering with the siting of a work of art; it would be reasonable in such a case for the college to order the stained glass window moved to a less conspicuous spot on the campus—especially when the window had been created by an employee of the college, and not just by any employee but by the chairman of the art department and gallery coordinator.

The relocation issue was actually a bit more complex. At the time of the dispute, the fourth-floor gallery site which the administration favored was in use. Thus the preferred alternative was not immediately available. But, as the court observed, Piarowski was both artist and gallery manager and thus (of all the players) the one best equipped to find alternative exhibit sites. In the end, an initially sympathetic court lost patience with an artist who seemed "to have been more interested in becoming a martyr to artistic freedom" than in resolving a practical but solvable dispute.

Judge Posner concluded with a retrospective comment about the University of Massachusetts case, which seemed to him a harder one than *Piarowski* because "the issue was removal, not relocation." The difference was not simply one of process or timing but also of substance: if the college administration had barred the display altogether, "Piarowski might have been discouraged from creating similar work in the future." In the actual case, by contrast, "the abridgment of freedom of expression is less, when the college says to him, you may exhibit your work on campus—just not in the alcove off the mall."

For Posner's court, location thus became an independent variable of some importance to recognition of artistic freedom. The reasoning was at least superficially persuasive; there is all the difference in the world between barring a work completely from the campus and limiting the places it can be displayed. The analytic problem is that the Supreme Court has dealt somewhat differently with the choice of location for expression in other settings. When the city of Chattanooga refused to permit the performance of the rock musical *Hair* in a municipal auditorium because city officials objected to the content, the U.S. Supreme Court found that to be an unconstitutional prior restraint. The city argued that the producers could have used a nearby private theater. But the high court dismissed this argument as of "no consequence," even if (and that was not clear) an equivalent private site existed. Quoting an earlier case on the location of demonstrations and marches, the justices insisted that "one is not to have the exercise of his liberty of expression in appropriate places abridged on the plea that it may be exercised in some other place."

The question of how far this precept governs geography in a case like Piarowski's is itself problematic, for the Illinois junior college situation differed in a couple of crucial ways. The original exhibit location, the court agreed, was not an "appropriate site." And unlike the Chattanooga ban on *Hair,* the college administration had not sent the artist out to find a private gallery somewhere that would accept his work. Instead, the college simply sought to shift the display from a highly visible site to one off the beaten path. That would be closely analogous to Chattanooga officials telling *Hair's* producers they were free to use a more remote and smaller city facility rather than the prime space they wanted.

Despite these analytic differences about the choice of expressive sites, some uneasiness remains about Posner's confidence in drawing so firm a line between "removal" (which is bad) and "relocation" (which is usually good or benign). Such issues have attracted the attention of others in the academic community and produced at least one serious proposal for standards to guide the handling of controversial campus art displays. In the spring of 1990, the American Association of University Professors and other groups convened a group of experts on art, law, education, and policy at Wolf Trap, near Washington, D.C. Their goal was nothing short of defining the appropriate scope and nature of artistic freedom in the academic setting. On the specific issue raised by the cases we have just examined, the conference offered this view:

> When academic institutions offer exhibitions or performances to the public, they should ensure that the rights of the presenters and the audience are not impaired by a "heckler's veto" from those who may be offended by the presentation. Academic institutions should ensure that those who choose to view or attend may do so without interference. Mere presentation in a public place does not create a "captive audience." Institutions may reasonably designate specific places as generally available or unavailable for exhibits or performances.

How might this view affect the outcome of cases like those at the University of Massachusetts and the Illinois junior college, if at all? Three points of possible contrast emerge. First, the conference urged that judgments about the suitability of display sites should be ones of general policy, made well in advance of contests over particular works. Thus the University of Massachusetts might well have decided years earlier to stop using the student union corridor as a gallery, or the Illinois junior college could have relocated the entire annual faculty exhibit to the fourth-floor gallery, farther from the central mall. But once a site has been designated as suitable for a general type of artistic display, individual works should not be barred or removed because they prove troublesome or offensive.

The Wolf Trap report leaves open an intermediate issue: whether a college could designate a particular gallery as suitable only for relatively innocuous works such as still lifes, landscapes, and portraits, while relegating racier material generally to the upper floors. The principal difficulty is that labels do not always work; there can be sexually explicit portraits, still lifes, even landscapes. The notion of classifying exhibit space according to subject matter may have some utility but will not necessarily avoid hard cases of the kind we have seen.

The Wolf Trap Conference statement offered a second guide to the courts: fear that some viewers might take offense, or even proof that some have already done so, would not justify removal of a work that is already on display. Thus the rationale cited by the courts in the Massachusetts and Illinois cases—impact on visitors and, in one case, special harm to student recruitment—sounds ominously like giving in to a "heckler's veto" that should not deprive others of the chance to see controversial work because some viewers find it objectionable. There is no question that some art patrons in western Massachusetts and downstate Illinois had their viewing options curtailed when federal courts sustained the challenged administrative actions. Whatever else may be said, it is clear that the "hecklers" in each case did get to exercise a type of "veto."

The Wolf Trap statement offers a third contrast: the presentation of a work in a public place does not, by itself, create a captive audience. But this statement talks of "those who choose to view or attend" and thus implies that colleges ought to be sensitive to the feelings of true "captives." Take, for example, a theater class at Pennsylvania State University, the members of which were warned by a graduate teaching assistant that their course grade would depend on seeing, among others, a sexually explicit play to which several students strenuously objected. It is one thing to say that the university ought not ban the play or even remove it from the course because some students find its language or nudity objectionable. But it is quite different and clearly unacceptable to compel any student to see the play in order to pass the course. Such coerced theatergoers would indeed constitute a captive audience, whose freedom to learn would be at risk. The institution bears the delicate task of balancing the artist's creative freedom against the need to protect the sensitive student's right not to be coerced into an unacceptable artistic experience.

• • •

That is precisely the dilemma that brings us to another current and difficult dimension of the arts on the university campus. It is the question of how far students should be warned—and professors required to warn—of controversial material contained in lectures and class presentations. Both Vanderbilt University and the University of Iowa have struggled with the issue, with somewhat different results.

In the spring of 1993, Vanderbilt's dean of arts and sciences directed one faculty member to warn his students, at the start of the semester, of any sexually explicit material he planned to use in class. Though the directive was addressed to a named individual, it left other faculty in the college wondering to what extent they might be seen to have a similar duty, even in teaching relatively innocuous material. Committee A of the American Association of University Professors, upon learning of the directive, expressed its concern about an apparent threat to the purest form of academic freedom (how and what a professor chooses to teach). Since Vanderbilt is a private university, no court challenge was possible, and the issue apparently remained between the dean and the one professor.

The Iowa situation was more complex. During 1992, the Iowa Board of Regents and even the governor received complaints about the use of certain films in classes at two of the state's three universities. Three incidents were cited, two involving films with apparent gay or lesbian content. At its February 1993 meeting, the board called on the faculties at all three universities to develop policies that would warn students of objectionable material in their classes. Failing such action, the regents threatened to impose a more draconian and content-specific warning policy of their own. Under this policy, a warning would be required "when course materials include explicit representations of human sexual acts that could reasonably be expected to be offensive to some students," with the understanding that an objecting student would be excused from the particular session and could drop the course if no alternative sufficed.

Such a policy would presumably create rather serious problems not only for teachers of art and art history or sex education, family life, and the like but also for those on medical faculties who might use such materials and illustrations in courses on anatomy or obstetrics and gynecology. Despite the regents' insistence that such a reading was not anticipated by the policy's framers, the language did nothing to allay the concerns of conscientious professors.

Even so, the faculties at Iowa State and Northern Iowa complied. Members of the University of Iowa faculty, however, demurred. In their view (and that of the university's president), general principles of faculty responsibility should suffice. The regents, still dissatisfied, pressed for a more focused policy. Eventually the president augmented the faculty senate policy by requiring only that professors give their students "adequate indication of any unusual or unexpected class presentations or materials." This alternative was soon accepted by the regents, and the drama seemed to have run its course. Any reference to "sexually explicit" or other categories of material was gone. The new rule was general and content-neutral.

Not everyone was satisfied, however, by these changes. Some Iowans launched the Campaign for Academic Freedom, charging that the new policy was no better than the one it replaced, or might even be worse because it was open-ended in regard to subject matter possibly covered. Critics also noted that the revised policy failed to say by whose views or standards material might be judged "unusual or unexpected."

The regents eventually concluded that the entire exercise had been misguided, or at least had created more problems than it had solved. In December 1995, the reference to "unusual or unexpected" was removed from the policy. Iowa's rules on course content thus became, once again, compatible with those of other states. The entire episode served mainly to suggest the sensitivity of interposing policies between teacher and student. Even proponents of such warnings would probably concede, after the dust had settled in Iowa, that the effort was not worth the modest benefit.

The warning issue is an inherently difficult one. Responsible faculty would be nearly unanimous on two points. The first is that professors have a duty not only to tell students early in the course what they plan to cover but also to stick fairly close to the announced coverage. The American Association of University Professors holds it "improper" for a faculty member

> persistently to intrude material that has no relation to the subject, or to fail to present the subject matter of the course as announced to the students and as approved by the faculty in their collective responsibility for the curriculum.

The other point seems equally well settled: that students should not be compelled to view or experience visual material they find offensive (not only on sexual grounds but for religious, racial, or other reasons as well). While education ought to be challenging and even unsettling, students need not be confronted with material abhorrent to their values. There is, however, an important corollary: if one student objects or even if many students object, the remedy is not to expunge the material but to permit objectors to satisfy the course requirements in some other way. Typically, professor and student would jointly seek an alternative path. If they could find no mutually agreeable substitute, as a last resort the student might be permitted to drop the course. An academic dean might have ultimate authority to approve such an exit; indeed, the exercise of this authority might alert an administration to a potentially problematic course.

• • •

Our focus to this point has been on the visual arts. A rather different set of issues arises with respect to the performing arts. Three relatively recent cases illustrate the contrasting approach. Of the first two, one involved a film and the other a play. In both, state university officials had canceled on-campus performances in response to off-campus criticism of content. In both cases, courts sustained the right to hold such performances, despite the pressures and concerns that led to the cancellations.

The first case involved a scheduled showing of a film, Jean-Luc Godard's *Hail Mary* in the art gallery at the University of Nebraska–Lincoln. Though acclaimed by film critics, the film was seen in some quarters as blasphemous because of its contemporary and irreverent portrayal of the birth of Jesus. Skeptics, including a prominent state senator, demanded that such a "sacrilegious" film not be shown. The director of the gallery balked, but his superiors soon stepped in and canceled the showing. A group of would-be viewers then took the issue to federal court.

The trial judge ruled against the university, finding that it had practiced what he considered unlawful censorship. The major precedent was a recent U.S. Supreme Court judgment that school boards and officials could not remove library books on the basis of personal whim or taste. The trial judge's ruling gave clear guidance to college officials in the handling of controversial films:

> Even if the cause [for the cancellation] had been only the fact of controversy . . . cancellation would not have been justified, because actions taken by an arm of the state merely to avoid controversy from the expression of ideas is an insufficient basis for interfering with the right to receive information.

Despite this ringing vindication of the gallery manager and the film, the case may portend less than a first reading suggests. For one thing, the unmistakable reason for the cancellation—bowing to pressure from an indignant legislator—was suspect at best. Regardless of the content or artistic merit of the target film, a court could have said simply that a state university's acceding to legislative threats by banning films is unconstitutional.

The other film case, the most recent involving campus arts, had a less satisfying outcome. When the regents of Oklahoma State University initially banned the on-campus showing of the Martin Scorsese film *Last Temptation of Christ* because of scenes that some critics found blasphemous, a group of would-be viewers went to court. The federal judge invited the regents to reconsider, which they did, rescinding the ban and leaving to the administration any further decisions. The administration then told the student sponsors to delete from ads about the film the usual phrase "brought to you by the students, faculty and staff of OSU . . ." and to insert a disclaimer that "the showing of this film does not reflect an endorsement of its contents by the OSU Board of Regents or Oklahoma State University."

The ads were changed, and the film was shown on the scheduled dates. But the plaintiffs returned to court and sought damages for what they claimed was still unlawful content-based censorship. They cited instances of the barring of controversial speakers in the 1960s as the basis of their claim that the free speech issues did not drop out when the film was shown. The trial judge dismissed the case as essentially moot, presuming "the parties will conduct themselves, constitutionally and morally, in an appropriate manner."

While the case was on appeal, the regents adopted a completely new policy on campus speech and artistic expression. Since this policy had not yet been applied and since its terms did not restrict speech, there was no basis for a First Amendment challenge. Moreover, the regents noted that *Hail Mary* (the film that had triggered the Nebraska ban) had been shown without objection at Oklahoma State. The appeals court did, however, find one small point in the plaintiffs' favor: they had sought nominal damages because of the regents' initial ban of the film, and this claim had now to be assessed; "if proved, a violation of First Amendment rights concerning freedom of expression entitles a plaintiff to at least nominal damages." The major issues, though, had come to rest.

Finally there is an intriguing California case from the late 1980s, involving a play. A junior college theater instructor had chosen for his class a play that treated race relations in a highly charged fashion. The script included "a flurry of racial slurs and epithets" just before the moment at which a black police officer fatally shoots a white suspect on stage. Community pressure, fueled in part by religious groups, caused the college administration to cancel performances of the play, even as a class exercise.

A group of would-be playgoers filed suit in state court to lift the ban. The court reached very much the same conclusions as had the federal court in the Nebraska case. Strong community pressure or controversial content, it cautioned, could no more justify banning controversial ideas from the campus stage than from the podium—especially when, as here, the play had been chosen and was to be presented as part of a drama class exercise. The case thus left open, and other courts seem never to have reached, the question of whether a *student-sponsored* play would fare differently. What we have is two dimensions of the issue in the cases that protect student-sponsored films, and the California judgment that protected the class-related play. Presumably the same standards would also apply to live theater under the aegis of student organizations.

● ● ●

The final issue that merits attention is that of federal restrictions on the funding of campus-based arts. In 1989 and 1990, all recipients of support from the National Endowment for the Arts were required to sign a pledge that many found abhorrent. As part of a request for advance or reimbursement, NEA grantees were required to certify that they would not use the funds to create works "which in the judgment of the National Endowment for the Arts . . . may be considered obscene, including but not limited to, depictions of sadomasochism, homoeroticism, the sexual exploitation of children, or individuals engaged in sex acts and which, when taken as a whole, do not have serious literary, artistic, political, or scientific value."

That requirement was contained in the Helms amendment, applicable to all NEA grants in fiscal year 1990. This amendment was a potpourri of constraints, a few of which might have made a claim for validity had they stood alone. Even ardent champions of free speech accept, for example, that Congress could refuse to fund works that a court had found to be legally obscene or to violate child pornography laws. On the other hand, Congress had no power to proscribe depiction of "individuals engaged in sex acts." And nobody really knew what the amendment's sponsor, Jesse Helms, had in mind when he barred funding of "sadomasochistic" and "homoerotic" works, since the terms were not defined in the amendment and (unlike "obscenity") were not familiar terms that had been fully defined elsewhere.

Several NEA grantees went to federal court seeking relief from the certification requirements. They came before a sympathetic judge, who held the Helms language violative of the grantees' First Amendment rights. He found in the statutory apparatus two fatal flaws: first, the vagueness of certain of the key terms to which a grantee must promise adherence; and second, the fact that any dispute over the meaning and scope of these terms would be decided not by a court but by the NEA, an agency without judicial process or powers. Thus it was hardly surprising that conscientious grantees might feel a "chilling" of their artistic expression and would resolve doubts by forgoing federal support to which they had every right. The combination—vague terms, the absence of any judicial process, and a consequent chilling—made this a relatively easy case for the vindication of the artists' speech claims. The court left open what would have happened if the Helms amendment had been confined to court-defined terms like "obscenity" or how the law would have fared if the interpretation even of questionable terms had been solely the province of the courts.

By the time this case reached decision, Congress had already replaced the Helms amendment. In its place came new and seemingly benign language. It came in two parts. The first charged the NEA to take into account, in its grant-making process, "general standards of decency and respect for the diverse beliefs and values of the American public." NEA officials tried to assure the artistic community that the language on "decency" was "nonbinding," whatever that meant. At least the new restrictions made clear that courts, not the NEA, would judge whether a work was legally obscene.

It did not take long for a group of four performance artists, whose grants had been withheld under this new language, to file a federal suit. This case was procedurally complex, raising still unresolved questions about the NEA chairman's duty to consult with the National Arts Council on awards. But on the key issue of freedom for creative expression, another sympathetic federal judge found the new language little better than the Helms formula his colleague had enjoined eighteen months earlier. While the artist was no longer required (as the Helms amendment demanded) to promise not to create suspect works, Judge A. Wallace Tashima found the force of the "decency" language in the preamble equally inhibiting.

This court also established that one who seeks government subvention may raise free speech arguments comparable to those that can be raised by civil and criminal defendants. He drew a striking parallel between protection of academic and of artistic freedom, quoting at length from the AAUP-sponsored Wolf Trap conference statement noted earlier. By analogy to the limits academic freedom imposes on government, Judge Tashima said,

> professional evaluations of artistic merit are permissible, but decisions based on the wholly subjective criterion of "decency" are not. . . . The right of artists to challenge conventional wisdom and values is a cornerstone of artistic and academic freedom. . . .

Thus the court held the new language, like the Helms amendment which it replaced, violative of artists' First Amendment rights. The government promptly appealed.

The case was pending in the circuit court of appeals at the time of the 1992 election. Many observers assumed the Clinton Administration, early in its term, would dismiss the appeal and leave the district court decree in force. For whatever reason, that did not happen. Indeed, the Clinton Justice Department initially filed a brief that seemed indistinguishable from what Bush Administration lawyers had been saying. A later reply brief took a more moderate stance but restated support for the challenged language. After four years, the judgment was affirmed on the day of the 1996 presidential election.

Senator Helms, undaunted, returned for yet a third round of content restrictions. In the 1995 reauthorization for a drastically shrunken NEA, he persuaded his congressional colleagues to accept new curbs. In addition to renewing the curbs against "sexually explicit" material, he exacted new language to forbid grants that "denigrate the adherents to a particular religion." While the testing of this new restrictive language will obviously take some time—and the number of individual grants may have been so drastically reduced that such a test would not even be of high priority to the arts community—the tension between those who grant and those who receive is certain to continue. There will also continue to be ample material of constitutional import for the courts.

The academic artistic community, though not a plaintiff in either of the earlier cases, was centrally involved in other ways. Early in the original Helms amendment era, the University of Iowa attracted national attention by refusing to sign the certificate, thus rejecting a small NEA grant to enable the university press to publish a poetry collection. Other universities shared Iowa's abhorrence of the Helms language, though no others appear to have declined NEA grants for similar reasons. Many university grant and contract officers routinely signed the required pledge, though apparently with no harmful effects.

The other impact was more direct. While the challenge to the 1990s restrictions was pending, the "decency" language was applied in somewhat oblique fashion to bar federal funding of art exhibits at Virginia Commonwealth University in Richmond and at the Massachusetts Institute of Technology in Cambridge. By this time a new NEA acting chair, Ann-Imelda Radice, had taken over in the waning days of the Bush Administration. Sensing that she would be challenged in court if she invoked the "decency" clause, she canceled grants for the two displays— which had been faulted only as venturesome or avant-garde—giving as her sole reason the failure of both shows to meet the statutory standards of "artistic excellence." Suddenly her negative judgments were beyond reach of the courts. The language about "artistic excellence" had always given the NEA's chair virtually unreviewable authority to refuse or withhold funds, even when the real (but unstated) reasons were in fact a concern about "decency." It was just that Radice was the first NEA chair to use the general language to accomplish a specific end.

Meanwhile, Both the VCU and MIT exhibits took place, funded by nonfederal sources. There was a special irony to the claimed lack of "artistic excellence." Just as the show opened, a work featured at MIT appeared on the cover of a preeminent national art journal. By then, it was of course too late to reopen the NEA request. Nor was it likely such an encomium would have made any difference anyway.

The academic community was involved in yet another and vital role.

Judge Tashima's use of the Wolf Trap conference statement and the close analogy the judge drew between academic and artistic freedom were not simply random events. In fact, the link between the campus gallery or stage and the outside arts world is as strong as one would find in almost any academic field. Many eminent composers, conductors, and visual artists are also college teachers. Much of the most vital creativity in our society occurs in campus studios and theaters. Thus the deep concern of the academy with restrictions aimed at the arts, as well as anxiety about the targeting of the campus creative community by foes of unfamiliar or disquieting forms of art, is quite natural and altogether predictable. What is less clear, given the paucity of cases that address the constitutional claims of the artistic community, is how much protection can be expected from the courts. The next decade will undoubtedly provide clearer answers.

The successful court challenges take on the quality of Pyrrhic victory. Though the National Endowment for the Arts survives in the final years of the twentieth century, its role and prospects are severely diminished in at least two ways that markedly affect artistic freedom in the campus setting. For one, the total level of support for the NEA and the National Endowment for the Humanities was reduced in 1995 and 1996 by roughly 40 percent. Even more serious, the NEA was virtually removed by congressional action from continuing to make grants to individual artists of the kind that had caused the initial furor. Thus whatever restrictions might be imposed on grantees (and Senator Helms did add some new ones relating to religious beliefs and views) would henceforth make relatively little difference, since so few individual grantees would remain. Artistic freedom, though the courts have recently given it strong endorsement, may exist mainly in the abstract.

VIII.

ACADEMIC RESEARCH AND
ACADEMIC FREEDOM

To: The Research Policy Committee
From: The Vice Chancellor for Research

The agenda for next week's meeting of the Research Policy Committee contains three of the toughest problems I've seen in decades of university experience. We'll need all our time to get through them. I hope the background memo, on which I had some help from our legal counsel, will be helpful.

Here's the agenda:

1. *Review of proposed grant from Pioneer Fund.* A senior behavioral scientist on our faculty sought, and has been offered, a grant from the Pioneer Fund in New York. Because this foundation has a long record of supporting primarily research that critics see as leading to "racist" outcomes, a group within our faculty has demanded we refuse the grant. The president has asked us to review the issue and advise him on whether to accept or reject the grant.

2. *Response to subpoena for data from scientific research now in progress.* The university just received a subpoena, in connection with a lawsuit to which it is not a party, for massive amounts of scientific data developed by a member of our faculty, who is also not a party to the suit. Compliance not only would be burdensome and disruptive to her; it might also bring about premature disclosure of important hypotheses that have not yet been fully tested. She wants our support in refusing to comply with the subpoena.

3. *Proposed city ordinance banning fetal tissue research.* The city council will consider next month a proposed ordinance that would ban research anywhere within the city (presumably including university laboratories) that involves any use of fetal tissue. The president would like our views on how hard we should fight this measure, and on what grounds.

BACKGROUND MEMORANDUM
FOR THE COMMITTEE

A. *The Pioneer Fund Grant*

The question could be posed with deceptive simplicity: may a public university ever reject a research grant offered to one of its faculty because it finds the sponsor's goals, the subject matter, or the potential uses of the results inimical to its values and interests? The short answer is probably no. But like many short answers, this one demands some rather complex analysis and involves some exceptions and qualifications.

Let's start with a few basic principles. Of all settings in which the content of research should be judged solely by the academic merit of the proposal and the credentials of the investigator, none would seem clearer than the university laboratory. Any notion of institutional control over the subject matter or mission of what professors do in the laboratory seems at variance with basic principles of academic freedom.

Of course, research is regulated in many forms we all accept, mainly through federal mandates and conditions that accompany government research grants. External regulation of research takes several familiar, and generally unobjectionable, forms. Grantees must, for example, certify their full compliance with nondiscrimination laws and rules and may incur extensive preaward reviews of large grants and contracts to ensure such compliance. The use of human subjects is extensively regulated and must be closely monitored by the institution through a congressionally mandated procedure. The welfare of laboratory animals has more recently become a major target of government safeguards.

In addition, and for quite different reasons, universities impose limits of their own. Many institutions forbid, and others sharply limit, acceptance of classified governmental research grants or of corporate-sponsored projects the results of which may not be freely published or must be delayed for long periods to permit sponsor review of possibly patentable technology. In these and other familiar ways, widely embodied in institutional policy or government directives, the academic community accepts extensive regulation of research activity, not all of it voluntary and some of it rather intrusive.

Such constraints as these focus on the means and manner of research. What is not at issue is the subject matter or anticipated applications.

Unlike the corporate or government laboratory, where a detailed research agenda is set and announced in order to ensure that what comes out of the laboratory will meet the goals of those who pay the bills, university professors largely shape their own research programs to reflect interests, experiences, and their own priorities. Others in the academy may find their colleagues' research interests to be arcane, silly, even potentially harmful. Yet the choice of what to explore is that of the principal investigator, not that of peers, much less of administrators or governing boards.

Institutions do of course make judgments about the *quality* of an investigator's research program, at the time of granting promotion, tenure, salary increases, and the like. Such a judgment is, however, quite different from approving or disapproving particular projects when they are proposed. It is widely assumed that each faculty member may select areas or objects of research, no matter how obscure or unpopular, and is in no way beholden to prove that the results serve the interests of the university or of mankind.

This much is conventional wisdom. Such familiar assumptions might be tested through an intriguing hypothetical case. Suppose a senior scholar in mechanical engineering, whose expertise includes weapons, had been asked by the South African government in the late 1980s to study the efficacy of various weapons used in riot control, the clear object being to develop a more lethal means to sustain apartheid. Such a project would be abhorrent to most members of the academic community, indeed to virtually all thoughtful people. But our callous researcher finds the project challenging and relevant to his research interests. Besides, the South African government is prepared to pay well and on time.

The engineering professor must be able and willing, of course, to comply with all university research policies, make full disclosure of the source of his support, etc. Let us suppose, indeed, that his treatment of human subjects and laboratory animals has been exemplary. The weapons research project would, in short, be objectionable on only one basis—the end or goal to which the results would almost certainly be applied.

The collective conscience of the academic community would be sorely tested by such a case. Colleagues and administrators would presumably seek some way to delay if not derail the project, perhaps on a technical or procedural ground. But if the project met all the rules, as we have assumed, the issues of content, application, and sponsorship would need to be faced. If, as we suggested earlier, such matters are not appropriate for university regulation, we face a severe dilemma. Those who wished to derail the project would be left to pursue such means as informal appeals to their colleague or self-help measures such as protests and demonstrations.

The case is not wholly fanciful. There is a strikingly close analogue in the form of the Pioneer Fund. Chartered in 1935 to provide scholarships exclusively for white students, the Pioneer Fund has developed an active research program which supports both university-based and off-campus projects. Much of the Fund-supported research has explored the nature and extent of interracial differences that relate to intelligence. Some Pioneer-sponsored studies have suggested a possible correlation between skin color and intellect.

In 1989 Dr. Linda Gottfredson, a tenured professor of psychology and an established researcher at the University of Delaware, sought and was offered support from the Pioneer Fund to continue her studies on race and intelligence. A primary focus of her prior research had been "the societal consequences of differences of ability between groups and individuals," with special attention to such practices as race-norming in the use of standardized test scores.

When her Delaware colleagues learned of the Pioneer Fund grant, several of them questioned the propriety of university acceptance of such support. The institution's president, Dr. E. A. Trabant, asked the Faculty Senate's Committee on Research to study the issue and to advise whether in its view the acceptance of such support would compromise the university's commitment to maintain a "multi-cultural and multi-racial environment." The committee sought, with limited success, to identify the precise goals of the challenged research and of the sponsoring organization. A representative of the Pioneer Fund, who came to campus and met with the committee, left most members of that body dissatisfied. Despite a recent revision of the language of the Fund's charter, the Research Committee remained skeptical whether any genuine or substantial change had occurred in focus or mission.

In the absence of clear proof of such a substantive change, the committee concluded that accepting Pioneer Fund support would compromise the University's commitment to equal opportunity, "as long as the Fund remains committed to the intent of its original charter and to a pattern of activities incompatible with the University's mission." Primarily on that basis, though with a peripheral concern about certain Fund procedures, the committee urged President Trabant to reject the grant, and the president accepted that advice.

The Research Committee could not have avoided issues of academic freedom and free inquiry, if only because the president had raised them in seeking their guidance. But in its report, the committee rejected Dr. Gottfredson's plea for recognition of an investigator's unfettered freedom to choose research areas and sponsors. The committee drew a distinction between two interests—"a faculty member's right to pursue research and a faculty member's privilege to seek funding for that research through the University." The latter interest (seeking funding through the institution) the committee felt was subject to conditions that could not properly be imposed on the investigator's choice of research areas or topics. In support of that distinction, the committee cited the myriad conditions that universities impose, and scientists accept, as part of the academic research enterprise.

In approving the report, President Trabant embraced the committee's qualified view of freedom in research. He added his own belief that "the University has a right to set its own priorities for support of scholarly activity." The Board of Trustees formally adopted the president's position as university policy. The Gottfredson grant had thus effectively been rejected, despite the presence of a willing grantor and a willing grantee. The particular grant languished. Subsequent applications from the University of Delaware for Pioneer Fund support were also blocked, since the ban reached any future faculty subvention by Pioneer, or presumably by any other grantor with similarly suspect views on racial questions.

Professor Gottfredson then took the issue before the Faculty Welfare Committee. There she challenged the Research Committee's distinction between rights and privileges in research, insisting that little would remain of the "right" if the "privilege" could be qualified or nullified on clearly ideological grounds. The core of her case was familiar on traditional grounds: if academic freedom would have been abridged by withholding a faculty benefit on the basis of a professor's scholarly views or interests—a premise unlikely to be seriously questioned—"restricting my funding on the basis of others' beliefs surely must do so"—the more clearly, she added, because the adverse action in her case had a kind of "guilt by association" quality. Moreover, despite the Research Committee's insistence that it meant to imply no pejorative view of Gottfredson's scholarship, one could not easily forget the disparaging references that had been made to her earlier publications.

Because the University of Delaware faculty was unionized, the issue was referred to an outside arbitrator. The faculty as a whole was now sharply divided. The president of the campus chapter of the American Association of University Professors (the bargaining agent) had as a scientist served on the Research Committee. In that role she joined other committee members in advising the president to reject the Pioneer Fund grant. She was thus in direct conflict with fellow AAUP officers who championed Gottfredson's efforts to reverse the committee's judgment. Such tensions among colleagues of normally harmonious views attested to the depth and intensity of conflict over a painfully divisive issue.

The ultimate goal of arbitration is to find a middle ground, and that is what happened here. The arbitrator ruled in favor of the researcher, but on narrow grounds that left open the ultimate question whether universities may ban research or reject external funding because the subject or application is at odds with institutional values. The Research Committee and the president had, the arbitrator believed, protested too much. While insisting they lacked either the power or the inclination to probe the quality or content of a professor's scholarship, that was precisely what they had done. Such an inquiry had taken place at two levels—one by examining Professor Gottfredson's own previously published scholarship and one by reviewing other research she had conducted with a former colleague.

The flaw in the committee's reasoning seemed axiomatic to the arbitrator: "The committee could not have found [the investigator's] work incompatible with the university's mission unless it had examined the content of the work." Because of this failure of process, a research grant (regardless of its source) could not be rejected for the reasons or in the way it had been rejected at Delaware. This narrow judgment left open many broader issues, especially on what substantive grounds, if any, a university might block such a grant if it had used impeccable procedures to reach this action.

The second part of the arbitrator's ruling came a step closer to that ultimate question. He implied that if he had had to reach the policy issue, he would have been sympathetic to Gottfredson's claims. The university, he noted, insisted it had the right to reject research grants from a sponsor that was publicly perceived as "racist," if that seemed necessary to protect its own credibility on racial issues. That was not so clear, cautioned the arbitrator: "Academic freedom is a contractually conferred right, and public perceptions alone, no matter how volatile, cannot suffice to overcome that right." Moreover, he added with just a touch of irony, "the university's commitment to racial and cultural diversity is an essential part of, and not a rival in conflict with, the university's commitment to academic freedom."

The point is basic, and it extends well beyond research. An embattled college or university may be tempted to invoke public image or perception as the reason for taking certain action. Courts sometimes even give tacit approval to image sensitivity or avoidance of adverse public perception. There may be certain actions that might be justified by such considerations. But when it comes to something as basic and as substantive as denying a research grant from a willing sponsor to an otherwise eligible investigator, this rationale seems highly suspect. Image sensitivity has rightly been rejected in other contexts, and the rejection by the Delaware arbitrator in the research context seems entirely consistent.

Apart from the Delaware case, there has been one other publicized skirmish with the Pioneer Fund. Smith College faced a similar dilemma. Professor Seymour W. Itzkoff, a senior faculty member in Education and Child Study, had sought and obtained an offer of Pioneer Fund support. When several colleagues protested the grant because of Pioneer's mission and reputation, the investigator offered to relinquish it. Smith's president, Mary Maples Dunn, was uneasy about such a resolution. She urged Itzkoff to change his mind and seek approval of the grant. But as he changed his stance, so did the college.

When processing of the grant was delayed, the investigator complained to the president. Dunn referred the matter to the academic dean, who responded that despite the dissonance between the college's values and Pioneer's perceived mission, Smith's commitment to academic freedom precluded rejection of the grant. The president so informed Itzkoff, cautioning that the Fund's goals "are intensely distasteful to the dean and me."

There the matter might well have ended had Itzkoff not wished to bring the issue to the attention of Smith's Board of Trustees. He wrote the trustees at length, charging that the administration had been hypocritical in judging the goals of the Pioneer Fund and his own quest for research support. Unlike his Delaware counterpart, who relied mainly on internal procedures, Itzkoff now launched a vigorous external defense of the Fund and its research agenda, adding that Smith's handling of the whole affair had "negatively affected my work both within Smith College as well as professionally in the world at large."

President Dunn (who at first had pressed Itzkoff not to renounce the grant) now felt she must clarify her role for the trustees. She reviewed Pioneer's stated goals, stressing the Fund's seeming commitment to support only studies of benefit to whites. Given the deep conflict between these goals and the college's commitment to equal opportunity, the president reaffirmed her conviction that Smith should not accept institutional support from such a source. She also recognized, however, that grants to individual investigators posed a different and far harder question. While the college did incur certain responsibilities by accepting grants for individual researchers, she would not on that basis alone limit the scope of scholarly inquiry:

> At the heart of any great academic institution is the freedom to pursue one's scholarly interests and I believe that the college should not restrict that freedom by placing any limitations on funding sources other than [procedural requirements for research].

Itzkoff had thus prevailed—or so for a time it seemed. But the Pioneer Fund learned about the controversy at Smith and, after paying the first installment on the grant, the Fund's president told Itzkoff that the board had decided to suspend further support for Smith faculty. The announcement suggested no conditions under which support might resume, and there is no evidence of subsequent Smith grants. Itzkoff's departure from the Smith campus apparently closed the chapter.

While the Delaware and Smith cases are unique, they illustrate an inherent tension between freedom in research and other central academic values. This conflict tests the limits of institutional responsibility for and authority over faculty scholarship. If there is any place to question the belief that academic researchers enjoy unfettered choice of subject matter, this is it. The boundaries of the debate are fairly easily marked.

On one hand, researchers must and do accept all sorts of restrictions and conditions. The effect of some such constraints on the scope of inquiry is not trivial. If laboratory use of certain hazardous materials is forbidden, for example, a chemist may be unable to conduct particular experiments. Extensive regulation of the use and care of laboratory animals may alter the direction and content of certain research. A ban on classified projects will affect relatively few investigators, but for those to whom support is not likely to come in other forms, such a ban may reduce the range of subvention.

If a university limits the permissible period of corporate prepublication review, the policy may effectively prevent a scholar from seeking support from certain industrial sponsors. Rules on conflict of interest may also preclude pursuing projects that investigators might wish to undertake. And so it goes, through an imposing list of research rules and regulations.

When it comes to the content or subject matter of inquiry, however, most universities shape faculty research only in peripheral ways. If a classicist wished to seek federal support for a complex chemistry project, the institution would raise basic questions, probably at a fairly low level. Such questions would imply no institutional disapproval of the content of the proposal or the use to which results might be put but would simply raise appropriate doubts about the investigator's competence in the field of proposed inquiry. Even then a university would be loath to object unless the mismatch were so obvious as to compromise both the institution and the individual. Extensive discussion and persuasion would likely precede any formal intervention.

The Pioneer Fund issue arises uniquely between these relatively easy extremes. The problem was not one of adherence to uniform rules and procedures; neither at Delaware nor at Smith was any question raised about the researcher's (or the sponsor's) willingness and ability to satisfy every requisite condition. Apparently, whatever one may have felt about Pioneer's historic mission and its research agenda, it was ready and able to make the requisite commitment to nondiscrimination. Nor was the problem remotely one of investigator competence; indeed, what made these cases painful for both institutions was the established status in the relevant subject matter of tenured professors who had sought Pioneer grant support.

The issue that both Delaware and Smith had to face was the one on which the two presidents differed—whether research support can ever be rejected because the goals of the sponsor or project or the potential applications of the results are profoundly at variance with the values of the institution itself. This issue remains unresolved and is ripe for general review.

A few general principles are helpful. Smith was right and Delaware wrong on the Pioneer Fund issue for at least two reasons. Neither institution had on its books any policy that would have justified rejecting research support for the reasons the Delaware Research Committee invoked. A few institutions do have such policies, though they have apparently never been applied. The University of Michigan's Board of Regents once declared that no research should be allowed on campus that would "be detrimental to the welfare of mankind." Neither Smith nor Delaware had made even so general a declaration. Thus, as the Delaware arbitrator found, nothing in institutional policy would support a subject-matter or sponsor-based ban on research support.

Suppose, however, that Delaware or Smith had a clear policy that covered the Pioneer Fund in all but name—for example, "No member of this faculty may receive external support for research the stated or manifest goal of which is to undermine or subvert the university's commitment to equal opportunity or affirmative action." The very task of framing a policy shows why the Delaware position is virtually untenable. Consider the potential reach of such a prohibition: a professor seeks a grant to probe the efficacy of the university's own affirmative action program. Another scholar requests support to determine whether the optimal student populations have been targeted for minority recruitment. Or an educational psychologist proposes to do, with support from, let us say, the Ford Foundation, just what Professors Gottfredson and Itzkoff proposed to the Pioneer Fund. These and other quite plausible variants suggest the folly of such an approach.

There are several other reasons why institutions ought not to limit scholarship on such substantive grounds. Even attempting to do so or claiming institutional authority to do so reflects a basic and obvious flaw—an assumption that universities may preclude their professors from doing or saying things that might embarrass the institution. If academic freedom means anything, it means that professors may speak out in institutionally embarrassing ways or in ways that may be at variance with institutional values and mission. This precept applies just as fully to speaking through a choice of research subjects as to using words in a letter to the editor or in a speech.

So selective an approach to the substance of research poses other serious concerns. What troubled critics at Delaware and Smith was the mission and the agenda of the sponsor (i.e., the Pioneer Fund has nurtured "racist" research elsewhere). Such a judgment comes painfully close to implying guilt by association. Moreover, it would be virtually impossible to impose such a ban without appraising the investigator's own prior research—something universities all do in judging *quality*, but not for assessing "worthiness" or "goodness" or value to humankind.

Finally, a policy of this sort would imply an institutional capacity to predict and thus to proscribe the uses to which research results might be put—i.e., this project can be forbidden because somebody might use the results to undermine affirmative action and equal opportunity. Such a process assumes that in any academic field—be it chemistry, geography, philosophy, or in this case educational psychology—certain applications are acceptable while others are not, presumably because there are truths so firmly settled that they may not be challenged, even by experts in the discipline. Or, alternatively, this approach assumes there are some scholars whose values and views are so dangerous or so at variance with the prevailing ethos of the academic community that they may not be allowed to use external support in pursuit of certain subjects for fear of what they may find or what use they would make of those findings. Again, to state the premises is to refute them, and in so doing to expose the illogic of so restrictive a view.

Before leaving the Pioneer Fund, consider one seemingly analogous case that will truly test the limits of tolerance. Suppose a deeply disgruntled alumnus wishes to finance research that would cause the demise of an institution he feels has wronged him. He finds a faculty member, recently denied tenure, who is equally disaffected. Together they concoct a plan to study the campus utility and communications systems, with an eye to planting explosives at key points that will cripple operations and effectively bring the institution to its knees. The professor prepares a research proposal and submits it to the grants office—where an eyebrow will quite likely be raised. But, consistent with the principles just outlined, can funding for such a purpose be refused?

The case differs from the Pioneer Fund cases in important ways. For one, the proposed activity is almost certainly criminal—a basis on which funding might be refused even without having on the books a formal policy against using external grants to facilitate breaking the law. There is also grave doubt whether what is proposed is research at all; this issue, too, could be raised without abridging academic freedom, but could not even have been contemplated in either of the Pioneer Fund cases. Beyond these two distinctions, there is serious doubt whether a college or university must serve as the medium of its own destruction. Such a criterion for barring true research would of course be risky; some critics at Delaware did in fact argue that taking Pioneer money would destroy the university's ability to recruit minority faculty and students and would thus forfeit major public financial support. Yet there does seem a clear difference between accepting funds that could hurt in such ways as these and carrying out an act of institutional suicide. Perhaps, in the end, some small measure of human judgment must be the critical guide.

B. Subpoena Demands for Research Data in Progress

Here too the question can be simply stated: may a court compel a university or one of its researchers, in a case to which neither is a party, to yield large amounts of research data in process, even though compliance would be disruptive and might (among other risks) reveal the identity of subjects who expected confidentiality? The short answer is probably, though the answer depends on numerous factors that need to be explored more fully.

Two recent cases offer a good starting point. A public heath professor at a midwestern state university received a demand that caused her great concern. Her recent research was on smoking cessation, its means and results. She and her university had been served with a subpoena seeking substantial amounts of her basic data. The information was apparently sought in connection with a lawsuit in which neither she nor the university was involved. The request came from a thinly disguised arm of the tobacco industry, which seemed to feel the professor's data might be useful.

The investigator was troubled by the subpoena for two reasons. Having to yield such data at this stage would disrupt her research program and might cause premature disclosure of findings and tentative hypotheses that were still very much in process. Moreover, she had promised confidentiality to many of her subjects, whose identity might now be disclosed—with immediate risk to them and even graver risk to her credibility as a researcher. So the investigator was most anxious to resist the subpoena, and in this goal she had the support of the university's lawyers.

A few months later a doctoral student at Washington State University was called before a grand jury investigating break-ins by animal rights activists (a major focus of his research) and was asked what he knew about the role of a named person in a particular incident at laboratories at his own university. The scholar refused to answer and was called before a federal judge, where he renewed his recalcitrance. His reason was clear and direct: "Activists within the environmental movement may refuse to speak to me if I testify. Other social scientists might find themselves less able to gain the trust of sources." He also expressed his fear that if such information could be freely compelled, social scientists "would be less willing to go out and do research which in some instances does require that we grant promises of confidentiality."

Despite the force of this plea and active support from civil liberties and scholarly groups, the judge was unmoved. He ordered the researcher to answer the grand jury's questions. This the student refused to do, and, as the judge had warned might happen, he was led to jail in handcuffs. He thus became apparently the first scholar incarcerated in modern times for refusing to reveal information he believed ought to be the object of legal protection against compelled disclosure.

The problem researchers face stems from the severely limited support the courts have given to comparable claims from scholars and other information gatherers. Judges have tended to be fairly generous to litigants who seek discovery, even from nonparty researchers and even where the materials being sought are highly sensitive. Researchers have never been able to establish a broad constitutional privilege to withhold such data. They lack the sort of legal shield that lawyers and accountants and members of the clergy enjoy in most states (and journalists in many states) to protect their confidential communications from forced disclosure. For the relatively few scholars who have tested the issue, the path has been rocky and uncertain at best.

The first such case came to the federal courts in the mid-1970s. A Harvard public health professor, Marc Roberts, had conducted interviews with many employees of Pacific Gas & Electric Company during a study of the way utilities reached environmental decisions. When a construction company sued PG&E for breach of a contract, its lawyer sought some of Roberts's data; he hoped it would document the process of making the corporate judgment that triggered the alleged breach. PG&E also sought access to Roberts's notes. The investigator resisted, counseled by the same lawyer who several years earlier had partially protected confidential sources of a Harvard political scientist doing research on Vietnam.

This court ruled in Roberts's favor, though on nonconstitutional grounds. The judge noted that the information could have been obtained from other sources in ways that would have been far less intrusive of the research process. There was also serious doubt whether Roberts possessed the kind of information the two parties sought. His status as a bystander, with no relationship to the parties, also helped. The judge took special note of "the importance of maintaining channels of communication between academic researchers and their sources."

Since that time there have been at most a dozen reported cases dealing with a scholar's claim of privilege. Seldom has the researcher been completely vindicated; in several cases, as with the Washington State University graduate student, such efforts have been unavailing. The nature of the research in issue and the nature of the threat, as well as the sympathies of the individual judge, have played a part.

Thus in cases involving a University of Wisconsin study of Agent Orange effects and studies of toxic shock syndrome at the Centers for Disease Control, researchers won at least partial victories—never on the basis of a complete privilege, but rather because of judicial concern about the potentially disruptive effects of forcing scholars to stop research and compile massive amounts of raw data.

Growing concern about confidential researcher-subject relations also played a role. In the CDC case, the court expressly noted the harmful effect that compelled disclosure of subject identity might have on "scientific and social research supported by a population willing to submit to in-depth questioning."

As the Minnesota medical researcher case suggests, the field of smoking and health has been a particularly lively area of dispute over access to research data. In a recent round of such litigation, a New York state court rejected cigarette manufacturers' demands for massive data, in part because of the scholar's "interest in academic freedom." The court accepted claims advanced by the American Cancer Society in support of researchers' freedoms:

> While these medical investigations are still in progress, they should not be subjected to examination and criticism by people whose interests are arguably antithetical to the medical scientists. It would have the effect of denying to these doctors the opportunity of first publication of their studies. It could also have a chilling effect and discourage future scientific endeavors.

One other recent case sheds some useful light. A graduate student at the State University of New York at Stony Brook kept a detailed journal in preparing his doctoral dissertation. His notes recounted experiences working at a Long Island restaurant which was later destroyed by a suspicious fire. A federal grand jury investigating the blaze subpoenaed the student, demanding that he bring his journal. He agreed to testify at length about his recollections of the restaurant and its employees but refused to produce the journal. The grand jury pressed for the journal, continuing to feel it would be vital to a complete inquiry.

The trial court ruled in the student's favor, partly because he had been so cooperative. The judge also recognized how harmful compelled disclosure of such materials might be to the scholarly process:

> Affording social scientists protected freedom is essential if we are to understand how our own and other societies operate. Recognized by cultural anthropologists since at least the turn of the century as a basic tool, fieldwork is used widely in other disciplines, particularly in sociology and political science. In order to work effectively researchers must record observations, communications and personal reactions contemporaneously and accurately.

The appeals court took a different and less sympathetic view, and in the end forced the student to turn over his notes to the grand jury. While the reviewing court recognized some potential basis for a scholar's privilege, this case did not offer the proper vehicle for its recognition. The court left open the possibility that a better claim in another case might warrant protection—for example, "where a serious academic inquiry is undertaken pursuant to a considered research plan in which the need for confidentiality is tangibly related to the accuracy or completeness of the study." Possibility of such protection was thus established in principle, the scope of any resulting protection left to be defined another day with a more deserving scholar.

Despite such reassuring words, the state of the law remains hazardous for the researcher. Few courts have recognized anything that could be termed a "scholar's privilege." Mention of academic freedom concerns has been sporadic. Yet scholars have nonetheless fared better in court than one might have expected in the absence of any privilege based either on statute or the Constitution. The scholar's experience substantially parallels that of reporters seeking to shield confidential sources or data. For years journalists had pressed in the courts without success for recognition of a constitutional privilege. The Supreme Court denied such a claim in 1973; such protection, said the justices, was a matter for legislators and not for courts. Yet in the years that followed, reporters have been surprisingly successful on nonconstitutional grounds, almost certainly having won more confidential source cases than they have lost.

So too scholars denied a constitutional basis for protecting or withholding sensitive research data have often managed on narrower grounds to avoid forced disclosure. The problem, then, is one of uncertainty; the scholar who guesses wrong may end up in jail. Even so, a few helpful and general principles emerge from the limited experience in the courts. Perhaps most appealing is the case in which the investigator's relations with research subjects invokes a well-established legal privilege comparable to that of the attorney's client, the physician's patient, and the priest's confessor. Such situations are rare. And even where some subjects in a given study may be protected in this way, the privilege will not likely apply universally; most persons interviewed or examined by a researcher who holds an M.D. or a J.D. degree would not be deemed "patients" or "clients."

Only slightly less promising are scholars' claims that research subjects may not have been promised but nonetheless reasonably expect confidentiality. There is special concern for subjects who were told before being interviewed that their identities or facts about them would not be revealed. Even when explicit assurances were not given, there may be grave risk of embarrassment or humiliation to the subjects or their families (e.g., the CDC toxic shock studies) or reprisal by an employer or by fellow workers (e.g., the PG&E environmental studies) if information of this sort suddenly became public.

An express promise of nondisclosure may not be essential. Several judges have found a basis to imply an expectation of confidentiality, not only in the subject's interests but also for the scholar's benefit—sensing the threat to the professional credibility of one whose sensitive research data turn up on the front page. Thus, even in a case where secrecy has not actually been promised or even discussed, a sympathetic judge may find an appealing basis for protection.

A third set of interests occasionally buttresses the scholar's claim. In one of the Centers for Disease Control cases, the court recognized a *public* interest in ensuring the smooth and uninterrupted conduct of the agency's health research mission, safe from the threat that compelled disclosure posed. If this interest depends on maintaining confidence and willingness to participate among the potential subject pool, then the value of confidentiality to vital national research needs becomes readily apparent.

Finally, there are a host of persuasive practical concerns. Several courts have been swayed by pleas not to disrupt or distort the research process at a critical stage. These courts have heeded claims of harm that could be caused by forcing the physical relocation of massive amounts of data, permitting insensitive hands to enter the laboratory or the data bank at a critical time, or risking the premature revelation of hypotheses and conclusions that are not yet ready for public discussion. Indeed, just such risks to research may be gravest of all, since the direct threat to the integrity of the scientific process is especially acute when such disruption impedes.

C. Local Regulation of Scientific Research

The last question on the Research Policy Committee agenda is quite different, but no easier: may local government ban the use in university research laboratories of certain materials, animals, or procedures, even if the effect of such a ban is to inhibit or foreclose a major area of scholarly inquiry? There is once again a short answer: such a ban shouldn't be legal. But the basis for this conclusion turns out to be surprisingly elusive.

Our inquiry begins in Cambridge, Massachusetts, the site of recurrent tensions between town and gown. For generations, Cantabrigians have been ambivalent about the two eminent universities that make their city unique in intellect. Away from the Boston area, they speak of Harvard and MIT with reverence. Yet at home, civic pressure occasionally overcomes civic pride to produce classic confrontations.

The tension and its portent for academic science seem to have intensified in recent years. Two actions, both seemingly unique to Cambridge, deserve closer attention. In the late 1980s, the Cambridge City Council adopted what seem to be the nation's first municipal limits on the experimental use of animals. The ordinance banned two widely used (though controversial) toxicological tests, LD and Draize. While the ban expressly exempted noncommercial research, the dispensation was a matter of grace rather than of legal right. The potential threat to the academic laboratory was inescapable. Two years later the City Council went a step further, this time not exempting the universities. In the summer of 1989, the council voted unanimously to create the position of commissioner to supervise all animal experiments done in the city.

The prelude to this action creates a useful context. When animal rights activists first brought their concerns to the council, a committee was appointed to assess the welfare of laboratory animals in local research facilities. The group included a veterinarian, a Harvard scientist, and an antivivisectionist lawyer. After extensive field study, the group reported that the laboratory animals they observed were well supervised and were housed in generally clean and comfortable conditions. But the absence of apparent problems did not deter the council from taking a further step. In midsummer, it adopted an ordinance which not only created the position of commissioner but also expanded upon federal regulations covering the care and use of primates in laboratories—compliance with which was to be monitored, not surprisingly, by none other than the new commissioner.

Across the Charles River in Boston, the Massachusetts legislature seemed bent on outdoing its cities. Under pressure from animal rights groups, Massachusetts joined seven other states in banning the use of pound animals for experimental purposes. Such a ban, by itself, would gravely inhibit laboratory research. But the Bay State's law was unique in its reach. It actually forbade the importation of pound animals for such purposes from any other state or from abroad. Thus it imposed a total ban on a major medium of research, not simply safeguards for the welfare of the state's own animals.

Universities and their faculties beset by such hostile and potentially crippling laws would hope to find redress in the courts. There ought to be some readily available legal checks on such local constraints, it would seem, at least if the status of research enjoys the degree of protection that seems warranted. Suppose the Cambridge ordinances had been challenged in court. Are there principles by which to vindicate and protect the researcher's interest?

Such principles are surprisingly few. As we have seen in the other two situations, there is modest legal recognition of research as an integral part of the academic enterprise. The basic charter of the American Association of University Professors, its 1940 statement on Academic Freedom and Tenure, confidently declares that "freedom in research is fundamental to the advancement of truth" and adds that "teachers are entitled to full freedom in research and in the publication of the results." Yale law professor Thomas I. Emerson, a lifelong guardian of both free speech and academic freedom, insisted there should remain "no doubt that the First Amendment provides extensive protection of freedom of scientific research." Yet virtually all the case law dealing with academic freedom has focused on other facets of scholarly activity, leaving protection for research largely to conjecture.

We might consider a classic situation in which some redress ought to be found, if ever it is available. It is the use for research of fetal tissue, the subject of the proposed local ordinance with which we began. Suppose that certain kinds of research—notably on Parkinson's disease—cannot be carried out effectively or would be meaningless without using fetal tissue. And suppose the reason for the funding ban is political opposition to abortion. (One could almost void the fetal tissue ban because it reflects a particular religious viewpoint and, rather like laws requiring the teaching of creationism in public schools, crosses the line between church and state and thus violates the establishment clause of the First Amendment.)

The federal fetal tissue funding ban (eventually rescinded by the Clinton Administration) was challenged several times in federal court, albeit on rather technical points of administrative procedure. Two courts rejected the challenges and one sustained, but none even came close to addressing the constitutional status of scientific research. Lawyers for the United Parkinson Foundation are not averse to seeking First Amendment protection for medical research; it was simply their practical judgment that such claims would have had so slight a chance of success that they would hardly have been worth the effort.

But is there no serious possibility of mounting a broader argument? If government action, marginally justified by traditional police power interests, effectively eliminates (or prices out of range) a whole field of scholarship or inquiry, might not a novel First Amendment claim be made? What if, for example, local government action made it impossible for researchers to obtain or to use a breed or species of animals without which a particular experiment could not be conducted? And what if scientists were legally barred from pursuing certain tests on these animals, which might hold the key to a promising line of medical study?

We might now invoke one improbable but nonetheless welcome ally. In the fall of 1991, California governor Pete Wilson vetoed a bill that would have banned the use of laboratory animals in conducting tests for certain cosmetic and household cleaning products. The governor, in explaining his veto, noted that despite his fondness for animals and his empathy with animal lovers, he was persuaded that "sufficient alternative testing methods are not available." While there may have been mixed motives for such a stand, the outcome and the rationale are potentially helpful.

One related set of issues may also be relevant. Most of the recent concerns stem from intense pressure by animal rights groups on the political process—perhaps most voluble in Massachusetts but felt in many other parts of the country. In addition to vigorous lobbying at several levels, there is also the physical intervention (e.g., raids on laboratories and holding areas) by animal rights activists that has occasionally brought the issue into the criminal courts. The whole subject of animal rights and animal welfare has played strange tricks on our legal system.

The harm from such actions is by no means speculative. Perhaps the most celebrated case was the decision several years ago of a Cornell

Medical School pharmacologist to forgo a major federal grant and redirect her research when animal rights groups protested her use of cats in the study of barbiturate addiction. The case is novel in two ways— first, because it is the first time the agency had known an investigator to give up a grant that had survived the rigorous process of peer review; and second, because some critics charged that the university had pressured the investigator to alter her animal-use practices—a charge the Medical School vigorously denied.

Examples abound of other pressures brought upon the academic research community by animal rights activists. Sometimes the results are direct, as evidenced by the number of uneasy scientists who may forgo any use of research animals simply to avoid controversy. The pressures may be felt less immediately through the courts, whether in decisions to ban certain procedures or to impose greater accountability on animal welfare committees. Whatever the means, there seems little doubt the animal rights movement has partly succeeded in its declared goal of stifling research to which it objects, regardless of the potential value of the research to human welfare.

Such forces obviously, directly, and seriously impair freedom of research on important topics. What, if anything, can either courts or universities do to check these forces and protect embattled scientists? Full and eventual protection must come through the political process. But courts might afford limited help. If, for example, there is evidence that an animal rights raid or vigilante activity was in any way condoned or encouraged by governmental authority—as one might possibly infer from enactment of laws like those in Massachusetts—a harassed investigator might possibly find redress in the courts.

More promising are the various avenues for strengthening institutional policy. Options would include instituting strong internal safeguards designed to shield campus research against external pressures, making a strong public commitment to deal firmly with any members of the academic community who disrupt research in any way (as by abetting the animal welfare groups), and promising special protection for animal research facilities whenever attacks are threatened.

There is one risk that ought to be noted, then avoided. It is the risk of excessive zeal in self-regulation that is designed to forestall or mitigate external forces. More than once, perhaps most dramatically in the handling of scientific fraud and misconduct, the academy has simply outdone the most zealous of regulators, all in the name of self-regulation. Policies we impose on ourselves are, among other factors, much harder to challenge in court than are the policies government visits upon us. So in the field of animal welfare as in others, universities should avoid doing worse things to themselves than their adversaries and nemeses would do to them.

Finally and most clearly, colleges and universities as institutions devoted to academic freedom must avoid any actions or even statements that might disparage the research goals and activities of its faculty, so long as these methods satisfy the procedural requirements imposed both by the grantors and the institution. Many within the academic community may see certain types of animal-based research as cruel or pointless or both. Yet as long as the general requirements have been met and information about the project is readily available, such matters as how the research is conducted and what effects it may have on animal subjects ought to be the object of neither governmental constraint nor collegial disdain.

IX

RELIGIOUS SPEECH ON THE PUBLIC CAMPUS

To: The Board of Trustees
From: President Carl Caper

Religion is always potentially controversial. Even in a secular university, it can cause conflicts. We've had more than our share of such tensions the past few months over religious issues. In this respect I doubt we are unique. Perhaps it's simply the nature of religion, and perhaps it is also a reflection of the times. In any case, we seem to have become a kind of battleground for controversies with religious roots. Let me review the critical issues, some of which we need to discuss and resolve at our next board meeting.

First, we've got a popular professor who brings more religion into the classroom than he should. I'm sure you've heard of Professor Paul Parable in physical education. He's won several teaching awards during the twenty years he's been on our faculty. His special field of study is human physiology. He has taught and published in that field since he came here. The problem is that recently he has begun sharing his deeply held religious views with his students. Part of the problem is the link between religious belief and his academic field; he occasionally suggests that the remarkable feats of the human body must reflect divine guidance.

There's more—quite a bit more, in fact. A group of students has threatened a lawsuit over our acclaimed religious studies program, since it has several ordained clergy on its faculty and offers special courses about various denominations and their beliefs. Some of the courses also use scriptures—the Bible, the Qur'an, and others—as assigned reading. We've always believed an elective religious studies program was appropriate for a secular university. But now this assumption has been challenged, and we need to revisit our premises.

As if this were not enough, we have two types of problems with student religious organizations (of which there are quite a few on campus, as befits so diverse a student body). Our policy is that student religious groups, even if they are recognized for other purposes, may not use campus facilities for their worship and devotional meetings. We adopted this policy some years ago in order to avoid proselytizing on university property. Now a Christian student group has challenged the rule, claiming it has been denied religious freedom, even though there are lots of other places near campus where these students could meet, such as local churches and the like.

Last week the Student Council refused funding from the student fee pool to Young Lions, a new religious group that's been making quite a name for itself by bringing noted evangelists to campus to speak. The group also publishes a magazine (*The Lion's Mane*) that covers current religious topics in a fairly direct way. It strikes many students and faculty as avowedly sectarian and rather unfriendly to other faiths.

We're fairly certain this issue will go to court if the student council doesn't reverse itself and reinstate funding for Young Lions. Student Council seems unlikely to budge; its members feel if they give in on this one, there are all sorts of other groups (religious and otherwise) they'd have to start funding. They're willing to risk the charge of being antireligious, though they insist that's an unfair view. I agree, but that won't necessarily keep us out of court on any of these tough issues.

What I would like to share with you is an analysis of these issues recently done by a member of our law faculty who specializes in the law of church and state and has followed such questions over the years. It may not provide all the answers but should at least get us started.

• • •

To: President Caper
From: Samuel Solon

You have identified some of the most analytically difficult and currently liveliest of issues in the field of church and state. Some historical background may orient our discussion. Today we view all state-supported colleges and universities as secular institutions, free of religious influence or involvement. It was not always so. When Thomas Jefferson founded the University of Virginia, it was the first truly secular institution of higher learning. His plan for a publicly supported college without a school of divinity or theology did not sit well in a state where organized religious bodies played a major role in civic life. Many powerful Virginians were so troubled by the absence of religion in the curriculum that Mr. Jefferson made several concessions, encouraging the first students to attend their own places of worship. His charter for the university stopped just short of giving religion a formal role in the academic program. Virginia marked a major break. Before and after that time, state universities elsewhere continued not only to teach about religion and require chapel attendance but also trained graduates for the ministry—a task which had been central to the founding of some of these institutions. The line between "secular" and "sectarian," like that between "public" and "private," remained elusive in higher education in this country for some time.

Not only was the practical role of religion quite different in earlier times. Equally important, the state of the law was also different. It was not until fairly recently that courts began to consider the place of religion on the public campus, returning to the issues that had troubled Jefferson but had been remarkably dormant for nearly a century and a half. Even today there have been remarkably few court cases defining the proper role of religion on the state university campus.

The twentieth century has brought many changes that shape these issues. The distinction between public and private higher education became much sharper. The task of preparing people for the ministry became exclusively the task of professional schools of theology and divinity, many of which retained close ties with private universities but would seem quite out of place on a state university campus. The closest we come today to the old model is the many consortia or course-sharing agreements between public and private institutions; such arrangements, in fact, enable public college students to pursue religious studies of a kind their own institution does not (and often cannot) provide.

Recently the law on church and state, especially in education, has evolved dramatically. Starting in the 1940s, the Supreme Court gave meaning to a dormant clause in the Bill of Rights which forbids government to "make any law respecting an establishment of religion." This clause, a vital corollary to the First Amendment's protection for the "free exercise" of religion, is unique to our Bill of Rights. The dual guarantees of religious liberty in our Constitution, traceable directly to the views of

Jefferson and James Madison, ensure a respectful distance between church and state, as much in education as in other facets of civic life.

The earliest religious freedom cases involved elementary and secondary education. The Supreme Court soon dealt with prayer and Bible reading in public schools and reviewed various forms of government aid to church-related schools. While most such forms of accommodation were enjoined under the establishment clause, the justices recognized the validity of certain practices, such as lending secular materials to parochial school students and granting parental tax benefits for the costs of attending such schools. Even in areas where the court spoke early and firmly—prayer in public schools, for example—some uncertainty persists; hardly a Supreme Court term passes without some new test of prayer or devotion in the school setting. These issues are not easily resolved and likely never will be put completely to rest.

The role of religion in higher education has been less often in the courts. When the issue did reach the Supreme Court, the justices stressed important differences between levels of education which may markedly alter the outcome. A pair of cases well illustrate the contrast. One concerned the constitutionality, under the establishment clause, of federal grants to church-related colleges and universities for construction and maintenance of physical facilities. The Supreme Court had held unanimously that the First Amendment barred state governments from offering such support to parochial secondary schools. Such grants, the justices said, constituted direct public aid to a religious institution. Funding in this form would breach the wall of separation almost as clearly as though such funds were given directly to the church with which the school was linked. Moreover, any public funds given to religious schools, even for a seemingly secular purpose, might offset and thus release other funds that could then be used for sectarian purposes. So the high court consistently invalidated such programs, however laudable the goal of aiding education.

When a similar issue arose a few years later at the college level, the outcome was markedly different. The Higher Education Facilities Act of 1963 authorized construction grants for buildings at private colleges that were used "exclusively for secular educational purposes." The grant program was challenged on the same First Amendment ground that had proved fatal to state support for parochial school facilities. Now the court took a different view, upholding the higher education grants program. Several factors defined the contrast. The court perceived the federally assisted facilities as physically separate from the sectarian parts of the campus and as being used solely for nonreligious purposes. Moreover, church-related colleges that were eligible for such funds had, through their commitment to academic freedom, convinced the court that they would separate the secular and the sectarian in their treatment of faculty, students, and curricula.

Finally, church-related colleges and universities were typically much larger and more complex institutions than the parochial schools that could not under the Bill of Rights receive building funds. Thus the Supreme Court observed, in giving constitutional stature to these differences, that

> there is less likelihood than in primary and secondary schools that religion will permeate the area of secular education. This reduces the risk that government aid will in fact serve to support religious education.

Perhaps most telling, the court was impressed by the greater maturity and the lesser impressionability of postsecondary students and by the separably secular nature of the academic goals most of them pursued in a religious setting:

> The skepticism of the college student is not an inconsiderable barrier to any attempt or tendency to subvert the congressional objectives and limitations. Furthermore, by their very nature, college and postgraduate courses tend to limit the opportunities for sectarian influence by virtue of their own internal disciplines.

For these varied reasons, the Supreme Court brought to bear on church-related colleges a far more lenient First Amendment standard than the one by which it had struck down most forms of aid to parochial schools. The contrast was almost certain to shape the resolution of other challenges that would soon reach the courts.

Less than a decade later, the court did revisit the issue. The occasion was a Washington State program to assist blind persons. Larry Witters chose to use public aid to pursue a degree in theology. His choice was challenged by state officials under the establishment clause and under Washington's constitution, which barred paying public funds for "a religious education." The state courts held that government funds could not be used to support Witters's goal, since the study of divinity or theology indeed amounted to a "religious education."

Witters appealed the denial to the United States Supreme Court, which unanimously reversed, holding that nothing in the establishment clause warranted such a ban. What the high court found compelling was the source of the payment; the choice that would send public money to a divinity school was that of a blind beneficiary, not that of government. Though the state remained free to withhold such funding if it wished to do so for its own reasons, the justices made clear that it need not do so.

The case then went back to the Washington courts, which reaffirmed their earlier view, leaving Witters still ineligible for state aid. This outcome reflected a far stricter standard of church-state separation in the state's own constitution, one which went well beyond the First Amend- ment and specifically enjoined the use of "any public money . . . for any . . . religious instruction." Many a program which might pass muster under the federal Constitution would fail under stricter language in the state charter.

Such a situation may seem anomalous. It is, however, explainable in ways that offer valuable insight into our federal system of rights and liberties. The U.S. Supreme Court has said from time to time that states may set *higher* standards on Bill of Rights issues if they wish; it is only *lower* standards that are unacceptable. So it is that some states guarantee their citizens broader freedom of speech and of the press than the federal Constitution ensures. Such variations have the highest court's blessing. The only limit on what states may do comes about if, in the process, some other federally protected right or liberty is undermined or nullified—a quite real prospect.

Several states, like Washington, do take in their own constitutions a stricter view of church and state than does the federal Bill of Rights. California is most notable in this regard, barring any public funding not only of religious schools but of private secular schools as well. Thus California has taken a quite austere view of religion on the public campus. Not only are there no chapels at any state colleges or universi- ties; even designating a room for private meditation proved deeply divisive at the University of California–Berkeley in the early 1960s. Yet at nearby Arizona State University, one finds at the center of a public campus a handsome chapel, which not only symbolizes but directly serves religious ends. Arizona has as much right, within a broad constitutional zone, to accommodate religion in this way as have California and Washington to keep religion far apart from public higher education. Such is the nature of a federal system, in which states retain broad latitude to define and apply basic human rights in rather different ways.

It is now time to look more closely at two facets of religion in the public university classroom. Recall, first, the troublesome case of the proselytizing professor. It is strikingly close to real life. Professor Philip Bishop had for many years taught physical education at the University of Alabama in Tuscaloosa. His special field was exercise physiology. In the spring of 1987, several of his students complained to the department chairman that Bishop occasionally injected his own religious beliefs into classroom discussions.

Four types of activity troubled these students. In class, Bishop sporadically cited his own religious values and beliefs, which he termed a personal "bias." He cautioned that he did not expect his students necessarily to share his views. Once or twice a month, in his lectures, he made passing reference to certain dimensions of human physiology which he felt revealed what he termed a "creative force."

More than once, Bishop told his classes that he sought to lead a "Christian life." He then invited the students to observe him and take him to task if they felt he failed to meet this goal—though with no hint that students would be rewarded or penalized for such admonition. Outside his regular courses, Bishop offered an optional class, in which he expounded his beliefs and theories about exercise physiology as a reflection of divine guidance and influence. No academic credit was given or expected for this supplemental class; nor did Bishop seek any salary or departmental recognition for offering it.

These four activities were the focus of the students' complaint. The department chair felt obliged to respond and did so soon after the meeting with the students, before the start of the next semester. Bishop was told he must refrain from "the interjection of religious beliefs and/or preferences during instructional time periods and the optional classes where a 'Christian perspective' of an academic topic is delivered." The chairman later gave his rationale for this directive: classroom discussion of personal religious belief, he felt, was not "appropriate for a public institution." He also feared such comments might harm the university's reputation, especially among colleagues at universities outside Alabama, who "consider this the Bible belt." Thus he felt he must take decisive action.

Bishop promptly appealed to the dean, who reviewed and affirmed the chairman's edict. Apparently on the advice of university lawyers, the dean added that a public university must take such cautionary steps to avoid condoning a violation of the First Amendment's establishment clause. Bishop then brought suit in federal court. He claimed that the chairman's and dean's directives abridged his freedom of speech, since he had done nothing that would warrant sanctions. On preliminary argument, the trial judge showed much sympathy to Bishop's plea. He enjoined the university from restricting Bishop's classroom speech or optional lectures on religious issues, at least so long as students had been assured they would be fairly evaluated by a blind grading system (which Bishop insisted he used anyway). The trial judge noted that Bishop's religious comments had apparently not interfered in any way with his teaching: "Faculty members are at liberty to divulge personal views in the classroom as long as they are not disruptive of classroom activities."

The judge rejected the university's claim that intervention was justified, much less compelled, by the establishment clause. To him there seemed no risk that others would view the university as having "established" Bishop's views by simply permitting him to express them occasionally in class. Because students understood Bishop's views to be purely personal, the in-class expression of these views could not be seen as advancing religion. Nor could such statements pose any risk of actual entanglement between church and state. The trial judge also remarked that Bishop's comments closely pertained to the subject of his physiology courses and seemed quite compatible with the university's overall educational mission.

The university appealed to a higher federal court, which reached a totally different result. Relying heavily on cases from elementary and secondary schools, the appeals court deferred to the administration's judgment of what ought to be done with a proselytizing professor:

> [Since] a teacher's speech can be taken as directly and deliberately representative of the school, [a university] necessarily has dominion over

what is taught by its professors. . . . The University's conclusions about course content must be allowed to hold sway over an individual professor's judgments.

On the religious freedom issue, the appeals court also sided with the administration. Whether or not Bishop had breached the wall between church and state, public universities should be able to take cautionary steps that would avoid any such inference, even if that included curbing professorial speech.

Bishop then sought review by the United States Supreme Court. His petition to the high court posed a dilemma for organizations like the American Association of University Professors—sensing that the appeals court had gone too far in its deference to the administration, but being nonetheless uneasy about the volatile issue of religious proselytizing in the state university classroom. The Supreme Court declined to grant review, and there the Bishop case came to rest.

The issues the case raised are, however, of broader significance. For different reasons, both federal courts stopped short of addressing the two most intriguing and difficult questions. The first was the "Bible belt" issue—whether a state university may ever limit what its faculty members say in the classroom on religious topics because of an "image" concern. The other issue was what steps colleges and universities may take to protect students from professors with views that may offend some in their classes.

The Bishop case itself was difficult for reasons that cut against one another. On one hand, the material he intruded into his lectures was unmistakably religious and, for this reason, deeply troubling to some of his students. Here the nature of the course may well make a difference; colleges ought to be especially sensitive to controversial material in a required course, though such concerns deserve attention even when they involve an elective or optional course.

Of all subjects, religion is the one of greatest concern in the classroom. Professors do and should enjoy broad latitude in commenting on topics ranging from weather to sports to politics to campus governance. Religion is, and should be, a different matter—different at least in degree if not in kind. For the potential harm to students from even a chance remark about matters of faith seems vastly greater than is true for any other subject. Thus, as the court of appeals suggested in the Bishop case, university officials should be able to enforce neutrality in the classroom to a greater degree on religious than on any other matters.

The relation between Bishop's comments and his academic field posed, however, a quite different issue. Relevant policies of the American Association of University Professors declare that a faculty member should not "persistently . . . intrude material that has no relation to the subject." For a mathematician or civil engineer to have spoken as Bishop did in class of divine inspiration would clearly breach this basic canon of professional responsibility. For a physiologist to postulate such a correlation is, however, a much more complex matter. Bishop's digressions could much less readily be dismissed as irrelevant. They were deeply troubling to some students, but at the same time arguably relevant to the subject of the course. Had either of the two federal courts reached the issues that lurked not far below the surface, the full complexity of the case would have emerged. In the absence of such inquiry, the most that one can safely do is speculate on how other courts might deal with classroom proselytizing.

We turn next to other aspects of religion in the classroom. While it is clear that public universities may no longer offer degrees in theology and divinity, as some once did, the academic study of religion poses a far different issue. Even in the elementary and secondary classroom, the Supreme Court consistently cautioned that a ban on devotional use of scripture does not foreclose study of the Bible in history and literature courses. What of religion as a theme in higher education? Curiously, the study of religion at the college level seems to have been tested only once in court. The challenge, appropriately enough, occurred at the University of Washington. Seattle church groups objected to the use of the Bible in an upper-level English course. Their concerns were of two distinct types—on one hand, that any use of scripture in a state university class might breach the separation of church and state; on the other, that the way the Bible was being used in the particular course "is contrary to the religious beliefs of plaintiffs—[indeed, that the Bible] cannot be taught objectively as a course in literature, for the attempt to do so violates their personal [sectarian] beliefs. . . ."

The Washington courts rejected both claims. The state supreme court was impressed that the focus of the challenged course was "the literary features of the Bible and . . . the authorship and treatment of the various books of the Bible, and their interpretation from a literary and historical point of view, employing the same techniques of scholarship used in the study of any other literary or historical text. . . ." The court also noted that the course was part of a secular degree program open to all students, that the instructors were all regular English professors, and that each of the several sections in the course used a different version of the Bible, chosen by each instructor "for his own professional reasons." Finally, the court offered this reassuring comment:

> There is no evidence that English 390, as taught at the University of Washington, is intended to affect the religious beliefs of students taking the course or indoctrinate them in any particular religious belief, or that it has had that effect.

For these reasons, Washington's high court denied any relief and allowed the course to continue. Indeed, the court worried that a judicial ban on such a course "would be catastrophic in the field of higher education" and would raise ominous portents:

> Would plaintiffs have us strike the works of Milton, Dante, and the other ancient authors whose writings have survived the ages because they wrote of religious theories with which plaintiffs quarrel? Our constitution does not guarantee sectarian control of our educational system.

The judgment was not unanimous, however. One member of the court sympathized with the plaintiffs' fear that any classroom use of the Bible risked intruding sectarian differences. For him, it was just such risks that had led the framers of Washington's constitution to build so unusually high a wall between government and religion. To this dissenter, English 390 was "religious instruction" and that was the end of the matter. Such a view might seem startling, even in dissent, in most states. In Washington, however, there was a context. The state's high court had some years earlier barred public schools from awarding any academic credit for home or church Bible study, a practice then common in other states though recently challenged elsewhere. Washington, like California, Missouri, and a few other states, has always taken a stricter view of separation and has enforced the stricter standard with special vigor in public education.

The dissenter's concerns found some support from the majority of judges, who added a few cautions of their own. A different curricular structure might have altered the equation. Had the challenged course not been part of a secular degree program, it might have been problematic. Had the instructors not been fully qualified, regular members of the English department, there might also have been problems. And had the use of the Bible in the classroom smacked at all of proselytizing, the court would have taken a closer look.

What guidance, if any, do we derive for state university programs in religious studies? At least three such programs, all of departmental status, are among the largest and most prominent in the nation—those at the University of California at Santa Barbara, the University of Virginia, and Indiana University–Bloomington. These programs meet at least two of the Washington court's criteria: they are housed within colleges of arts and sciences, and they lead to secular degrees at both graduate and undergraduate levels. But the size and scope of such programs far surpass the one or two courses with which the Washington court was dealing. Moreover, the faculties of these large programs include many ordained clergy, who offer courses dealing with Catholic, Protestant, Jewish, and non-Western theologies.

Should so comprehensive a religious studies program be tested in a state like Washington, the Bible course case would be helpful but hardly dispositive. Yet the constitutionality of state university religious studies programs should remain clear—at least as long as the courses are adopted through the regular curricular review process and are open to students of all faiths (or of no professed faith), and as long as those who teach the courses are members of the regular faculty.

The status of clergy on state university faculties deserves a further comment. Not only does the appointment of a minister, priest, or rabbi to a publicly supported teaching post breach no First Amendment precept. For a public employer to bar a member of the clergy, otherwise qualified, from a government job solely on ground of the person's ordination actually abridges the free exercise of religion. That much the Supreme Court made clear two decades ago in affirming the constitutional right of clergy to hold elective public office. All the major state university religious studies programs meet these criteria, and for this reason should pass constitutional muster. Only where there is a genuine risk of proselytizing or of sectarian discrimination or exclusion should such programs risk legal challenge. And, as we observed in the case of

Professor Bishop, such risks are not confined (nor indeed most likely to arise) where the formal subject is religion.

The role of religion outside the classroom has also assumed greater importance and visibility. Not surprisingly, after the Supreme Court had held that clergy could not be invited to deliver invocations at public school graduations, comparable practices at the university level were soon challenged. A federal judge in Indiana declined to extend the high school doctrine to benedictions and invocations at public university graduations. There were two crucial differences. One was the absence at the university level of the type of "coercion" which the Supreme Court had found compelling at the high school graduation; it seemed highly improbable that adult students and their families were so impressionable that they would be constrained against conscience by a religious element in the ceremony. Indeed, "the very mission of higher education is to challenge basic values instilled during childhood at a time when the individual student has the intellectual maturity to choose between competing beliefs." Second, the setting posed a dramatic contrast:

> The atmosphere of a university graduation is also different from that of a high school graduation. The ceremony, both by its size and program content, is impersonal. Thousands of graduates do not attend. In a stadium filled with thousands of graduates, a non-adherent could dissent without being noticed and without fear of being identified as a non-conformist.

Controversy over the role of religion has also spilled onto the athletic field and court. The rapid recent growth of organizations such as the Fellowship of Christian Athletes has created new points of possible tension—team prayers before and after games and religious observances of other types. Through the 1995 season, the University of Florida's star quarterback clasped his hands in prayer after each touchdown, while his counterpart at Florida State pointed to the heavens following every score. Many other players have not only acknowledged the role that faith plays in their lives on and off the field but have also been increasingly demonstrative in ways that trouble some fans and teammates. Though the issue has not yet reached the courts, an NCAA rule against postgame team prayers almost did incur such a challenge at the behest of Liberty University's football team. The matter was resolved through interpretation in such a way as to avoid any threat of formal sanctions—though the growth of visible religious devotion on the part of college athletes makes an early court test almost inevitable.

We turn next, and quite logically, to the status of student religious organizations. It would be surprising if students coming to the public campus from myriad religious backgrounds did not seek congenial communities of faith. And it would be perverse for any public university to inhibit their quest. The issues are of a different order: the degree to which student religious groups may—or even must—be treated differently from other student organizations. Until these questions began reaching the courts in the late 1970s, institutional practice and policy ran the gamut.

Most state universities have given formal recognition to student religious groups that sought it. There the pattern has, however, diverged. Some public universities have conferred extensive benefits, treating religious clubs essentially like secular groups. Only the campus affiliates of mainstream religious faiths—Hillel for Jewish students, Newman for Catholics, Wesley for Methodists, etc.—remained aloof, and quite as much by their own wish as because of university policy. In such a setting, Bible study clubs, fellowships of Christian athletes, and a host of other groups with an undeniably religious perspective appear on the roster of recognized organizations and simply blend in for virtually all purposes.

Elsewhere the relationship was less uniform. Certain state universities had policies that would deny some or all campus perquisites not only to the Newman-Hillel-Wesley type of group but also to less formally religious organizations. It was such a policy that brought this issue to the United States Supreme Court. The University of Missouri once treated religious clubs just like other student groups. But in the early 1970s the university's Board of Curators revised the policy to bar the use of any campus facilities "for purposes of religious worship or religious teaching." This change reflected the special strictures of the state's constitution; Missouri has always separated church and state more strictly than called for by the First Amendment of the United States Constitution.

Under the new policy, an evangelical student group named Cornerstone was told it could no longer meet in the Student Union on the Kansas City campus, even when space was available, because its mission was religious. A group of students took the issue to federal court. The university successfully argued in the trial court that state law as well as the federal establishment clause required it to act as it had; allowing such a group to use public facilities would have breached the wall of separation.

Cornerstone appealed, however, and found a more sympathetic panel at the next level. The appeals court rejected the university's establishment claim, finding no possible breach in simply permitting a student religious group to use campus facilities. In fact, the appeals court added, the denial of such access would actually abridge the student group's free speech on the basis of its message or content. That was something the federal Bill of Rights did not permit, no matter how strong might be the state's commitment to separation.

The university then sought and obtained Supreme Court review. There were three possible options. The high court could affirm the district court on the ground that (as the trial judge ruled) such a ban was required by the establishment clause. Or the justices could agree with the appeals court that free speech entitled student religious groups to equal treatment. As a middle ground, the court could allow the university broad latitude to decide either way, acceding to the state's separation clause, if it wished, or giving the students maximum free expression.

In the end the middle ground got only one vote. Justice Byron White, dissenting alone, argued that university officials should be free to go either way on so sensitive a matter, especially when they felt constrained by the state constitution. The other justices accepted the Cornerstone position and affirmed the appeals court's judgment. Student free speech was at issue, the majority said. A public university could not limit such expression because of its content, even if the "content" was as sensitive as promoting religion. Recalling its earlier judgment on the right of student political groups to be recognized by state colleges, the justices found this case subject to the same First Amendment principles. No university interest that was less than "compelling" would justify denial of campus access on the basis of a group's mission or program.

The court then addressed the university's claimed basis for its denial of space. Like the appeals court, it found no possible violation of the federal establishment clause in granting all groups equal access to campus facilities. The only way in which an establishment violation might occur, under the court's recent religious freedom cases, would be if the access policy specifically "advanced religion." This risk seemed remote here, though the court did recognize that "religious groups will benefit from access to University facilities." It added:

> The question is not whether the creation of a religious forum would violate the establishment clause. The university has opened its facilities for use by student groups, and the question is whether it can now exclude groups because of the content of their speech. . . . In this context we are unpersuaded that the primary effect of the public forum, open to all forms of discourse, would be to advance religion.

There remained the novel question of the role of the Missouri Constitution, the separation clause of which had shaped the university access policy in the first place. The student group argued that federal rights must trump even a state constitution if the two were in conflict. The Supreme Court would have resolved the conflict in this way had it not found a less drastic means of accommodation. The court stopped just short of holding that states could never limit federal constitutional rights by provisions of their own. The issue had not quite arisen here because Missouri's courts never held that student religious groups *must* be denied access to campus meeting rooms. Such a policy might be desirable under state law but had not been deemed mandatory. Thus, the high court was "unable to recognize the State's interest as sufficiently 'compelling' to justify content-based discrimination against . . . religious speech."

That resolved the issues that had to be decided. But before leaving the case, the majority added one important qualification. Harking back to the issue of campus recognition for political groups, the justices reaffirmed the legitimacy of rules governing the time, place, and manner of campus speech, recognizing "a university's right to exclude even First Amendment activities that violate reasonable campus rules or substantially interfere with the opportunity of other students to obtain an education." Beyond time, place, and manner was the issue that much troubled Justice White in his dissent—a state university's need to differentiate between meetings that quietly discussed religious themes and outright services of worship or proselytizing activity. Lacking the authority to draw such lines, White argued, "the majority would have to uphold the University's right to offer a class entitled 'Sunday Mass' . . . [since] such a class would be indistinguishable from a class entitled 'the History of the Catholic Church'." Justice White offered his own response to this dilemma: deny full free speech protection, if necessary, to a service of worship as such—a position the majority rejected in a footnote as illogical and unworkable.

This issue remains troublesome and has never been fully addressed. Clearly there are situations where "speech" on religious matters could, and even must, be kept out of public educational facilities—as a unanimous Supreme Court had recognized shortly before the Missouri case in holding that private groups could not use private funds to post copies of the Ten Commandments in every public school classroom in Kentucky. There simply was no secular purpose for such a display of scripture; a court need not even reach issues of whether such action served to "advance religion"—though unquestionably it did.

That judgment did not answer the issues that the Missouri case left open. The difference lay not in the grade level of the classroom; had the issue been posting the commandments in classrooms at the University of Kentucky, the outcome would have been no different. Thus there remain, as Justice White cautioned, a set of questions about the capacity—even duty—of state universities to avoid making facilities available for constitutionally forbidden religious activities and exercises. The Missouri decision simply left these issues for another day.

What administrative options, if any, did survive the Missouri decision? In what respects might a public institution deal specially or differently with a student religious organization? Several options come to mind. First, there is the ruling's recognition that a state university may bar expressive activity which "substantially interfere[s] with the opportunity of other students to obtain an education."

Might that language allow the institution to deal with religious proselytizing that threatened to impede student access to classroom and laboratory buildings? Undoubtedly it would, though only through uniform, content-neutral rules that apply equally to political party recruiters and proselytizers for secular causes as well.

The problem of overly aggressive and disruptive solicitation is hardly unique to religious zealots; it occurs in other contexts as well. Campus rules designed to keep the plaza free of religious proselytizing must be uniform and comprehensive in application. They must be applied as energetically to Republicans and Democrats, to Greenpeace or Common Cause, to Young Americans for Freedom. Here the Missouri mandate serves us well: campus rules that affect speech or expressive activity must be content or viewpoint neutral.

What about off-campus or outside religious groups? Again, the answer depends chiefly on the scope and generality of the rule. If the policy is to deny campus status to all external organizations, political and social as well as religious, there would be uniformity. If, however, religious groups faced barriers that Democrats or Republicans or others from outside would not face, the focus of any such rule would at once make it inherently suspect.

There may, however, be one permissible difference. Suppose a religious group requests the use of the stadium for a rally featuring its spiritual leader. If the stadium is not for rent to anyone, that would be the end of the matter. But suppose student groups can lease such a facility when it is not in use. Is there no basis on which the administration could reject a request for a stadium event featuring a highly visible sectarian leader? Such a case might well meet the test of perceptibly "advancing religion" which the Supreme Court recognized in the Missouri case and elsewhere. To many campus observers, making prime space available for a manifestly sectarian event might seem to go beyond the accommodation or evenhanded access that Widmar demands. "Advancing religion" is of course a subjective standard. Later cases have refined its meaning through concepts such as "endorsement" and "sponsorship" that would surely apply here even though they postdated the Missouri case. Thus, if the event and its site are widely publicized—"Pope to Address Huge Rally at State U. Stadium"—there might be a hint of an institutional imprimatur. Obviously any such judgment would depend on factors special to the situation. Not all religious rallies, even led by spiritual notables, cross the line between equal access and religious endorsement or sponsorship. The point is simply that the Missouri case did not leave the public university powerless to avoid being placed in a position of "advancing . . . [or seeming to advance] religion." What the Supreme Court said is that access rules may not be invoked to deny all religious uses, out of concern or fear that any and all religious activities would compromise the institution's secular character or its neutrality. Only a grave particular threat would justify an exception.

Finally, we come to what may seem the most obvious of the Missouri ruling's concessions. The court was at pains to assure administrators that the judgment "in no way undermines the capacity of the University to establish reasonable time, place and manner regulations." This reassurance seems obvious and familiar. Such policies abound. Campus rules typically require student groups to file charters, submit lists of officers, and commit themselves to abide by a set of standards and principles. Religious groups seem no different in this regard from political or social clubs. Requiring a pledge not to discriminate on racial grounds seems routine, and is universal. But what if university policy also tells student organizations they may not discriminate on religious grounds? May a religious club, as a condition of recognition, be required to agree that it will admit members of all sects (and nonbelievers) without regard to faith or belief? Or may a group drawn from a denomination that abhors and condemns homosexuality be forced to welcome gay and lesbian members? Ordinarily, there would be no doubt about the enforceability of such an obligation; political and social organizations must fully meet such university standards. But the case of student religious groups is problematic. One could argue that to force a Muslim student group to admit Jewish and Christian students as members would take the heart out of the organization and undermine its very reason for existence.

Surprisingly, there seem to be no court decisions on this point. There is, however, one protracted case which may shed some light. Georgetown University, a Catholic bastion, struggled with the government of the District of Columbia over the application of an ordinance that forbids any educational institution from discriminating on the basis of sexual orientation. Two gay student groups claimed that Georgetown had violated this law by refusing to grant them recognition and access to campus facilities. (Gay students had been informally acknowledged and been allowed to meet on campus and invite speakers, had received support services and engaged in various other activities, but had consistently been denied formal recognition.) The university forcefully defended its refusal to recognize these groups; since recognition (under university policies) would imply a religiously guided "endorsement" of any student group that was recognized, Georgetown officials claimed that forcing such action would abridge the university's religious freedom.

A trial judge found in the university's favor and dismissed the complaint. Forcing recognition, she concluded, would compel Georgetown to act in a manner "inconsistent with its duties as a Catholic institution." The student groups appealed and found a more sympathetic panel at the next level. The appeals court first acknowledged that an equal rights law could not be so applied as to compel the university's "endorsement" of a group with a mission that was abhorrent on ground of religious principle. But the appellate court did not agree that the gay rights law compelled ideological acceptance of abhorrent causes. Thus the judges held that Georgetown could, despite the nature of its objections, be legally required to give equal benefits to a student gay or lesbian organization. Such a mandate, said the appeals court, would not abridge anyone's free exercise of religion, even though a requirement of full recognition (with "endorsement") might well do so. Thus emerged a distinction that helped to resolve the case: "Georgetown's obligation under the statute is not to express a particular point of view. It is to make tangible benefits available to its students without regard to their sexual orientation."

Finally, the court addressed Georgetown's free exercise claims. The core of this claim was the conflict between Catholic tenets and the action required by the human rights law. In nonreligious contexts, courts had begun to resolve conflicts between nondiscrimination and First Amendment freedoms in favor of the former—for example, by consistently upholding laws that required social and service clubs to accept women or minority members despite claims of freedom of association and choice. When there was a direct conflict in this area, expressive or associational freedoms had almost invariably come out second best.

This case was, however, different on both sides. It was the first to pit antibias laws against a religious belief or principle. It was also the first case in which the forbidden bias involved sexual orientation rather than race or gender. Nonetheless, the court of appeals resolved the issue consistently with the nonreligious cases. The District's interest in ensuring equality for gays and lesbians was "compelling" enough to override all but the most basic of liberties. Yet here the university's religious freedom interest seemed "relatively slight"—an interest which, ironically, had been attenuated by how far Georgetown had willingly, if informally, accommodated so many of the gay and lesbian students' needs. Thus the balance now tipped decisively in favor of requiring equal access to all tangible benefits, while stopping short of the "endorsement" that full recognition would imply, since such an imprimatur was not vital to meet the goals of the human rights law.

What bearing might the Georgetown case have on the fate of a student religious group faced with an abhorrent duty as a condition of university recognition? At first blush, the parties and the interests would appear to be reversed. At Georgetown, the *university* invoked religious freedom, while the *organization* argued for equality. Here the *institution* would be seeking to impose policies designed to ensure equality, while the *student group* would be resisting these policies on religious grounds. But in fact the principles that emerged in the Georgetown case may be quite helpful.

On the student group's side, we might assess the religious freedom claim much as the courts assessed Georgetown's interests. In both situations, religious liberty has undeniably been affected—here, by telling a student organization to admit members of different faiths or to tolerate homosexuality directly contrary to its religious beliefs and principles. While the sanction may be less direct—denial of recognition rather than the penalties imposed by the D.C. antibias law—the effect of noncompliance would be similar enough to constitute a serious threat to religious liberty.

Such a finding does not, however, end the inquiry here any more than it did with respect to Georgetown. It simply shifts the analysis to the other side—the strength of the government's interest and the alternative means (if any) of serving that interest. It seems long past the time when a state university would be required to prove the importance of ending racial and religious bias among recognized student groups. In many states and possibly even under federal law, the institution would be legally culpable if it allowed such bias to persist. One aside is important: religious exemptions do exist in certain areas. The Federal Equal Employment law, and laws of many states, contain very narrow exceptions for certain hiring by religious entities. A Catholic diocese cannot, for example, be found to have "discriminated" unlawfully for refusing to hire a non-Catholic as a priest. When it comes to hiring clerical or custodial personnel, though, the exemption does not apply; qualified persons of all faiths must be considered. That is about the extent of the dispensation; it has never gone beyond the core needs of the faith. Thus, in the campus setting, the university could not force Hillel to hire a non-Jew as its spiritual adviser, but that is about as far as the statute (or the Constitution) extends. No statutory exemption or exception of this type would remotely cover the matter at hand.

When it comes to gender or racial membership barriers, the student religious group's claims would probably be controlled by Supreme Court cases that have required social clubs to admit persons with whom they strenuously do not wish to associate. There are differences on both sides, but these differences do not seem sufficient to shift the constitutional balance.

When it comes to requiring a student group to accept gay and lesbian members, the issue is more complex. The basis for banning antigay bias is statutory, not constitutional. It exists only in a small number of states that have added sexual orientation to other forbidden grounds of discrimination. Until and unless the Supreme Court extends the equal protection clause to include sexual orientation, the outcome will depend upon the state of the local law, and thus will vary widely across the country.

Finally, we reach the related issue of university funding for religious student groups. Patterns have varied substantially—some public colleges providing such support from general student fee pools, others broadly barring such support, and still others supporting certain kinds of student religious activities but not all. Until early 1994, there was no directly applicable law. Then two major cases emerged almost simultaneously in federal appeals courts at opposite ends of the country, challenging funding denials by the University of Hawaii and the University of Virginia.

The Hawaii case was the earlier and less portentous of the two. In 1989, the University of Hawaii student government approved funding for activities of several religious student groups, including Maranatha, Campus Crusade for Christ, Hawaii Youth for Christ, and Champions for Christ. The planned events were to include "campuswide Bible studies" and other programs designed to bring religious messages and themes to various parts of the campus. Soon after the funding for these programs had been approved, the Hawaii ACLU threatened to sue for a violation of church and state law. University officials promptly agreed to rescind the appropriations. They added that they would henceforth make no grants to the named organizations or to "any other groups which would use the funds to promote a particular religious point of view even if in a secular context." The religious groups remained free, however, to seek funds for secular activities.

Maranatha and the other organizations, led by a student named Greg Tipton, now went to federal court, where they sued the university and the ACLU for abridgment of their religious liberty. The trial judge dismissed the suit on the ground that "Tipton had no right to government-subsidized speech." The appeals court reached a similar conclusion by a more elaborate route. It agreed that state universities had no duty "to fund the exercise of constitutional rights," but went on to note the rather diffuse nature of Tipton's complaint. Since the complaining students had cited no specific constitutional violations, they could prevail only if the university's funding policy were incapable of any valid interpretation. That was more than the religious groups were able to demonstrate.

What the university had said, in effect, was that student groups could not receive funds the transfer of which would violate the establishment clause as construed by the Supreme Court. So far, so good, the courts would agree. But the administration had gone a bit further and had said it would also bar funds that might be used "to promote a particular religious point of view. . . ." It was not obvious that the Supreme Court would enjoin a state university from granting such funds. Nonetheless, the appeals court sided across the board with the administration. Even a policy that might be broader in scope than necessary would be upheld "so long as it is evenly applied to all student groups seeking funding in support of nonsectarian events." Such uniformity seemed to prevail here; not only did the policy apply alike to all student groups, but the university had gone further and had "made accommodation for funding certain activities of religious organizations."

That settled the immediate issue in the court of appeals. The judges recognized it had managed to avoid two much harder questions—whether a state university "could outright refuse to fund all student religious organizations while funding the activities of other student groups" and "whether the University could fund purely religious events or 'pervasively sectarian' student groups." These more difficult questions remained for another day and a different case.

Meanwhile, in another federal court the University of Virginia was coming closer to at least one of these open questions. A university-approved student group sought funding for continued publication of a magazine called *Wide Awake: A Christian Perspective at the University of Virginia*. The magazine's declared goal was to "challenge Christians . . . [by encouraging] students to consider what a personal relationship with

Jesus Christ means . . . and [by offering] a Christian perspective on both personal and community issues, especially those relevant to college students at the University of Virginia." Early issues of the magazine contained indisputably religious material in both editorial and contributed form, even in advertising.

A longstanding university policy barred the use of student fee funds to support (among others) "religious activities." Relevant guidelines defined this phrase as referring to "an activity which primarily promotes or manifests a particular belief(s) in or about a deity or an ultimate reality." When funding for *Wide Awake* was sought and denied under the guidelines, a student group led by Ronald Rosenberger went to federal court. Its claim was not that the policy had been misapplied; it conceded that publishing *Wide Awake* was clearly a "religious activity." But it argued that any policy which would deny funding solely because of the content or viewpoint of such a publication would violate both the free speech and religious freedom guarantees of the First Amendment. It also claimed the university's action violated the principle set out in the Missouri decision; student activity funding, like access to meeting space, represented a public forum from which religious speech could not be excluded.

The district judge rejected all of the group's claims and dismissed the suit. He found that the funding mechanism did not create a public forum, which made the Missouri ruling inapplicable. He refused to find any content or viewpoint discrimination or any other abridgment of religious or expressive freedoms. The court of appeals reached the same result on similar grounds, though requiring some sixty-five pages to address what it recognized at once to be novel and difficult questions of constitutional law. (Free exercise of religion issues had been abandoned on appeal; that left only the alleged bias against religious speech and an equal protection argument unlikely to survive if the First Amendment issues did not.)

The appeals court noted that in all ways, except funding for publications, student religious groups at Virginia fared no less well than political or other organizations. Moreover, the judges agreed with the court in the Hawaii case that state campuses "are under [no] affirmative duty to ensure that university students' expressive activities are funded." Even so, the denial of funding imposed a troublesome condition; the *Wide Awake* group had been told, in effect, that they must forgo "constitutionally protected religious expression" as the price of obtaining student fee support. Had such a condition been imposed on expression of any other type, the policy would almost certainly have violated the First Amendment. So the question for this court was how differently religious messages could and should be treated.

The appeals court's answer was "quite differently." The court was convinced the university had sought in good faith to avoid violating the establishment clause. Under the Supreme Court's recently refined establishment standards, "an award of SAF funds to defray publication costs of *Wide Awake* would 'convey a message of endorsement' of Christianity to non-Christian members of the University of Virginia community." This court insisted it "would be difficult to view awarding SAF monies to *Wide Awake* as anything but state sponsorship—and therefore advancement— of religious belief." The recurrent nature of such funding and the likelihood of continuing controversy over it gave this issue a politically divisive character, recalling the fear of "entanglement" that underlay the Supreme Court's consistent refusal to allow state support for parochial schools.

One might well ask, as did Rosenberger and his fellow plaintiffs, "But what about the Missouri decision?" The *Wide Awake* case had seemed to them on all fours with the Supreme Court's judgment that state universities must give religious groups equal access to meeting space. The appeals court found several vital differences. First, the University of Virginia had met the spirit as well as the letter of the Missouri ruling, having granted all benefits except funding for religious publications. Second, the Missouri ruling was based on a finding that campus meeting space was a public forum, to which rigorous free speech standards applied; this court took a quite different, nonforum, view of student activity funding for publications and the like. Third, the "advancement of religion" which had been deemed absent in Missouri was unmistakably present in Virginia, if only because paying for an avowedly Christian magazine creates a stronger inference of institutional support than simply opening the doors of student union meeting rooms.

Thus the suspect "condition" which this court saw in denial of funding was, in the end, justified by a compelling university interest—avoiding what might otherwise have been an unconstitutional advancement of a religious viewpoint. The challenged policy was no broader than needed:

"government is left no choice but to forswear financial support of the myriad forms of religious endeavor in which a student organization might engage."

The *Wide Awake* plaintiffs now sought the Supreme Court's attention, and got it. The case, heard in the late winter of 1995, was decided on the last day of the term. Arguments that had been rejected by both lower federal courts now prevailed, though by the narrowest of margins. Avoiding the religious freedom claims, the majority rested its judgment in favor of *Wide Awake* squarely on grounds of free speech. To refuse funding for publications because they treated "religious" topics was discrimination against content that the First Amendment did not permit. Since any similar nonreligious publication would have been funded, the university's treatment of *Wide Awake* singled out and disadvantaged a particular viewpoint.

Had the issue been one of access to physical space, the Missouri ruling would have controlled. The lower federal courts had agreed with the university that funding publications was different, partly because funds were limited in ways that space was not and partly because funding publications might imply a degree of endorsement that opening meeting room doors could not. But the Supreme Court majority saw no such distinction between funds and space. The Missouri ruling had done more than simply open the doors of meeting rooms; the access claim had in fact been broadened, most recently to bar a public school system from refusing to pay an interpreter for a deaf student attending a parochial school.

The majority then addressed and rejected the university's concern about establishment—a concern so strong that the appeals court said the university had no constitutional choice but to refuse funds for a religious magazine. In contrast, the majority now felt this issue too had been settled against the university by the Missouri ruling. So long as the program of supporting student activities was essentially neutral and did not "advance religion or aid a religious case," the establishment concern seemed misplaced. Cases that involved taxes for the support of religious activity were thus inapposite. Nor was there any greater concern because mandatory fees were the source of the funding; the actual payment, said the majority, would be to a commercial printer and not to a church or religious group.

Thus each of the grounds on which the university and the lower courts relied was in turn rejected. The distinction between funding and facilities, which had seemed vital in the decade and a half since the Missouri ruling, was swept aside. To refuse funding for such a category of expression was, purely and simply, an abridgment of free speech.

The court was, however, sharply divided. The four dissenters took direct and strong issue with the majority:

> The Court today, for the first time, approves direct funding of religious activities by an arm of the State. It does so, however, only after erroneous treatment of some familiar principles of law implementing the First Amendment's Establishment and Speech Clauses. . . . [We] would hold that the University's refusal to support [*Wide Awake's*] religious activities is compelled by the Establishment Clause.

The balance of the dissent amplified the depth of division between the two wings of the court. The dissenters sharply criticized the majority's "novel" view that "only direct aid financed with tax revenues is barred" and went on to identify several risks and hazards of such a judgment. The dissenters also had a somewhat different view of the contents of *Wide Awake:* "The subject is not of the scholar's study or the seminar room, but of the evangelist's mission station and the pulpit." What the majority had now forced the university to subsidize was, in the dissenters' view, "nothing other than the preaching of the word. . . ." What ensued were sharp differences between majority and dissent over both First Amendment precedent and such particulars of the case as the challenged university guidelines which had triggered the dispute.

Finally, the dissenters ridiculed the majority's assumption that constitutional problems were avoided by paying a printer rather than a church to put out an avowedly Christian magazine; by that theory, "the State could simply hand out credit cards to religious institutions and honor the monthly statements (so long as someone could devise an evenhanded umbrella to cover the whole scheme)."

Where does the Virginia case leave the public university and religious activity? Since the Missouri decision, it has been clear that public institutions can draw few lines between religious and other student groups. What *Wide Awake* did was to narrow still further the permissible range of distinctions—indeed, perhaps to moot the issue entirely. What remain open to institutions are those options we noted earlier during our analysis of the Missouri case—content-neutral time, place, and manner rules and other policies aimed at disruptive behavior rather than at message or content or affiliation.

Thus a state university may still control fraudulent religious solicitation under general rules that protect students and faculty against phony schemes and scams of all types. The ritual sacrifice of a live animal in married student housing can be regulated, so long as nonreligious animal slaughter would be treated the same way. If incense or candles used in a dormitory room during a worship service pose a fire hazard, general rules presumably afford the institution adequate recourse.

In fact, funding of publications was about the only issue of importance that remained in genuine doubt after the Missouri decision. Such funding was virtually the only benefit that Virginia and other public universities had withheld from student religious groups in recent years. Thus one might well ask whether settling this one remaining issue deserved the heavy constitutional artillery both sides of the Supreme Court brought to bear. Back on campus, life continues with remarkably little change for most members of the academic community.

X

FREE SPEECH ON THE PRIVATE CAMPUS

To: The Board of Trustees
From: Charles Gold, President

You have read in the last few weeks about a series of anti-Semitic incidents that have taken place on our campus. Swastikas appeared on several bulletin boards in residence halls. Some Jewish students received vicious personal attacks via e-mail. Graffiti appeared last weekend on the front of the new campus Hillel Jewish Student Center. Two recent speakers appearing at campus forums spewed some vicious and hateful statements. The unofficial student weekly, the *Daredevil,* contains a column devoted to "exposing truths" about such issues as the alleged role of Jews in the slave trade, "Jewish domination" of the film industry, and so on.

We could respond in any of several ways. One approach, which some of you probably favor, would be to ignore the attacks and hope the perpetrators (who probably crave attention) will eventually go away. Another possibility would be to convene campus forums to discuss these issues and build a sense of community—though I have little hope any of the hatemongers would attend. Or we could launch a counterattack, designed to get out to the campus community the real story of the role of Jews in the history of this country (and for that matter of this university).

Let me suggest a different and bolder approach—one that may contain some risks but in the long run could prove more satisfying than the others I just outlined. Of course we respect academic freedom and protect free speech; one would expect no less of a great and distinguished university. On the other hand, we are a *private* institution. We are thus not bound by the constraints of the First Amendment. So if there are areas of expression where our mission and character might warrant different standards, we should feel free to impose these standards even though a state university could not do so.

What we now face is just such an issue. We attract a large number of outstanding Jewish students; if the campus climate remains as it is now, I fear for the level and quality of our applications this fall. We draw a substantial portion of our private gift and endowment support from Jewish alumni, several of whom called in the past week to express their dismay and alarm at what they heard about campus anti-Semitism. About a fifth of our faculty are Jewish, and the group includes some of our most eminent scholars and best teachers. So it seems to me we can make a case for special treatment of one category of expression.

In much the same way and for similar reasons, I have always assumed a Catholic university would be free to deal differently than other institutions with sacrilege, blasphemy, or advocacy of abortion. A historically black private college ought to be able to be tougher on people who make racist statements than would other institutions. So it is with us. Given our special relationship with the Jewish community and our special level of concern, I propose that we develop standards dealing directly and firmly with anti-Semitic statements and acts.

Before we discuss this proposal at next week's board meeting, we need some legal background. I have asked our general counsel to prepare such a paper, and it is enclosed. As you will see, he cautions that this issue may be more complex than I had initially assumed. In the end, though, he supports the legality of the action I envision. I hope you will also be prepared to support our moving in this direction.

MEMORANDUM OF THE GENERAL COUNSEL

The issue of free speech on the private campus is more difficult and complex than a lay observer might expect. In a simple world, public colleges are fully bound by the First Amendment, while private institutions are entirely free to deal with speech however they wish. The problem is that such a neat and simple world does not exist, and really never has existed.

Part of the current confusion is deeply rooted in our history. In the first judgment involving a private institution of higher learning, the famous Dartmouth College case in 1819, the United States Supreme Court proclaimed a clear distinction between "a civil institution to be employed in the administration of government" on one hand and, on the other, "a

private eleemosynary institution." Dartmouth, falling in the latter category, persuaded the court (or at least Daniel Webster did so on its
behalf) that the New Hampshire legislature could not constitutionally
alter the college's basic charter. Moreover, Chief Justice John Marshall
declared that private colleges "do not fill the place, which would
otherwise be occupied by government, but that which would otherwise
remain vacant."

Even back in the early nineteenth century, though, the actual differences were far less distinct than was Chief Justice Marshall's vision. Many
universities that we would today consider totally private—Harvard and
Yale, for example—began with such generous public support of land and
funds that their founders would have been puzzled by labels like
"independent." (Yale, in fact, still includes the governor and lieutenant
governor of Connecticut on its governing board.) Other universities that
started out in one mode later completely changed character. The classic
examples are Tulane, which began as the public University of Louisiana
but became fully private through endowment, and Rutgers, which was
fully private for much of its history but today proudly (and accurately)
calls itself "the State University of New Jersey."

Many blended models exist in between—public-charter institutions
like the Universities of Delaware and Vermont, which have many private
qualities, or private-charter universities like Howard, Pitt, and Temple,
which receive essentially public funding. Then there is the unique case of
the Massachusetts Institute of Technology; it is private for virtually all
purposes but since 1862 has been a recipient of federal land-grant
support. There is also Cornell University, which, though a private Ivy
League university for most purposes, contains four "statutory" or "contract" colleges that are state-funded as part of the State University of New
York. So it goes through a fascinating litany of variations and hybrids.

In fact higher education in the United States offers a continuum of
institutional types, from most clearly "public" to most clearly "private."
Save for completely public community and junior colleges, which
receive little nonpublic support, hardly any real campuses neatly and
cleanly reflect the prototypes. Few state universities derive anything like
full support from government; little more than a third, sometimes a
quarter or less, of the budgets of the great public research universities
comes from state legislative appropriations. The balance of their budgets

draws upon myriad sources, many of them quite private (such as the individual and corporate donations they seek as vigorously as their private peers).

Conversely, the major private universities get massive research funding from the federal government—in fact, far more on a per-capita basis than what state universities receive from the same agencies. Many also receive substantial state and local public support as well. There may be a handful of small colleges so aggressively "private" they even refuse to enroll students with government aid; they may succeed in avoiding all federal regulation, but only at a price few others can afford. The balance of so-called private (or "independent") institutions are hybrids, with a complex array of funding sources.

Our own university is of course very much in that mode. Our charter legally vests authority in a self-perpetuating board of trustees, which is a preeminently private body. Yet there are various indicia of our complex and hybrid character. We receive tens of millions of federal research dollars each year, and we draw substantial state support for our hospital and our other health science programs, among others—not to mention the thousands of students we enroll each year who bring with them federal and state financial aid. We are thus quite typical of most institutions of private or independent higher education. We are private in form and name (and history), but in reality we are able to operate only with the addition of some indisputably public elements.

What does all this tell us about free speech? May we adopt and enforce policies which would violate the First Amendment if they were imposed by state universities? The short answer is that we almost certainly may do so. But short answers have little virtue beyond brevity. As you will see, the qualifications and cautions are many, and in the event of legal challenge the status of such a policy would be less clear than one might like or expect. Let me explain these vagaries and complexities as best I can.

We have no final or definitive authority on these issues. The Supreme Court once agreed to address the status of speech on the private university campus, but the case was dismissed and never decided. In that case the lower courts did address the merits, giving us some valuable guidance, and we could do no better than to start with that case.

In 1978 a political organizer named Chris Schmid was arrested for handing out political leaflets on the Princeton University campus. He was charged with the misdemeanor of trespass, since as a nonstudent he was not authorized by campus rules to distribute such materials. The lower courts treated the case as fairly routine, and sustained a trespass conviction. The New Jersey Supreme Court recognized, however, that the case was anything but routine. A majority of the court eventually reversed Schmid's conviction on free speech grounds, relying on the state constitution rather than on the First Amendment. (States may, the U.S. Supreme Court has said, grant protection under their own constitutions to speech which the Bill of Rights might not protect. The Bill of Rights, in other words, establishes a floor but not necessarily a ceiling when it comes to defining the scope of individual rights and liberties.)

Before turning to the state constitution, the New Jersey court gave close attention to Schmid's federal First Amendment claims. For this reason, the case remains the most thorough analysis of the status of free speech on a private university campus. After noting that the Bill of Rights does not normally extend to private property, the court took account of two important exceptions—private entities that were either closely entwined with or were extensively regulated by government. The actions or policies of such otherwise private entities might be treated as "state action" and would thus be judged by those constitutional standards normally reserved for actions and policies of government itself. In the Princeton trespass case, however, the New Jersey Court found neither of these analogies persuasive. Though Princeton "is involved in a continuous relationship with the State" for accreditation, bonding and other beneficial purposes, the court concluded:

> Princeton University is, indisputably, predominantly private, unregulated and autonomous in its character and functioning as an institution of higher education. The interface between the University and the State is not so extensive as to demonstrate a joint and mutual participation in higher education or to establish an interdependent or symbiotic relationship between the two in the field of education.

One other possible basis of "state action" drew the court's attention. The U.S. Supreme Court had once held that a "company town" could not bar speakers or pamphleteers because a corporate enclave of this type so closely resembled a city government that it should be so treated by the courts. Later the high court extended this theory to shopping centers and malls, though by the time the Schmid case developed, protection had been confined to distributing messages and materials that pertained directly to the mall's policies. Thus it was still an open question whether a major private university campus should be treated like a company town for speech purposes.

There were some fairly obvious points of similarity, given the range of services a private university offers its students and staff. After acknowledging these parallels, however, the New Jersey court found dispositive two types of differences. Unlike people who inhabit a company town, university staff and students may and do receive information through myriad alternative communication channels. Moreover, the university does not play in the lives of its students the role of "a government substitute or surrogate" to nearly the degree the company town and its managers did in the lives of residents. Thus Schmid's attempt to impose First Amendment obligations on the university by this route proved no more successful than had the nexus-and-regulation theory he had tried and found wanting earlier in the case.

There remained the New Jersey Constitution, and it proved to be Schmid's trump. Noting that states have constitutional power to protect more speech than the federal Bill of Rights demands, the New Jersey court reviewed instances in which the state's judges had in fact been more expansive. What needed reconciliation here was a subtle tension between two constitutional interests of a high order—the use of private property on one hand and the exercise of political expression on the other. Several factors must be weighed in the balance—the nature and normal use of the property, the extent and nature of the public's invitation to use the property, and the purpose of the expressive activity.

Under this formula, Princeton had effectively provided its own answer: a strongly stated university commitment to "free inquiry and free expression within the academic community" seemed at variance with a claimed need to evict a political pamphleteer simply because he was not a student. Schmid's expressive activities seemed neither incompatible with Princeton's goals nor disruptive of any of its normal activities. To the extent that disruption might be feared, the university's needs could be met through narrow "time, place and manner" rules (of a kind that did not exist when Schmid arrived but were later adopted). Thus, after such a careful balancing of interests, the court concluded that Princeton

University had abridged Schmid's state free speech rights. On this basis the state's high court reversed the conviction.

Princeton and the prosecutor now sought U.S. Supreme Court review. The justices agreed to hear the case, and briefs were filed. While the case was pending, the applicable campus trespass rules were revised. When the new rules were brought to the attention of the judges in New Jersey, they saw no need to comment on them. But the U.S. Supreme Court dismissed the case because the facts on which the case turned had changed. What remains, then, as the final judgment is the New Jersey Supreme Court's holding that the old rules (which lacked, among other features, any detailed procedural standards) violated the state constitution's free speech clause. At the same time, the New Jersey judgment also stands for the view that Schmid had raised no First Amendment issue because the Bill of Rights did not apply to a private institution like Princeton. Should the same issue arise later in New Jersey, at Princeton or another private campus, one can only assume that the state's courts would review the compatibility of the rules with the state constitution under standards similar to those it would apply to a public campus like Rutgers.

What would have happened if Schmid had taken his case to federal court rather than being brought into state court by the arresting officer? Most of the private college cases have in fact arisen in federal courts. Since the 1960s, when student litigation really began, many plaintiffs have sought to bring the Bill of Rights to bear on the actions of private institutions of higher learning.

An important distinction needs to be made before examining the federal cases: such claims have arisen only in the absence of legislation. Where Congress has enacted a law that expressly covers private universities, like the laws barring race and gender discrimination or laws that regulate research involving animals or human subjects, the only constitutional issue facing a court is whether Congress has power to extend its laws to private campuses. This issue is meaningful only for the handful of militantly private colleges like Hillsdale and Grove City that refuse any form of federal aid, direct or indirect. It is not an issue for the vast array of institutions that receive federal support in various forms. For the vast majority of private campuses, the only issues are those of scope and interpretation, not of constitutional reach.

Many questions about federal rights arise, however, in areas where Congress has not acted. That is clearly the case with most speech and expressive activity, where Congress has not imposed rules on private colleges and universities. Though there have been recent efforts to make private campus speech a federal matter, any free speech claim in the federal courts would have to be based on the First Amendment. Such a claim would succeed only if a court found "state action" on the private university's part—something the New Jersey Supreme Court refused to find of Princeton University in the Schmid case. Just this question came before federal courts a number of times in the 1960s and 1970s (and only occasionally since then), with varying results that may be useful to summarize here.

Most of the earlier cases challenged Vietnam-era penalties imposed on student demonstrators on private campuses. All but a few federal courts found no basis for "state action" and thus dismissed such suits for lack of federal jurisdiction. The Bill of Rights simply did not apply of its own force to the typical private campus. This view prevailed even when the university received massive federal funding—as at Stanford, Columbia, and New York University (all successful litigants on this very issue)—and even more clearly when the institution was less substantially impacted by federal funds and policies.

Occasionally a court would narrow or qualify the ruling; the judge who dismissed the suit against Columbia, for example, stressed the absence of any link between the specific discipline and the federal money, thus hinting that if the plaintiff had been summarily dismissed from a *federally funded* research project or a *state-supported* health facility, the court might then have taken a different view of the case. Yet time and again during these years and even more clearly in later years, most federal courts declined to take private college suits.

A few notable exceptions and one fascinating hybrid deserve attention. The exceptions involved nominally private campuses where a finding of "state action" with respect to the whole institution seems obvious. The classic cases are those of Temple and the University of Pittsburgh. Both institutions were once as private as, let us say, Haverford and Duquesne. For some purposes (collective bargaining, for example) they remain no less private today. But massive state funding transformed both institutions into commonwealth universities. This metamorphosis invited federal judges to find enough "state action" to impose constitutional obligations. Thus, even though Pitt and Temple remain private in charter and governance, the major share of funding that is public and other mutually beneficial links with the commonwealth pushed the case across the line.

A much harder case was that of the state's other major private campus, the University of Pennsylvania. Penn had sought and obtained sharply increased support—roughly a quarter of its operating budget—from the commonwealth. The amount included direct and major support for the health sciences, accompanied by requirements on such policies as preferring in-state applicants for professional programs that one would associate with the public sector. Penn had assumed a major role in the Philadelphia redevelopment project, for which it received substantial funding as well as a significant voice in the program. The university also received much direct state funding for buildings and research projects and of course enjoyed extensive tax exemptions. Many of its students were able to attend an expensive private institution only with sizable loans or grants from federal and state government. Thus, the judge concluded, there had developed a "symbiosis" between Penn and government (at several levels) that justified a finding of state action in a dismissed faculty member's suit for reinstatement.

The Penn case was the highwater mark of "state action" on the private campus. Unlike the Columbia case, this court treated the university as governmentally impacted for all purposes. The judge did not ask whether the aggrieved professor had worked on publicly funded research; in his view, there need be no link between the source of the claim and direct government subvention. Yet the case bears two important qualifications. The first is obvious: Penn was more deeply allied with and dependent on government (at several levels) than most major private universities. With the possible exception of Cornell (with its four state university colleges), no other Ivy League school would likely have been forced to respond in federal court to the merits of such a claim.

The other factor is harder to assess but is crucial for us and brings us back to our theme. The claim against Penn was one of *discrimination,* an area of redress which would soon thereafter be covered by specific act of Congress. Had the plaintiff instead claimed her free speech had been abridged, the court might have been less ready to find enough "state action" to support federal jurisdiction. Nothing said in the Penn case implies such a subject-matter limitation on the state action finding; it is only a caution worth raising in the absence of a clearer guidance.

In fact, one other case involving campus speech was working its way through the federal courts about the same time. A group of students at Alfred University had taken part in an anti-ROTC demonstration, for which they were suspended. They went immediately to federal court, seeking reinstatement. Though they had demonstrated as a group and were charged under the same rule, some of the students prevailed while others did not. How, one may ask, could that happen?

Alfred University is no ordinary private institution. It is a classic hybrid. Though mainly a private liberal arts college, Alfred is host to the State University of New York College of Ceramics, which enrolls about a third of the student body. About a fifth of Alfred's total budget at that time came from the state, which employed a quarter of the faculty. The ceramics students received Alfred degrees, though they paid much lower tuition. SUNY provided pro-rata support for various Alfred services, including the dean of students' salary. (The arrangement in some ways resembles that at Cornell, the other SUNY college host, though Cornell receives a per-student payment on a different formula.)

When the students' case reached federal court, the trial judge dismissed the entire suit; it was, in his view, no different from the others filed against private liberal arts colleges. But the court of appeals saw the case as far more complex and split the student body down the middle. The SUNY ceramics students, it held, had the same due process rights as those at regular SUNY campuses, while the liberal arts students were no different from those at Colgate or Sarah Lawrence. (The liberal arts students argued they too should benefit from Alfred's hybrid character; both courts declined to go that far despite the unique nature of the institution.)

The Alfred case seems almost to have been designed to test easy assumptions about federal law and the private campus. Two student demonstrators, who might have shared a room and taken many courses together, would have fared very differently—one reinstated and the other out—on the basis of a choice of academic major. This result is at least anomalous, if not bizarre. Yet consider the alternatives. To do as the district judge did and dismiss the whole case would be to overlook the special status of SUNY students whose academic field is offered and supported by New York State only at a private host campus. Conversely, to reinstate the liberal arts students because certain other Alfred programs received state funding would have transformed Alfred University's character to a greater degree than the federal constitution warrants. Solomonic solutions usually leave both sides dissatisfied, though sometimes the measure of wisdom is the degree to which unhappiness is shared.

It may now be time to summarize where we are, before tackling the next set of issues. There has been relatively little litigation over these issues in recent years—partly because campuses have been quieter, partly because more of the constitutional claims of the 1960s find statutory support in the 1990s and partly because (as we have seen) the results in court have not greatly encouraged those who were aggrieved by private institutions. Those who prevailed did so under unusual conditions.

Take Chris Schmid, for example; had the case come up differently, the outcome could have been quite different. Suppose, for example, Schmid had not been brought into court to answer a criminal trespass charge, but had instead petitioned a state court to compel Princeton to waive its rules and allow him free range on the campus. In that posture, the issues would have been quite different, and so quite probably the outcome. Indeed, courts have more than once sustained trespass rules of *public* universities under conditions not that different from those in Princeton in 1978. Of course we will never know what the U.S. Supreme Court would have said about the case had Princeton not changed the rules in midstream; nor do we know how the New Jersey courts would view the new and more precise campus speech policies. In short, the Schmid case may be (as Justice Holmes once quipped of a precedent he would confine narrowly) "a ticket for this day and train only."

For the longer term, the private campus federal cases may also tell us less than a quick review might suggest. Decisions involving genuinely hybrid institutions—Pitt, Temple, or for that matter Alfred—should not be generalized beyond the relatively small universe from which they arise. Thus if the Temple-Pitt issue arose at Howard or Gallaudet, a similar jurisdictional ruling would be expected. And if SUNY students at

Cornell, or maybe even ROTC students at MIT (with its land-grant legacy) were suspended, they could presumably take advantage of the Alfred ruling.

Such cases, however, give little guidance for the general run of private colleges and universities. The threshold for federal jurisdiction over nongovernmental entities has risen considerably in the last decade or so. Thus federal judges would be far less likely to find "state action" at a campus like Penn than they would have a quarter century ago. While many more private universities now resemble Penn in their degree of financial interdependence with and regulation by government, this very fact would probably diminish the likelihood of a similar ruling today.

Thus the assumption with which we began is probably sound and should be restated: except for special circumstances or governmental impaction, most private colleges and universities are probably free to control campus speech in ways the First Amendment would forbid at a public institution. There are, however, several other elements we need to examine before making a final judgment.

We have been looking only at the courts. Clearly legislatures may and do play a substantial and growing role in the process. The policies and actions of private colleges and universities are in fact extensively regulated by federal, state, even local laws. Congress has imposed on all institutions of higher learning an increasingly complex web of rules, standards, and obligations. These rules typically draw no distinction between public and private campuses. Thus all colleges are forbidden to discriminate in employment and other areas, all are required to disclose data about campus crime and other matters of interest to potential students, and all are required to treat human subjects and laboratory animals humanely in their research programs.

In fact, campus expression has, until quite recently, been one of the few areas that lawmakers have left alone. But the growing concern about campus speech policies was bound to attract interest on Capitol Hill, as it did in the spring of 1991. In mid-March, Representative Henry Hyde, a conservative Republican from Illinois, introduced what he termed the Collegiate Speech Protection Act of 1991.

Lamenting that "free speech is under siege . . . at our universities" and charging that "the demands of political correctness are casting a pall of intolerance over American universities," Hyde touted his bill as a way to restore free inquiry and open debate. The law he proposed was striking for its brevity and simplicity. In a single page, it declared that any higher education institution already covered by federal civil rights law (and that meant virtually all)

> shall not make or enforce any rule subjecting any student to disciplinary sanctions solely on the basis of conduct that is speech or other communication protected from governmental restriction by the first article of amendment of the Constitution of the United States.

The bill contained only two other provisions. Institutions "controlled by a religious organization" would be exempt, though only to the extent that the law would "not be consistent with the religious tenets of such organization." The other section created a civil remedy for any student at an institution that violated the bill's basic sanction—a remedy that was not confined to students affected or inhibited by the forbidden policy.

While the text took but a single page, the accompanying press release offered many pages of rationale. Its central section was a litany of incidents of repression and restraint of expression, drawn from campuses across the country. More than half the examples, though, came from public universities and were thus irrelevant to a law addressed only to private campus speech. Indeed, the variety of state university incidents raised doubt whether First Amendment standards—the Hyde bill's central core—were nearly as clear as its sponsor assumed. Of the incidents drawn from private campuses—Hampshire, Smith, Clark, Vassar, and others—most dealt with classroom or extracurricular climate, not with formal speech codes or rules of the sort the Hyde bill targeted. Even so, the supporting statement gave cause for concern about the current state of campus speech.

Hyde's espousal of such a bill surprised few observers. His name had been closely tied to a rider some years earlier that forbade use of federal funds for abortions. What did raise eyebrows, though, was the person who shared the podium at Hyde's press conference. Professor Nadine Strossen had, only weeks earlier, assumed the presidency of the American Civil Liberties Union. A scholar of First Amendment law and policy, she had written and spoken of her deep dismay with campus speech codes. She now joined with Hyde in calling for federal legislation that would do to private campuses what the federal courts seemed to be doing to public university codes. The ACLU rationale differed little from Hyde's: speech codes stifle debate, and the intervention of Congress was vital to guarantee "students of every background and ideology a means to challenge efforts at enforced orthodoxy of any stripe."

Media reaction, even from sources not usually Hyde champions, was generally sympathetic. The *Washington Post* editorially lamented the popularity of campus speech codes and warned that if private universities did not see the folly of their own ways, the Hyde bill "will gain, and deserve, support in Congress."

Missing from the initial response was any recognition of the profound differences between public and private institutions. These differences began to emerge a few weeks later—for example, in a statement by the National Association of Independent Colleges and Universities that was highly critical of the Hyde bill for its assumption that speech on public and private campuses was essentially fungible. Yet there was remarkably little concern about the parity of treatment of institutions that might have strikingly different needs and missions.

During the summer, desultory hearings were held, but the Hyde bill never got out of committee. Meanwhile a similar bill surfaced in the Senate with Idaho Republican Larry Craig as its sponsor. Despite strong expressions of support from members of both houses, momentum stalled by late 1991 and neither bill reappeared in ensuing sessions. Nonetheless, the prospect of a federal speech-code ban was quite real at the time. Since it might recur, the legal issues deserve our attention.

There seems little doubt that Congress has constitutional power to do what Hyde and Craig proposed to do to private campus regulation of speech. By amending Title VI of the 1964 Civil Rights Act, these bills would simply have added expression to the grounds (race, religion, gender, age, and others) on which colleges and universities that receive federal funds may not discriminate against their students. Private institutions have already been told they must observe Fourteenth Amendment standards of equality in dealing with their students, faculty, and staff. Adding First Amendment speech rights to those already covered seems well within the scope of congressional power over the use of federal funds. While some sticky issues could arise at church-related colleges, the Hyde bill's exemption avoided this problem.

The intriguing question, then, was not whether Congress *could* act in this way but whether it *should* do so. The case for intervention was appealing: speech codes existed on many private campuses and were probably spreading. Some of these codes were excessively vague and broad and would clearly not have passed muster at state universities. The potential threat of a speech code to free discussion and debate did not vary with the source from which the institution drew its primary support. So long as some of this support came from the federal government, the argument ran, Congress had as clear a responsibility to protect free speech on the recipient campus as it does to protect equal opportunity.

The leap from race or sex to speech, however, deserves closer analysis. Racial and gender bias have always been a paramount concern. Even before Congress passed civil rights laws in the 1960s, federal courts had said that private recipients of federal funds would violate the Constitution if they discriminated in using the funds. Thus a person who had been denied equal treatment by a federally aided private entity might have had an actionable claim even without the statutes that made such relief explicit (and of course clarified in myriad ways the duties that accompanied federal funding).

On the other hand, no court ever suggested so broad a reach for the First Amendment. There has been no hint that a private entity, simply because it receives public funds, must treat equally all expression that would be protected by the First Amendment on public property. Such a duty could arise only if Congress imposed it, as the Hyde and Craig bills threatened to do. That is a vital difference between restricting speech on one hand and denying equal opportunity on the other. What the civil rights laws forbade was discrimination, much of which was already vulnerable under the Constitution by the time Congress acted to make the ban explicit. That could never have been said of the way private entities dealt with speech. The distinction is a central one, bearing on the policy judgment.

Doubts about the wisdom of the Hyde-Craig bills require careful development and delineation. Granting that speech codes are bad and should be avoided, it does not necessarily follow that Congress is the proper body to bar such codes at private educational institutions. After all, there are many constitutional safeguards Congress has not felt compelled to extend to nonpublic universities. Due process is a prime example. If Rutgers wishes to expel a student, it must follow procedures less elaborate than those of a criminal trial but far more rigorous than the exit interview with a stern dean of students that once sufficed. Princeton, however (at least as far as the federal Constitution goes), may use whatever process it wishes to dismiss a student—and may act against the student for any reason that is not expressly barred by federal law (e.g., racial bias). In fact there are many differences between public and private campuses in the current reach of federal law. The case for treating speech the same at both requires more than noting the existence of federal power that has not been fully exercised.

There are several other, deeper policy concerns that go to the heart of speech on the private campus. The Hyde and Craig bills would bind private universities to First Amendment standards. The implication is that state universities know precisely what student speech is and is not protected. But this premise is doubtful. It has already taken four federal court suits to define the scope of public campus power, and we have surely not heard the last of such litigation. So the beguiling notion that private campuses now need only follow their public peers suggests a degree of clarity that simply does not exist and is not likely to exist.

There is another serious problem of interpretation. The proposed exemption for church-controlled institutions would apply only where a federal ban "would not be consistent with the religious tenets" of the church. If, let us say, a Catholic college adopted a special rule barring blasphemous or sacrilegious speech, the exemption would almost surely apply. But such bans are not the real-world issue. Rather, the issue is how Catholic colleges may deal with such unsettling speech as advocacy of abortion or of gay and lesbian rights. College administrators would presumably claim that they must be free to deal with such speech in accordance with church tenets; whether a court would accept this claim under the exemption is far less certain.

There is even grave doubt whether, given our tradition of separation of church and state, secular courts in this country have any business at all probing such questions as the "consistency" of policies with "the religious tenets" of a religious organization. Courts must, for example, keep out of internal church disputes unless the case can be resolved entirely on such secular grounds as property or contract law. If issues of theology or religious doctrine arise, then the power of secular courts has reached its end.

There is one special irony about the attempt to regulate private speech codes through Title VI of the Civil Rights Act. This law and its many implementing regulations obligate private as well as public universities not only to avoid overt discrimination but also to combat harassment and take other steps to ensure equality. Most speech codes have been designed to serve precisely those interests. Their goal has been to create a more welcome campus environment for vulnerable groups. Had Hyde-Craig passed, it would have left Title VI telling private colleges what they must do to combat bias while removing a specific tool some institutions may have considered useful for just that purpose.

The Title VI link and the irony of the Craig-Hyde approach resurfaced in March 1994 when the federal Office for Civil Rights released a staff memo labeled Investigative Guidance on Racial Incidents and Harassment against Students. The memo spoke of the duty imposed on federally funded colleges and universities by Title VI to combat harassment. In addition to physical conduct, harassment was defined to include "verbal, graphic or written" assaults so "severe, pervasive or persistent" as to "interfere with or limit" a student's ability to "participate in or benefit from" the institution's services or activities. If a racially hostile environment were found to exist at a recipient institution, some response would be expected. Among the corrective elements to be reviewed would be "applicable anti-harassment policies"—harassment having been defined to encompass "verbal, graphic or written" forms. Some solace came from an accompanying footnote: "Of course, OCR cannot endorse or prescribe speech or conduct codes or other campus policies to the extent that they violate the First Amendment of the United States Constitution." This disclaimer was comforting to a degree. Yet the statement as a whole strongly implied federal administrative support for campus policies directed at verbal as well as physical harassment. And while the footnote might give a public institution useful guidance, its value to a private campus (where the First Amendment does not apply of its own force) was far less clear. Then add to the equation the possibility of something like a new Hyde-Craig bill. The quandary for the private college intensifies.

The concern here is not simply one of interpretation. This discussion goes to the very heart of private higher education and its right to be distinctive. At issue is quite as much what speech standards private institutions should impose upon themselves, whether or not government decrees such standards. Many private universities proclaim their adherence to maximum freedom of expression. Harvard's Faculty of Arts and Sciences, for example, assures students that any regulation of expression "will be consistent with established First Amendment standards." Similar commitments may be found in the handbooks or codes of most other prestigious private universities. Such policies may, however, concede more than is necessary or wise at the core of private higher education.

Regulating speech is not like regulating race or sex discrimination. When it comes to barring bias in admission or employment, private institutions as well as public regulators long ago recognized the primacy of equal opportunity as against a private college's claim for different treatment (except for the special case of a religious institution's choice of persons to teach theology or divinity). What may have escaped those who insist on uniform treatment of speech is the special relationship of expression to the character of private higher education. Vital differences and interests may occasionally warrant restrictions that would be unacceptable on a public campus. Parents may well have chosen a private campus, at substantial added cost, in part to place their children in a more congenial and protective environment. One means the institution currently has to enhance its environment is dealing more harshly with threatening speech. Accordingly, a historically black private college may feel it should combat racial slurs and epithets in ways the First Amendment would deny to its public counterparts. A single-sex college that recently became coeducational may wish to deal more harshly with gender-based remarks. And a university with many Jewish students and faculty may wish to single out anti-Semitic speech for harsher treatment. They have always been free to do so. There is a good argument that they should not only remain free to do so but also should not disable themselves from dealing differently with speech that touches these special interests. Harvard law professor Randall Kennedy has thought-fully questioned the notion that private universities must conform fully to First Amendment constraints:

> I can easily imagine a vibrant, rigorous, intellectually distinguished college whose governing authorities reject such a notion. I have in mind a college whose authorities focus on something else: a core set of values and knowledge that is inculcated and transmitted by a carefully and tightly planned program of instruction.
>
> I can easily imagine, that is, a first-rate Catholic or conservative or feminist or socialist university at which the curriculum, hiring of faculty, and rules regarding access to the campus by outsiders were governed by policies aimed at infusing the student body with the college's overarching religious or ideological commitments.

Whether or not one shares Professor Kennedy's view, it is hard to avoid the logic of letting private colleges and universities make such choices free of government constraint. Although most private institutions pride themselves on voluntary adherence to First Amendment standards, the option of shaping rules to meet special needs has always been there. Public colleges are, and should be, fully bound by the First Amendment quite simply because they are part of government. For those institutions that are not public, the option to deal differently with campus speech seems a tolerable distinction.

And so the law now permits, with one notable exception. As in many other areas, the exception is California. Soon after Congress failed to act on the Craig and Hyde bills, California's lawmakers adopted a strikingly similar measure, which soon became known (for its sponsor) as the Leonard law. Its central section declares that

> no private post-secondary educational institution shall . . . make or enforce any rule subjecting any student to disciplinary sanctions solely on the basis of conduct that is speech or other communication that, when engaged in outside the campus . . . is protected from governmental restriction by the First Amendment to the United States Constitution [or the free speech clause of the California Constitution].

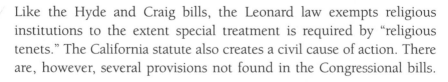

Like the Hyde and Craig bills, the Leonard law exempts religious institutions to the extent special treatment is required by "religious tenets." The California statute also creates a civil cause of action. There are, however, several provisions not found in the Congressional bills.

"Nothing in this act," declares the Leonard law, "prohibits the imposition of discipline for harassment, threats, or intimidation, unless constitutionally protected." This California statute also makes clear it does not bar campus rules "designed to protect hate violence" so long as they are consistent with the free speech guarantees. Finally (and inexplicably) the Leonard law assures Californians that it "shall not be construed to authorize any prior restraint of student speech."

Thus California did just what Congress declined to do. The Leonard law binds private universities to public-sector standards in dealing with student speech. A few early skirmishes suggest what might be in store. The law was invoked against a deferred rush policy at the University of LaVerne; the rule there forbids fraternities from promoting their houses to freshmen before rush begins and thus arguably inhibits student speech. Several months later, there was another early test, at Occidental College. An Occidental fraternity had circulated to its members a limerick that campus women's groups found offensive. These groups complained to the administration, and the fraternity was suspended for having released the limerick.

The Individual Rights Foundation, a conservative watchdog group, then went to court on the fraternity's behalf. The college soon agreed to settle the case, reinstating the fraternity and granting its members complete amnesty. But the saga did not end there. The women's groups complained to the federal Office for Civil Rights, which began investigating the college's response to the incident as a possible violation of Title IX (the sex discrimination section) of the 1964 Civil Rights Act. Now reenter the Individual Rights Foundation, this time suing the federal agency for threatening to force a private college to abridge students' free speech rights. At this point the agency backed down, apparently conceding it might have gone too far in placing Occidental in an impossible dilemma. (Of course in the event of a showdown between federal and state law, the former would prevail under the supremacy clause; if the Leonard law prevented a California private college from doing what federal law compelled it to do, then state law must yield. But neither side seemed anxious to press the contest that far.)

The ultimate battleground was almost certain to be Stanford University, since Stanford's speech code inspired the Leonard law in the first place. In May 1994 a group of Stanford students filed suit in state court, asserting that the speech code violated the Leonard law. The code's architect, law professor Thomas Grey, responded that Stanford "could be liable for harassment if we didn't provide some kind of enforcement against students being harassed"—an obvious reference to the very recent OCR guidance memo. Some months later, a California Superior Court judge agreed with the students and enjoined enforcement of the code. He faulted the code in two respects. He found its key terms overly broad; the code banned "stigmatizing" insults and slurs that would not meet the "fighting words" test. The judge also faulted the code for its selectivity; it banned insults about certain personal qualities (such as race and gender) but not other-directed epithets. Had the University of California adopted such code language, it would have failed the First Amendment test—and that really was the only issue under the Leonard law. Professor Grey felt the judge had "missed the main thrust" of the code's key section, which should be seen as "part of a comprehensive prohibition of discriminatory harassment'" and not as a freestanding speech code. But the Stanford administration decided not to appeal. In explaining this decision, President Gerhard Casper (a distinguished constitutional scholar) underscored the dilemma that such private institutions face:

> I do, indeed, believe that Stanford should voluntarily agree to be bound by the principles of free speech. However, such voluntary agreement to principles is not the same as being ordered by the state legislature to follow every twist of case law.

Ironically, in four years the Stanford code had never been enforced. Yet it had evoked much contention, on campus and beyond. The code offered a highly visible example of two conflicting phenomena—on one hand, the institutional urge to restrict offensive speech on matters of race and gender; and on the other, the governmental urge to limit the power of private universities to deal differently with student speech. In the end, when the Stanford code passed into history, it was far from clear which force had prevailed. Stanford's students were no longer constrained (if ever they had been) in speaking of race and gender and other sensitive personal qualities. Whether the level of discourse on the Stanford campus will change remains to be seen. Meanwhile, private colleges and universities remain free, outside California, to adopt speech codes if they wish and to restrict expression in ways that public colleges may not. What other states may do and whether Congress will ever revisit the Hyde-Craig issue remain matters of keen interest for observers of campus speech.

The ultimate issue for private institutions remains one of policy. Perhaps the wisest course, except in the most unusual and compelling situations, is for private universities to act as though they were subject to the First Amendment while rightly insisting that in fact they are not. Such a course is likely to create the soundest balance between the unique character of the private university on one hand and the realities of an increasingly regulated world on the other.

XI.

POSTSCRIPT

Office of the President
Beacon State University
Beacon, IA 57709

Dear Colleagues:

As this academic year comes to a close, I thought we might reflect on some of our shared experiences. We survived a visit by the most inflammatory and racist of speakers, who withheld little of his usual venom. We also survived our first crisis in computer speech, following the arrest of a senior faculty member for downloading quite sexually explicit images on his campus computer. (We also learned we urgently need new policies on acceptable use of computers, and such policies are now in preparation.) We granted recognition to the new gay and lesbian student organization, and, I hope, explained to skeptics in the larger community why we had done so. And we managed to keep open at the university art gallery that controversial exhibit which seemed to feature works that would offend just about every group on campus.

Along the way we decided we didn't need and in fact didn't want a speech code, partly because our existing policies would cover most situations people cite when they seek a code. We also avoided adopting any policy that would prevent faculty from engaging in sponsored research projects, no matter how alien or abhorrent their goals might seem to most of us.

This has, therefore, been a year of dealing with, reassessing, and protecting free expression in numerous forms. Among the lessons I hope we have learned has been the incredible variety and diversity of the ways in which free speech issues arise on a university campus. Most of us tend to think of "speech" and "press" in the relatively traditional modes of the spoken and printed word. Increasingly we will be dealing with issues of free expression in other media—controversial art works, research on uncongenial topics, electronic affronts, and still other forms we may not yet envision. As we face these new challenges, we do have some experience (and a substantial body of constitutional law) on which to draw. We should bear in mind that whatever the framers of the Bill of Rights may have expected, the First Amendment has adapted over the years to telephones, motion pictures, radio and television broadcasting, fax, cable, and is now just beginning to take the measure of digital communication. It would serve us well to stay ahead of the game in this regard as well as others.

The most valuable lessons of this past year reflect the centrality of free expression in a campus community such as ours. Several premises are vital. First, a university should, of all institutions in our society, welcome a broad range of views and ideas, including many that may be unpopular, unsettling, or even unacceptable to many on and off campus. In this sense a university is preeminently an open forum where, as Thomas Jefferson once said of the university he founded in Virginia, "error is to be tolerated so long as reason is free to combat it." We do not, as a community, pass judgment on the value or merit of ideas. As individuals, we may of course agree or disagree and make known our views. But as a community, we do not condemn—nor, for that matter, do we praise or acclaim. Rather, we provide a forum which is open to the broadest possible range of views and values.

Second, we must never lose sight of our primarily educational mission. What is so fundamentally wrong with a university suppressing ideas—through speech codes, research bans, and other means—is the kind of lesson that action teaches our students. Moreover, resorting to such measures as curbing views or ideas implies that we lack (or failed to use) subtler means of persuasion. What a university does best is to teach—whether to improve racial or religious or ethnic understanding, or to expand cultural and intellectual horizons, or for myriad other purposes. When a university decides the need is so great or the alternative means so weak that it must resort to stifling ideas, that is a sad day indeed.

Third, the vitality and strength of universities as places of free inquiry depend heavily on their vigilance in maintaining freedom. The institution that claims the need, or even the right, to pick and choose among viewpoints runs a grave risk that others will in turn force their views on the institution. Whether in the 1950s or the 1990s, the surest way to invite political pressure on such matters as off-campus speakers was for a university to pick and choose among viewpoints. If the campus administration could impose its own standard and differentiate between "acceptable" and "unacceptable" views, then why (asked governors and legislators) may we not do likewise? Conversely, those universities that most firmly maintained neutrality in such matters also proved most effective in deterring intervention. Vigilant protection of free expression thus offers an especially effective form of self-regulation, a powerful and eloquent antidote to political intrusion.

Fourth, as a practical matter, restraints on speech may prove counter-productive to the interests of those who sought them. So it is with groups who have recently pressed for speech codes and other curbs on insensitive speech; the history of repression suggests that such groups are the very ones that have most often suffered when speech curbs gain legitimacy. Whatever may appear today as the potential short-range benefits, proponents of restraint would be well advised to consider far graver long-term risks.

Fifth, also a practical concern, the drawing of distinctions between speech that is "acceptable" and speech that is "unacceptable" is a highly elusive process. While we may, as Justice Potter Stewart once said of obscenity, "know it when we see it," translating intuition into precedent is a daunting process. In each of our difficult experiences this year, we would have been hard pressed indeed to explain in a principled way why we turned away a speaker, took down a painting, rejected a research proposal, or barred a student organization. If we insist on the uniform application of content-neutral principles wherever speech is at stake, we will find ourselves consistently upholding free expression.

Sixth, the process of undermining or diluting basic freedoms is an inescapably corrosive one. James Madison wisely warned his Virginia colleagues in 1785 that "it is proper to take alarm at the first experiment on our liberties." The concept of partial or limited suppression is a mischievous one—barring just one speaker whose views everyone abhors, closing just one art exhibit that exceeds the bounds of propriety, or denying recognition to just one especially provocative student group. Such action, however reasonable and principled, creates a most dangerous precedent, of precisely the sort Madison feared in his reference to a "first experiment." Consistency in such matters is not always easily achieved, but serves far better in the long term.

Finally, lest I sound naive, let me acknowledge that there are times and situations where speech, even on a university campus, may not be completely free. Even the staunchest of First Amendment absolutists concedes exceptions. As the courts have consistently recognized, speech that poses an immediate threat of imminent lawless action—the "clear and present danger" test—may lead to sanctions, though seldom to prior restraint. Where a private person has been defamed, actual damages may be recoverable from a campus newspaper quite as much as from the outside media. The display (or even possession) of child pornography is criminal everywhere; clearly the campus affords no sanctuary. These few well-defined limits have as much force with the academic community as they do in the larger community. The exceptions serve in large part to prove the rule; they create a powerful presumption that speech beyond the exceptions must be free.

We at this university feel a special responsibility as guardians of academic freedom and free expression. We do not claim to have all the answers; nor have we encountered the full range of forces that may test our consistency and our vigilance. We do pledge, however, that as a community of learning we will continue to provide maximum freedom for expression and inquiry. We believe the university will be a better place for our commitment to these views.

With best wishes for the coming summer and the next academic year, I am,

Very sincerely,

Peter Parable
President

SOURCES AND REFERENCES

Introduction

The most comprehensive treatise on legal aspects and issues in U.S. higher education is William A. Kaplin and Barbara A. Lee, *The Law of Higher Education* (Jossey-Bass, 3d ed., 1995). Each chapter contains a detailed bibliography of legal and nonlegal references pertaining to the specific topic under discussion. The most focused of regular periodicals is the *Journal of College and University Law*, published quarterly by the National Association of College and University Attorneys. Current developments are noted, along with regular opinion and editorial comments, in the weekly *Chronicle of Higher Education*. Most campus legal developments of major importance are noted in the general media, particularly the *New York Times*, the *Washington Post*, and the *Los Angeles Times*. From time to time general law reviews arrange special issues or symposia on such current and lively higher education topics as speech codes, academic freedom, and sexual harassment.

I. Who Needs a Speech Code?

By far the most detailed survey of actual institutional practice in the regulation of campus expression is Arati R. Korwar, *War of Words: Speech Codes at Colleges and Universities in the United States* (Freedom Forum First Amendment Center, 2d ed., 1995). An earlier edition, published in 1992, surveyed speech policies of public campuses; the second edition added a section on private colleges and universities. The major articles cited in the chapter are Robert C. Post, "Racist Speech, Democracy and the First Amendment," *William & Mary Law Review* 32 (1991): 267; Mari Matsuda, "Public Response to Racist Speech: Considering the Victim's Story," *Michigan Law Review* 87 (1989): 2320; Nadine Strossen, "Regulating Racist Speech on Campus: A Modest Proposal," *Duke Law Journal* 1990, 484. The early U.S. Supreme Court case sustaining a conviction for "fighting words" was *Chaplinsky v. New Hampshire*, 315 U.S. 568 (1942); though this case has never been overruled, it has not been followed by the Supreme Court, which has struck down later "fighting words" charges, e.g., *Gooding v. Wilson*, 405 U.S. 518 (1972). The Supreme Court's somewhat uncomfortable distinction between regulating "hate speech" and "hate crimes" comes in *R.A.V. v. City of St. Paul,* 505 U.S. 377/508 (1992), and *Wisconsin v. Mitchell,* U.S. 476 (1993). The lower court cases dealing expressly with and uniformly invalidating campus speech codes are *Doe v. University of Michigan,* 721 F. Supp. 852 (E.D. Mich. 1989); *UWM Post v. Board of Regents,* 774 F. Supp. 1163 (E.D. Wis. 1991); and *Dambrot v. Central Michigan University,* 839 F. Supp. 477 (E.D. Mich. 1993), affirmed, 55 F.3d 1177 (6th Cir. 1995). For a special insight on the Michigan and Wisconsin cases by the lawyer who successfully represented the Michigan plaintiffs, see Robert A. Sedler, "The Constitutionality of Campus Bans on 'Racist Speech': The View from Without and Within," *University of Pittsburgh Law Review* 53 (1992): 631. The Stanford and Connecticut cases are unreported. The most recent development is a federal appeals court judgment setting aside sanctions under a California junior college sexual harassment policy which bore some resemblance to a speech code, *Cohen v. San Bernardino Valley College,* 92 F.3d 968 (9th Cir. 1996). For the views of one thoughtful college attorney on the options facing universities that wish to regulate campus speech by valid means, see Lawrence White, "Hate Speech Codes That Will Pass Muster," *Chronicle of Higher Education,* May 25, 1994, A48.

II. The Outspoken University Professor

For a general collection of essays on the subject of academic freedom and professorial speech in the college community, see William W. Van Alstyne, ed., *Freedom and Tenure in the Academy* (Duke University Press, 1993). Three other recent and helpful symposia are Ernst Benjamin and Donald Wagner, eds., *Academic Freedom: An Everyday Concern* (1994); Robert K. Poch, ed., *Academic Freedom in American Higher Education: Rights, Limitations and Responsibilities* (ASHE-ERIC Higher Education Reports, 1993); and "Focus on Academic Freedom," *College and University Journal* 22, no. 2 (Fall 1995). A principal source of policy is the "redbook" of the American Association of University Professors, formally titled *AAUP Policy Documents and Reports* (1995); the basic 1940 Statement on Academic Freedom and Tenure has received the endorsement of over 150 organizations across the academic spectrum. The case of Professor Philip Levin is reported as *Levin v. Harleston,* 770 F. Supp. 895 (S.D.N.Y.), affirmed, 966 F.2d 85 (2d Cir. 1992). The case of Professor Dube is *Dube v. State University of New York,* 900 F.2d 587 (2d Cir. 1990). The complex and protracted saga of Professor Leonard Jeffries is *Jeffries v. Harleston,* 820 F. Supp. 741 (S.D.N.Y. 1993), 21 F.3d 1238 (2d Cir. 1994), 52 F.3d 9 (2d Cir. 1995). The case of Professor Ron Silva is *Silva v. University of New Hampshire,* 888 F. Supp. 293 (D.N.H. 1994); the latest chapter involves facts strikingly similar to those in Silva, resolved similarly at the appellate level, *Cohen v. San Bernardino Valley College*, 92 F.3d 968 (9th Cir. 1996). The case of Professor Graydon Snyder has produced no reported judgment.

III. Free Speech and New Technologies

Case and other legal materials are spare in the field of new technologies, though the courts are beginning to grapple with the issues and to forge analogies. The Supreme Court judgment that defined the current standard for "clear and present danger"—incitement to imminent lawless action—is *Brandenburg v. Ohio*, 395 U.S. 444 (1969). The case of Jake Baker, decided by the district court and pending on appeal, is *United States v. Baker*, 890 F. Supp. 1375 (E.D. Mich. 1995). The first computer obscenity case, decided by the same appeals court in which the Baker case is pending, is *United States v. Thomas*, 74 F.3d 701 (6th Cir. 1996). The three-judge district court case striking down provisions of the Communications Decency Act is *ACLU v. Reno*, 929 F. Supp. 824 (E.D. Pa. 1996). See also, for a recent case dealing with digital expression and encryption policies, *Bernstein v. U.S. Department of State*, 922 F. Supp. 1426 (N.D. Cal. 1996). The two computer libel cases are *Cubby, Inc. v. CompuServe*, 776 F. Supp. 135 (S.D.N.Y. 1991), and *Stratton-Oakmont, Inc. v. Prodigy Services*, 1995 N.Y. Misc. LEXIS 229 (Sup. Ct. 1995).

IV. The Constitution and the Off-Campus Speaker

An early and prophetic analysis of the First Amendment issues posed by campus speaker bans is William Van Alstyne, "Political Speakers at State Universities: Some Constitutional Considerations," *University of Pennsylvania Law Review* 111 (1963): 328. A good and practical summary of current issues involving the handling of volatile off-campus speakers is Council for Advancement and Support of Education (CASE), "Coping with Controversial Speakers," CASE Paper for Advancement Professionals, no. 17, May 1994. The early State University of New York case is *Egan v. Moore*, 36 Misc. 2d 967, 235 N.Y.S.2d 995 (Sup. Ct. 1962). William Buckley's challenge to a rare encounter with a campus speaker bar is reported as *Buckley v. Meng*, 35 Misc. 2d 467, 230 N.Y.S. 2d 924 (Sup. Ct. 1962). The later and more successful challenge to Herbert Aptheker's exclusion from the University of North Carolina at Chapel Hill is reported as *Dickson v. Sitterson*, 280 F. Supp. 486 (M.D.N.C. 1968). Several months later, another federal judge struck down Illinois's Clabaugh Act and its bar to speakers in *Snyder v. Board of Trustees*, 286 F. Supp. 927 (N.D. Ill. 1968). Other cases are *Evers v. Birdsong*, 287 F. Supp. 900 (S.D. Miss. 1968); *Brooks v. Auburn University*,

296 F. Supp. 188 (M.D. Ala. 1969); *Smith v. University of Tennessee,* 300 F. Supp. 777 (E.D. Tenn. 1969); and *Molpus v. Fortune,* 311 F. Supp. 240 (N.D. Miss. 1970), affirmed, 432 F.2d 916 (5th Cir. 1970).

V. Gays, Greeks, and Others

The basic Supreme Court case defining the relationship between the public university and student organizations, albeit in the context of recognition, is *Healy v. James,* 408 U.S. 169 (1972). The major cases involving recognition of gay and lesbian student groups are *Gay Student Organization of the University of New Hampshire v. Bonner,* 509 F.2d 652 (1st Cir. 1974); *Gay Student Services v. Texas A & M University,* 737 F.2d 1317 (5th Cir. 1984); *Gay and Lesbian Students Assn. v. Gohn,* 850 F.2d 361 (8th Cir. 1988); and *Gay Lesbian Bisexual Alliance v. Sessions,* 917 F. Supp. 1558 (M.D. Ala. 1996). The challenge to the mandatory University of North Carolina fee (and specifically the *Daily Tar Heel* component) is *Kania v. Fordham,* 702 F.2d 475 (4th Cir. 1983). The Rutgers University fee controversy is reported in *Galda v. Rutgers, the State University,* 772 F.2d 1060 (3d Cir. 1985). The two recent cases on the validity of mandatory student fees, reaching quite different results in New York and California, are *Carroll v. Blinken,* 957 F.2d 991 (2d Cir. 1992), and *Smith v. Regents of the University of California,* 844 P.2d 500 (Cal. 1993). An especially helpful analysis of the issues may be found in Christina E. Wells, "Mandatory Student Fees: First Amendment Concerns and University Discretion," *University of Chicago Law Review* 55 (1988): 363. In the fraternity area, the old standard of deference was set by the Supreme Court's decision in *Waugh v. University of Mississippi,* 237 U.S. 589 (1915). The major transitional case was *Sigma Chi Fraternity v. Regents of the University of Colorado,* 258 F. Supp. 515 (D. Colo. 1966). The most recent, and drastically different, approach is embodied in *Iota Xi Chapter of Sigma Chi Fraternity v. George Mason Univ.,* 993 F.2d 386 (4th Cir. 1993).

VI. Free Press on the College Campus

For a helpful recent overview of the legal issues raised by restrictions on the campus press, see Greg C. Tenhoff, "Censoring the Public University Student Press: A Constitutional Challenge," *Southern California Law Review* 64 (1991): 511. The Supreme Court's one decision involving the student press, though at the high school level, is *Hazelwood School District v. Kuhlmeier,* 484 U.S. 260 (1988). The University of Minnesota newspaper funding case is *Stanley v. Magrath,* 719 F.2d 279 (8th Cir. 1983). For a very recent *Minnesota Daily* case on a slightly different issue, see *State v. Knutson,* 539 N.W.2d 254 (Minn. 1995). The Colorado junior college newspaper case is reported as *State Board for Community Colleges and Occupational Education v. Olson,* 687 P.2d 429 (Colo. 1984). The earliest of the advertising-rejection cases was *Lee v. Board of Regents,* 441 F.2d 1257 (7th Cir. 1971), involving a public campus newspaper in Wisconsin. The Mississippi case is *Mississippi Gay Alliance v. Goudelock,* 536 F.2d 1073 (5th Cir. 1976). The much later case involving submission of controversial material to a Nebraska public university newspaper is *Sinn v. The Daily Nebraskan,* 829 F.2d 662 (8th Cir. 1987). The denouement of the *Dartmouth Review* controversy is reported in *Dartmouth Review v. Dartmouth College,* 889 F.2d 13 (1st Cir. 1989). The general legal status of off-campus publications on the state university campus is discussed in *Hays County Guardian v. Supple,* 969 F.2d 111 (8th Cir. 1992); *Spartacus Youth League v. Board of Trustees,* 502 F. Supp. 789 (N.D. Ill. 1980); *Solid Rock Foundation v. Ohio State University,* 478 F. Supp. 96 (S.D. Ohio 1979); and *New Times, Inc. v. Arizona Board of Regents,* 519 P.2d 169 (Az. 1974).

VII. Artistic Freedom on Campus

For a more detailed review of many of the issues discussed in this chapter, see Robert M. O'Neil, "Artistic Freedom and Academic Freedom," *Law and Contemporary Problems* 53 (1990): 177. A thorough and helpful insight into the San Francisco State mural controversy from the university president's perspective is Robert Corrigan, "Diversity, Public Perception and Institutional Voice," *Liberal Education,* Spring 1995, 20-31. The case triggered by the removal of the unflattering portrait of Mayor Harold Washington is *Nelson v. Streeter,* 16 F.3d 145 (7th Cir. 1994). The University of Massachusetts–Amherst case is reported at two levels, *Close v. Lederle,* 303 F. Supp. 1109 (D. Mass. 1969), reversed, 424 F.2d 988 (1st Cir. 1970). The more sympathetic view of college gallery displays that provoke or offend is in *Piarowksi v. Illinois Community College District 515,* 759 F.2d 625 (7th Cir. 1979). The inconclusive California State University case is *Applegate v. Dumke,* 25 Cal. App. 3d 304, 101 Cal. Rptr. 645 (1972). The University of Nebraska film case is reported in *Brown v. Board of Regents,* 640 F. Supp. 674 (D. Neb. 1986), and the California community college play controversy led to *DiBona v. Matthews,* 269 Cal. Rptr. 882 (Cal. App. 1990). The Oklahoma State University film case is *Cummins v. Campbell,* 44 F.3d 847 (10th Cir. 1994). The two cases striking down successive congressional content restrictions imposed on funding for the National Endowment for the Arts are *Bella Lewitsky Dance Foundation v. Frohnmayer,* 754 F. Supp. 774 (C. D. Cal.

1991), and *Finley v. National Endowment for the Arts,* 795 F. Supp. 1457 (C.D. Cal. 1992). The Finley decision was finally affirmed by the court of appeals on November 5, 1996.

VIII. Academic Research and Academic Freedom

While there are fewer articles or comments on these issues than most others, one excellent analysis is Rebecca Eisenberg, "Academic Freedom and Academic Values in Sponsored Research," *Texas Law Review* 66 (1988): 1363. Neither of the Pioneer Fund disputes led to any reported litigation, though the outcome at the University of Delaware was widely noted in the *National Review,* March 18, 1991, 32; *Washington Times,* May 1, 1992, A3; and Net Hentoff, "Against the Odds: A Historic Free Speech Victory," *Village Voice,* May 2, 1995, 20. The issue of demands for research in progress or for unpublished data has led to a number of cases. The early case involving the Pacific Gas & Electric interviews is *Richards of Rockford, Inc. v. Pacific Gas & Electric Company,* 71 F.R.D. 388 (N.D. Cal. 1976). The Agent Orange controversy is resolved in *Dow Chemical Company v. Allen,* 672 F.2d 1262 (7th Cir. 1982). For two dimensions of the growing controversy over demands for research involving cigarettes and tobacco, see *R. J. Reynolds Company v. Fischer,* 207 Ga. App. 292, 427 S.E.2d 810 (1993), and *Application of American Tobacco Company,* 880 F.2d 1520 (2d Cir. 1989). See also *Deitchman v. E. R. Squibb & Sons, Inc.,* 740 F.2d 556 (7th Cir. 1984). The Jeep rollover research saga is reported in *Wright v. Jeep Corporation,* 547 F. Supp. 871 (E.D. Mich. 1982), and *In re Snyder,* 115 F.R.D. 211 (D. Ariz. 1987). The Stony Brook graduate student's travails with the law are reported in *In re Grand Jury Subpoena Dated Jan. 4, 1984,* 583 F. Supp. 991 (E.D.N.Y. 1984). The later and less sympathetic view of an asserted scholar's privilege is *Scarce v. United States,* 5 F.3d 397 (9th Cir. 1993). On the final topic in this chapter, that of local regulation of research, there is surprisingly little material and no reported court decisions.

IX. Religious Speech on the Public Campus

The Supreme Court's sharp separation of lower and higher public education for church and state purposes took place in *Tilton v. Richardson,* 403 U.S. 672 (1971), and *Hunt v. McNair,* 413 U.S. 734 (1973). The decision allowing Washington State to fund a blind student's study of divinity is *Witters v. Washington Department of Services for the Blind,* 474 U.S. 481 (1986). The case of the proselytizing University of Alabama professor is *Bishop v. Araonov,* 926 F.2d 1066 (11th Cir. 1991). The challenge to the University of Washington English course that included the Bible as a text and basis for discussion was rebuffed in *Calvary Bible Presbyterian Church of Seattle v. Board of Regents,* 436 P.2d 189 (Wash. 1967). Quite recently and comparably a federal judge dismissed objections to benedictions and invocations at state university graduation ceremonies in *Tanford v. Brand,* 883 F. Supp. 1231 (S.D. Ind. 1995). On the use of state university facilities, the Supreme Court granted equal access to student religious groups in *Widmar v. Vincent,* 454 U.S. 263 (1981). The Georgetown University dispute with the District of Columbia over recognition and benefits for gay and lesbian organizations is reported in *Gay Rights Coalition of Georgetown University v. Georgetown University,* 496 A.2 567 (D.C. Ct. App. 1985). The recent and widely publicized dispute over other forms of support for student religious groups led to two major cases—*Rosenberger v. Rector and Visitors of the University of Virginia,* 115 S. Ct. 2510 (1995). The other case, which stopped at the court of appeals level, was *Tipton v. University of Hawaii,* 15 F.3d 922 (9th Cir. 1994).

X. Free Speech on the Private Campus

Since the Bill of Rights of the Constitution applies only to government, the reach of the First Amendment to private institutions is of course quite limited. Not surprisingly, there are few pertinent cases. There is, however, the early case that broadly defined relations between government and private higher education, *Trustees of Dartmouth College v. Woodward,* 17 U.S. 518 (1819). The most important recent case was clearly the trespass case at Princeton University, *State v. Schmid,* 423 A.2d 615 (N.J. 1980), which the Supreme Court had agreed to hear but then dismissed after Princeton made major changes in its access rules. The other recent case that explores these issues is *Powe v. Miles,* 407 F.2d 73 (2d Cir. 1968), involving the contrasting legal claims of students enrolled on the same campus in privately and publicly supported degree programs. Professor Randall Kennedy's thoughtful comments appear in "Should Private Universities Voluntarily Bind Themselves to the First Amendment? No!" in *Chronicle of Higher Education,* September 21, 1994, B1. Comments and arguments from Henry Hyde, the principal congressional proponent of forcing private colleges to adhere to First Amendment standards for student speech, appear in Henry J. Hyde and George M. Fishman, "The Collegiate Speech Protection Act of 1991: A Response to the New Intolerance in the Academy," *Wayne Law Review* 37 (1991): 1469. The Stanford suit brought by a group of anti–speech code students under California's Leonard law was extensively covered in the Bay Area press but produced no reported court decision.

INDEX

ROBERT M. O'NEIL
is Director of the Thomas Jefferson Center for the
Protection of Free Expression and author of *Classrooms in the Crossfire:
The Rights and Interests of Students, Parents, Teachers, Administrators,
Librarians, and the Community.* He is also former President of the
Universities of Virginia and Wisconsin.